Jean Baudrillard

Key Contemporary Thinkers

Jean Baudrillard

From Marxism to Postmodernism and Beyond

DOUGLAS KELLNER

Stanford University Press
Stanford, California

Stanford University Press
Stanford, California
Copyright © Douglas Kellner
Originating publisher: Polity Press, Cambridge
   in association with Blackwell Publishers, Oxford
First published in the U.S.A. by
   Stanford University Press, 1989
Printed in Great Britain
Cloth ISBN 0–8047–1738–9
Paper ISBN 0–8047–1757–5

Original printing 1989

Last figure below indicates year of this printing:

00 99 98 97 96 95 94 93 92 91

Contents

Contents

But certainly for the present age, which prefers the sign to the thing signified, the copy to the original, fancy to reality, the appearance to the essence . . . illusion only is sacred, truth profane. Nay, sacredness is held to be enhanced in proportion as truth decreases and illusion increases, so that the highest degree of illusion comes to be the highest degree of sacredness.

Ludwig Feuerbach

As long as humanity has existed, its progress, its acquisitions have all been of the order of sensibility. Each day, it becomes nervous, hysterical. And in regard to this activity . . . are you certain that modern melancholy does not result from it? Do you know if the sadness of the century does not come from overwork, movement, tremendous effort, furious labor, from its cerebral forces strained to the breaking point, from overproduction in every domain?

The Goncourt Brothers

'Why so hard?' the charcoal once said to the diamond; 'for are we not close relations?'

Why so soft? O my brothers, thus I ask you: for are you not – my brothers?

Why so soft, unresisting and yielding? Why is there so much denial and abnegation in your hearts? So little fate in your glances?

And if you will not be fates, if you will not be inexorable: how can you – conquer with me?

And if your hardness will not flash and cut and cut to pieces: how can you one day – create with me?

Friedrich Nietzsche

All things considered, the century of the end will not be the most refined or even the most complicated, but the most hurried, the century in which, its Being dissolved in movement, civilization, in a supreme impulse toward the worst, will fall to pieces in the whirlwind it has raised.

E. M. Cioran

'Le cristal se venge'.

Jean Baudrillard

Acknowledgments

For discussion and helpful critical remarks on earlier versions of this text I am grateful to Robert Antonio, Stephen Bronner, Judith Burton, Harry Cleaver, Robert Fernea, Beldon Fields, Gloria Gannaway, Robert Goldman, Catherine Ploye, Jonathan Ree, Rick Roderick and Michael Ryan. Mike Featherstone encouraged me to write a critique of the English-language reception of Baudrillard's work for *Theory, Culture and Society* which helped mobilize and organize my thoughts for this project. My appreciation and critique of Baudrillard's theory of the consumer society is indebted to Robert Goldman's work and our discussions on these topics, while discussions with Harry Cleaver helped clarify the limitations of Baudrillard's interpretation of Marx. Discussions with Mark Poster, Jacques Morrain, Arthur Kroker, Charles Levin, Scott Lash, Jonathan Friedman, Gail Faurschou and Steve Pfohl helped clarify my understanding of Baudrillard and provided useful information and illuminations of 'the Baudrillardian scene.' Jean van Altena performed superb copy-editing. I am especially indebted, however, to Steven Best, with whom I struggled to come to terms with Baudrillard in our discussions and collaborations over the past three years.

I have dedicated the book to T. W. Adorno, whose critical and polemical spirit animated my encounter with Baudrillard.

The author and publishers are grateful to Editions Grasset and Fasquelle for permission to reproduce material from Jean Baudrillard, *La gauche divine*, Paris, 1985.

A Note on Sources and Abbreviations

I will refer to Baudrillard's major writings within the text using the
abbreviations listed below. I shall use English translations where they exist,
though I occasionally modify them. Citations and page references from the
French are from the original publication, and all translations from French,
German and Spanish texts not yet translated are my own.

A	America
ALM	L'autre par lui-même
CM	Cool Memories
CPES	For a Critique of the Political Economy of the Sign
EC	The Ecstasy of Communication
ES	L'échange symbolique et la mort
FF	Forget Foucault
GD	La gauche divine
MoP	The Mirror of Production
S&S	Simulacres et simulation
SC	La société de consommation
SED	De la séduction
SF	Les stratégies fatales
SIM	Simulations
SO	Le système des objets
SSM	In the Shadow of the Silent Majorities
SW	Jean Baudrillard: Selected Writings

In the spirit of T. W. Adorno

Introduction

Signs of the times: a new wave of New French Theory has appeared. After the often fervent reception and heated debates over the works of Sartre, Lévi-Strauss, Barthes, Derrida, Foucault and others, Jean Baudrillard is now sliding toward center stage of the cultural scene in some circles. In a number of 'postmodern' journals and grouplets, Baudrillard is being proclaimed as a fundamental challenge to our orthodoxies and the conventional wisdom in Marxism, psychoanalysis, philosophy, semiology, political economy, anthropology, sociology and other disciplines. A growing number of books and articles contain copious references to his work, and it is *de rigeur* in some cultural and art journals to cite Baudrillardian quotes and references. A Canadian journal devotes a special issue to him, and presents Baudrillard as 'a talisman: a symptom, a sign, a charm and above all, a password to the next universe.' An Australian anthology introduces the 'Baudrillard scene,' and a German text presents a transcription of discussions with Baudrillard and celebrates him as the theorist of 'the death of modernity.' Journals and publishers throughout the English-speaking world rush his work into translation in a variety of journals, including *Semiotext(e)*, *Telos*, *October*, *Artforum*, *The Canadian Journal of Political and Social Theory*, *Thesis Eleven*, *Z/G*, *On the Beach*, *Theory, Culture and Society* and others. Baudrillard's name appears ever more frequently in the cycle of conferences promoting postmodernism, and a Baudrillard reader is produced in a co-publication by Stanford University Press and Polity Press.[1]

Although English-language translations of Baudrillard's texts are rapidly proliferating, few, if any, serious critiques of his work have appeared in English.[2] Thus questions arise: is Baudrillard simply the latest faddish import from France, or is he an important theorist whose novel and provocative ideas deserve serious study? Is his current vogue a quick blip on the cultural screen, soon to be replaced by the next turn of cultural fashion, or has he posed problems and offered positions that are likely to concern us for some time? Does Baudrillard provide new beginnings and perspectives for our contemporary theoretical and political concerns or merely a series of ultra-radical gestures that portend the collapse of both critical social theory and radical politics?

Baudrillard has certainly produced an imposing and impressive body of work during the past twenty years, which has opened up new lines of thought and discourse, while putting in question many of the Marxian, Freudian and structuralist positions which characterized the previous era of radical social theory. Today, Baudrillard is being celebrated as one of the master thinkers in the discourses of poststructuralism and postmodernism. Yet reception of his thought has been remarkably uncritical and resolutely ahistorical. There has been little analysis of his complex intellectual trajectory, his involvement in a series of debates within the French post-May 1968 intellectual scene or the dramatic transformations in his writing and thinking in the 1970s and 1980s. Instead, Baudrillard appears as if by magic on the 'postmodern scene' to do battle with the Marx, Freud, Foucault, French feminists, Socialists and Communists.

In this book I will begin the process of mapping out, contextualizing and critically appraising Baudrillard's work as a whole. First, I will indicate how Baudrillard's thinking and writing were deeply influenced by a certain style of radicalism that appeared in France in the 1960s. The 1960s rebellions against the established society included revolts against the disciplines, methods, theories, styles and discourses of the university intellectual establishment. 1960s radicals both attacked conventional wisdom, and sought new critical theories and discourses. This led to a positive appropriation of Marxism, which, along with anarchism, emerged as a dominant critical discourse. It also led to a concern with Freud and sexuality, culture and everyday life, as well as to syntheses of Marx, Freud and the new cultural and political theories which proliferated in the highly volatile situation of the period.[3]

Baudrillard was part of this movement of French thought. Trained as a sociologist, in his 1960s and early 1970s work, he merged the Marxian critique of capitalism with studies of consumption, fashion, media, sexuality and the consumer society in texts which can be read as updating and reconstructing Marxian theory in the light of the new social conditions then appearing in France. From this perspective, Baudrillard's early work can be interpreted as a response to neo-capitalism, which, in the 1960s, came with a vengeance to France, with contradictory consequences. The Monnet Plan of the 1940s had inaugurated state planning, and by the 1960s modernization, technological development and the growth of both monopoly firms and a technocratic state sector were evident.[4]

In addition, new architecture, commodities and expressions of the consumer society such as drugstores, advertising, ubiquitous television and mass media were transforming everyday French life, and appeared to be ushering in a dramatically new social order. Social theorists and historians of a wide variety of tendencies agreed that the France of the 1960s was qualitatively different from the France of the 1950s.[5] Baudrillard called the new social formation 'the consumer society,' while others referred to it as the 'technological society' (Ellul), the 'post-industrial society' (Aron and Touraine), the 'society of the spectacle' (Debord), or the 'bureaucratic society of controlled consumption' (Lefebvre).

These socioeconomic developments stirred a remarkable series of attempts to reconstruct radical social theories to account for the changes in social conditions and everyday life, and spawned many new critical discourses. Roland Barthes explored the new consumer and media culture in his studies of 'mythologies.' Influenced by the French semiologist Ferdinand de Saussure's call. to study 'the life of signs in society,' Barthes analyzed the ways that the 'mythologies' of advertising, fashion, popular culture and the mass media attempted to transform 'petite-bourgeois culture into a universal nature.'[6] Barthes saw these mythologies as naturalizing contemporary bourgeois society, making it appear that a historically produced society was an expression of nature by erasing and covering over nasty historical conflicts and conditions or making them appear accidental and 'normal.'

At the same time, new theories of language and culture were being developed to analyze various forms of discourse and culture. These theories ranged from Lévi-Strauss's structural anthropology to Lacan's structural psychoanalysis and from Althusser's structural Marxism to the theories of textuality and deconstruction advanced by Jacques Derrida. The new structuralist, semiological and deconstructive theories focused attention on language, representation and the importance of discourses, images, codes and culture in everyday life. In particular, the new theories of representation and signification broke with conventional views of the relationship between language and reality. Drawing on Saussure's structural linguistics, the semiological theories of language problematized relations between language and reality, words and things. Saussure saw the linguistic sign as consisting of a signifier (the acoustic or visual component) and a signified (the conceptual component). On this theory, meaning was primarily determined not by referring language to the world, but through differences within a system of language and with the structures and rules of signification responsible for the production of meaning. Relationships between words and things, signifiers and what they signify, were conceptualized as strictly arbitrary, there being no 'natural' links between language and the world. The statement 'The sky is blue today' relates an arbitrary signifier 'sky' to the heavens above, and uses the signifier 'blue' to denote the difference between the sky on a particular sunny, cloudless day and its grey, cloudy or nocturnal appearance.[7]

Whereas previous approaches to linguistics theorized language in diachronic, or historical, terms and as an aggregate of distinct words, Saussure argued that language should be studied as a synchronic structure, as a system whose individual parts function relationally, within the system of language. Semiology was conceived as a science which would study the system of language, and Saussure proposed that it be extended to social systems of signification, to study of 'the life of signs within society.' Barthes and others took up Saussure's challenge, and applied semiological principles to the study of myths, ideologies, fashion, the media, images and other aspects of social life. Baudrillard was deeply influenced by the semiological revolution, which articulated the importance of signification, representation and systems of signs in social and domestic life. The semiological turn forced his generation to rethink relationships between language and other systems of representation like painting or cinema, as well as those between representation, language, power and social reality. These developments were part of a process of questioning the fundamental premises of language and thought, and contributed to the subsequent reconstruction of the disciplines of linguistics, anthropology, sociology, political economy, philosophy and cultural studies.

In addition, French theorists began taking seriously phenomena from everyday life which had been neglected previously and which tended to remain segregated from the domain of 'high culture.' Since the 1940s, Baudrillard's sociology teacher, Henri Lefebvre, had been calling for a 'critique of everyday life' and the expansion of Marxism toward theorization of the conditions, problems and possibilities for change within everyday life.[8] Lefebvre had published a whole series of volumes on Marxism, including early texts written while he was a member of the Communist Party and later texts which attempted to reconstruct and develop Marxism in a creative way after his expulsion from the Party in 1956.[9] He greatly expanded the Marxian theory through his studies of consumption, architecture, urbanization and the multifaceted roles of language and culture in contemporary neo-capitalist societies.

Lefebvre's project deeply influenced Baudrillard, though we shall find that the latter's approach to these phenomena differed significantly from that of his teacher. Baudrillard was much more sympathetic to structuralism and semiology than Lefebvre, whose Marxism was more orthodox and more critical of competing theoretical systems.[10] During the 1960s, other French radicals were questioning and, in many cases, moving beyond the Marxism that remained the theoretical framework for Lefebvre and for Baudrillard's early works. The group of theorists associated with the journal *Arguments* were studying the impact of new technologies on the labor process, class structure and political system, and were rethinking Marxism in the light of these transformations. New theories of class and the new working classes emerged along with new theories of technology, the media, language and culture. These theories also considered new strategies of social transformation, and ranged from class theories of social change which looked beyond the Marxian proletariat to the 'new working class' to the works of

Guy Debord and the 'situationists', who were developing theories of 'the society of the spectacle' which focused on image production, spectacle and new forms of domination and alienation in the consumer society. The situationists searched for new strategies of revolt and revolution, while criticizing Marxist-Leninist theories of the party and holding on to the proletariat as the revolutionary subject.[11]

The period was a time of ferment, experimentation, novelty and synthesis that combined theories from diverse fields. At the time, Baudrillard was a teacher of sociology at Nanterre, and was seriously engaged in the study of Marxism, anthropology, history, culture and politics. During the 1960s, before publishing his first book on *Le système des objets* (see 1.1), he translated some plays by Peter Weiss, Brecht and others, a book on Third World revolution and a collection of photographs of Germans.[12] He was on the Left politically and supported the established and emerging revolutionary tendencies in France and elsewhere in the world.

The revolutionary ferment in the intellectual world exploded in the political and social sphere in France, in May 1968, when for a few heady weeks it looked as if revolution was in the making for the first time in an advanced capitalist country.[13] Students began agitating for reforms in March, and went on strike and took over their universities in early May; their example was followed by the workers, who occupied their factories in mid-May. Production and the routines of everyday life came to a halt. De Gaulle mysteriously left the country at one point, and it appeared that a radical overthrow of the entire system was taking place.

By June, however, 'normality' had returned. De Gaulle promised new elections and reforms, the workers returned to work (with the support of the Communist Party and the trade unions); and the students went on vacation. Some reforms were effected, but by and large, France returned to business as usual and the old routines. Still, the events deeply influenced their participants, who for some years after continued to live and think in their revolutionary and utopian ambiance. Although Baudrillard was part of this situation, he has never really analysed or discussed how all these contradictory factors and influences shaped his thought and writings. Indeed, simply to list the 'influences' on a complex thinker like Baudrillard is itself misleading. My purpose here is simply to enumerate some of the forces in the intellectual and political field that constitutes Baudrillard's 'scene,' forces that are evident in his writings. To continue the list would require discussion of Jacques Derrida's deconstruction, Andy Warhol's pop art, Marcel Mauss's theory of the gift, George Bataille's theory of expenditure and symbolic exchange, Lacan's revision of Freud, Lévi-Strauss's structuralism, Althusser's structuralist reading of Marx, the work of American writers on the consumer society and Critical Theorists like Herbert Marcuse, T. W. Adorno and Walter Benjamin. A full inventory of the influences on Baudrillard, however, would not only be tiresome, but would be beside the point, since Baudrillard increasingly came to think against and oppose most of the major influences on his early work. By the 1970s, it appeared to one interpreter that 'Baudrillard is against any thinker whose ideas he takes seriously.'[14]

Still, Baudrillard's texts emerged from a specific historical matrix, and it is useful to recall this matrix before beginning to analyze and criticize the texts themselves. The following chapters, then, will start with Baudrillard's early writings, although the organization will not be strictly chronological. After attempting to establish his early problematic and examining his studies of the 'system of objects' and the consumer society, which form the original matrix of his thought, I will proceed thematically, albeit without ignoring chronology and context. In particular, I will analyze his early exercises within neo-Marxian social theory, his break with Marxism, his turn to 'postmodern' positions and the surprising developments in his works of the 1980s. Throughout I will attempt to contextualize, present and critically appraise the works discussed. Since Baudrillard's project remains unfinished, I cannot claim to present final perspectives on his work, though I do hope to provide comprehensive critical views of the entirety of his published work to the present time.

1

Commodities, Needs and Consumption in the Consumer Society

Baudrillard's first two published works, *Le système des objets* (hereafter *SO*) and *La société de consommation* (hereafter *SC*) explore the system of objects structured into a 'consumer society'; whereas his third book, *Pour une critique de l'économie politique du signe* (hereafter *CPES*), attempts to reconstruct political economy and Marxism on the basis of semiological theories of the sign.[1] At their best, these early texts provide the sort of critical theory and concrete analysis of everyday life and the social world produced by Roland Barthes, Henri Lefebvre and the situationists. They also contain explications and critiques of some of the central concepts of both Marxism and bourgeois political economy and social theory.

Baudrillard's first books appeared at a time when the importance of *culture* for the reproduction and expansion of capitalist societies was being perceived in a variety of quarters. Within the Social Democratic and Communist traditions, Marxists tended to separate culture from politics and economics; on the whole, traditional Marxists perceived only these latter domains as the proper areas of study and intervention for those seeking revolutionary social change. Consequently, radical cultural theory was neglected by comparison with the domains of history, politics and economics, which were taken to be both more 'real' and more important than the 'superstructures' of culture.

The neglect of culture had been challenged by German Marxists like Ernst Bloch, Walter Benjamin, Bertolt Brecht and the Frankfurt School, as well as by Lefebvre, Barthes, the situationists, Sartre and others. The dramatic emergence of the consumer society after World War II made it even more important to conceptualize the central roles that culture was playing in the reproduction of contemporary capitalist societies. As Fredric Jameson put it, in 'late capitalist' social formations, culture, 'far from being an occasional matter of the reading of a monthly good book or a trip to the drive-in' is 'in the very element of consumer society itself; no society has ever been saturated with signs and messages like this one.'[2] On this view, the cultural sphere – mass culture, advertising, information and communication technologies and so forth – had a direct role in production and economic management, as well as in socialization, education, acculturation and leisure.

Baudrillard, anticipating this trend, made the role of the cultural sphere in everyday life the main focus of both his earlier and his later work. His first three books focus on the ways in which culture, ideology and signs functioned in everyday life, while his later work continues his groundbreaking forays into the life of signs in society. His early investigations ranged from explorations of the consumer society to study of a wide variety of cultural phenomena within social life, especially the media, art, sexuality, fashion and technology – which themselves were becoming forms of commodification and consumption.

Lefebvre, Baudrillard and others claimed that the contemporary stage of capitalism is distinguished from earlier socioeconomic formations precisely by the increased importance of commodity culture within both production and social reproduction – the ways in which society reproduces itself in individual thought and behavior. On this view, one cannot properly understand history, politics, economics or any social phenomenon without grasping the role of culture and commodification within the social logic of contemporary capitalist societies.

1.1   STARTING POINT: *THE SYSTEM OF OBJECTS*

Baudrillard's first published book, *Le système des objets* (1968), investigates the new world of objects bound up with the explosive proliferation of a brave new world of consumer goods and services. The project operates within the framework of a subject-object dialectic in which the subject faces a world of objects which attract, fascinate and sometimes control his or her perception, thought and behavior. The analyses given presuppose the theory of the commodification of everyday life under capitalism advanced by Marxists like Lukács and semiological theories in which objects are interpreted as signs which are organized into systems of signification.[3]

The ambitious task which Baudrillard set himself was to describe the contours and dominant structures of the new system of objects and at the same time indicate how they condition and structure needs, fantasies and behavior. The book itself is highly systematic; it starts with an exploration of the system of *functional objects* (consumer goods), then proceeds to a series of studies of systems of seemingly *nonfunctional objects* (antiques, collections) and *metafunctional objects* (gadgets and robots), and concludes with an inquiry into 'the socio-ideological system of objects and consumption.'

Baudrillard combines structuralist analysis of systems of objects with Freudian analysis of the hidden meanings in the life of objects and Marxist ideology critiques of dominant ideological legitimations of the consumer society.

Le système des objets is animated by Baudrillard's sense that he is describing a *new* social order, one which he variously describes as a 'new technical order,' 'new environment,' 'new field of everyday life,' 'new morality' and new form of 'hypercivilization.' He frequently uses the terms 'modernity' and 'modern' to describe the new environment; thus he interprets the rise of the system of objects and consumer society under the sign of *modernity* (whereas later he will describe the genesis and contours of what he will eventually call a 'postmodern' world). The text is full of interesting insights and anticipations of his later work. Indeed, the framework of a perceiving, desiring subject facing a world of objects and signs defines the trajectory of Baudrillard's thought right up to the present. Thus his first book begins his project of describing the ways in which subjects relate to, use, dominate or are dominated by the system of objects and signs which constitute our everyday life.

The starting point of Baudrillard's oeuvre is thus our familiar system of objects. Individuals in all societies have always organized their everyday life through the production, arrangement and use of objects, and Baudrillard describes what he sees as the characteristic features of our contemporary system of objects and what distinguishes it from that of previous societies. He begins by describing the structures of organization of the objects of everyday life (*SO*, pp. 21ff.). Furniture in a traditional environment tended to be personalized, expressive and symptomatic of familial history, taste and tradition. Modern furniture, by contrast, he claims, is more functional, mobile, flexible and stripped of depth, symbolism and personal style. Modern interiors 'liberate' objects from expressive functions, and allow them to be arranged in various functional combinations; thus a table can be eaten on, written on or used to organize books and papers, whereas a multipurpose couch can be used to seat guests or to sleep on as a bed. New functional interiors and furniture displace the enclosed space of walls through the arrangement of objects, windows and lighting. Thus, modern home environments open up functional space by creating diffuse zones of angles and combinations of objects illuminated by new sources of lighting and more and larger windows which open up the closed and well-ordered space of the bourgeois interior which had previously constituted domestic space (*SO*, pp. 27–30).

The reduction and diminution of mirrors and the decline in the presence and prominence of family portraits are also indicative of a new style and 'modern order,' as is the disappearance of large, ticking living-room clocks (*SO*, pp. 31–4). In the new organization of objects and interiors, objects are no longer as subjective, expressive, familial, traditional and decorative as they once were. They are more functional, more homogeneous, artificial and without depth. The new world of objects requires an 'organizational man' who is able to master, control and order the objects in varying combinations and permutations (*SO*, pp. 37ff.). The new 'mode of living in the technical era' (*SO*, p. 38) calls for individuals capable of manipulating objects, arranging them and producing systems of order which are themselves replicative of social models and systems (in technical discourses, home fashion magazines, architecture and design and so on).

The technical order requires a technical language to describe the new system of objects and their relations, their organization into ensembles, structures and significations. This system of technical objects, Baudrillard claims, is 'essential' by comparison with the subjective system of needs and values (*SO*, pp. 12ff.), although he frequently interprets the creation of the object world in Freudian terms, as the projection of subjective impulses, wishes and so on. The thrust of Baudrillard's analysis is that the new technical world of objects leads to new values, modes of behavior and relations to objects and to other people. The modern individual is portrayed as a 'cybernetician' (*SO*, p. 41) who is induced to order objects into environments and to produce new ambiances and styles in accord with the imperatives of the technical world. After describing the structures of organization of objects, Baudrillard then describes the 'structures of ambience' (*SO*, pp. 42ff.). Here he discusses how color, material, form and style are combined to produce a new mode of living and a new type of environment. While traditional colors were expressive, much like traditional furniture, more modern pastel colors are detached from nature and are more artificial and free from traditional systems of signification. Thus colors too are more functional and lose their singular value by being organized into systems that are relative to each other and to the ensemble as a whole (*SO*, p. 49). New artificial materials like plastic, synthetics, stucco and glass replace natural, 'living' material like wood or cotton; they are 'homogeneous as cultural signs and can be instituted in a coherent system. Their abstraction permits combining them as one wishes. . . . The entire modern environment thus passes globally into a system of signs' (*SO*, pp. 54–5). We see here how Baudrillard uses semiological theories of the sign to interpret the structure of everyday life. Henceforth the organization, nature and effects of the life of signs in society will be a major focus of his work.

To the technical organization of objects there corresponds a systematic cultural organization of ambiance, which imposes a 'new morality,' which in turn structures modern life in its totality, with regard to eating, sleeping, procreating, smoking, drinking, receiving people, communicating, observing, reading and so on (*SO*, p. 65). In short, the system of objects leads people to adapt to a new, modern world which represents a transition from a traditional, material organization of the environment to a more rationalized and cultural one. Baudrillard provides a multidimensional analysis of this new world, and attempts to elucidate the ways in which objects and individuals are 'liberated' from traditional systems and usages, yet constrained by the technical imperatives of the new environment.

Although Baudrillard describes the system of objects as a system of commodities which constitute a consumer society, and focuses his description on types of commodities, advertising, credit, modes of consumption and so on, there is little discussion of the emergence of the system of objects in the course of the development of capitalism. In several discussions (*SO*, pp. 175ff., 204ff., and *passim*), Baudrillard poses the question of whether it is the imperatives of production, technical imperatives or psychological projections – or a combination thereof – which is the motor behind the proliferation of the new world of objects. On the whole, he seems to give more weight to technical imperatives and psychological projections than to production itself in the creation of the system of objects, although he claims that it is an 'open question' as to what forces are primary in overthrowing one mode of civilization and producing another (*SO*, p. 188). In any case, Baudrillard's analysis suggests that the Marxian problematic of revolution is severely undermined in a technological society in which change and revolution are integral to the system itself: 'Everything is in motion, everything is changing, everything is being transformed and yet nothing changes. Such a society, thrown into technological progress, accomplishes all possible revolutions but these are revolutions upon itself. Its growing productivity does not lead to any structural change' (*SO*, p. 217).

Baudrillard's *Le système des objets* is thus closely related in spirit to the theories of the 'technological society' which were circulating in France at the time.[4] On this model, the rapid development of science and technology was the prime motor of social development, and the result was a qualitatively new form of technological society. Baudrillard's study is distinguished from these studies by a critical scrutiny of the structure of the system of objects and the ways in which it differs from the traditional object worlds. He also carries through cultural analyses of the mythologies surrounding such objects as mirrors, clocks, colors, glass, collections, automobiles, gadgets, robots and so on. Also of interest in his discussion of the ways in which consumption, credit and advertising have produced a new morality, one based on a consumerist (leisure) ethic of fun and gratification rather than a productivist (work) ethic. These analyses permit discussion of the subjective projections and responses involved in the system of objects, and provide a framework for the analysis of the consumer society which would occupy him in his next book.

1.2 THE CONSUMER SOCIETY

Baudrillard's second book, *La société de consommation*, continues his systematic theoretical and empirical investigations of objects and activities in the new world of consumption and technique. Whereas his first book contains rather theoretical studies of the world of objects, his second book presents a sketch of the nature and structures of the new worlds of leisure and consumption for a more popular audience. The book begins with a preface by the social theorist J. P. Mayer, who compares the work to Durkheim's *The Division of Labor in Society*, Veblen's *Theory of the Leisure Class* and Reisman's *The Lonely Crowd*. Advertising hype aside, the book is probably both Baudrillard's most accessible text and the one most easily assimilated to conventional (or Marxian) sociology. Baudrillard draws on such theorists of the consumer society as Daniel Boorstin, Guy Debord, John Kenneth Galbraith, Henri Lefebvre, Herbert Marcuse, Marshall McLuhan, Edgar Morin, Vance Packard, David Riesman and Thorstein Veblen (all cited, with others, in the bibliography of his book, pp. 317–18).

La société contains analyses of the structure and nature of commodities and objects, a theory of consumption and studies of the mass media, sex and leisure; it concludes with some observations concerning the nature of contemporary alienation. The project is animated by the conviction that a deeper understanding of consumption is needed to comprehend the fundamental dynamics of neo-capitalist societies. Whereas capitalism focused its energies on developing a system of mass production during the nineteenth and early twentieth centuries, beginning in the 1920s the issue of mass consumption and the management of consumer demand became an issue of paramount importance.[5] Although the introduction of a consumer society was postponed by the Depression and World War II, its emergence after the war was one of the defining features of the contemporary situation which Baudrillard undertakes to theorize.

His analysis begins with a description of the new world of consumption: 'We are surrounded today by the remarkable conspicuousness of consumption and affluence, established by the multiplication of objects, services and material goods, all of which constitutes a sort of fundamental mutation in the ecology of the human species. Strictly speaking, these affluent individuals are no longer surrounded by other human beings as they were in the past, but by *objects*' (SC, p. 17; SW, p. 29). Everyday life, Baudrillard suggests, is determined more by the manipulation of commodities and messages and the organization and display of domestic goods – hence by interaction with objects – than by social interaction with other people. This continual interaction with objects has a powerful impact on human life:

Just as the wolf-child becomes a wolf by living among them, so we are ourselves becoming functional objects. We are living the period of objects: that is, we live by their rhythm, according to their incessant succession. Today, it is we who are observing their birth, fulfillment and death; whereas in all previous civilizations, it was the object, instrument and perennial monument that survived the generations of men. (*SC*, p. 18; *SW*, p. 29)

Baudrillard's key point is that commodities are part of a *system* of objects correlated with a *system of needs*:

Few objects today are offered *alone*, without a context of objects to speak for them. And the relation of the consumer to the object has consequently changed; the object is no longer referred to in relation to a specific utility, but as a collection of objects in their total meaning. Washing machine, refrigerator, dishwaster and so on have different meanings when grouped together than each one has alone, as a piece of equipment. The display window, the advertisement, the manufacturer and the *brand name* here play an essential role in imposing a coherent and collective vision, of an almost inseparable totality. (*SC*, p. 20; *SW*, p. 31)

Participation in the consumer society thus requires systematic purchase and organization of domestic objects, fashion and so on into a system organized by codes and models.

In this society, *consumption* has become the center of life:

We have reached the point where 'consumption' has grasped the whole of life, where all activities are connected in the same combinatorial mode. . . . In the phenomenology of consumption, this general climatization of life, goods, objects, services, behaviors and social relations represents the perfected, 'consummated' stage of evolution which, through articulated networks of objects, ascends from pure and simple abundance to complete conditioning of action and time and finally to the systematic organization of ambience, which is characteristic of the drugstores, the shopping malls, or the modern airports in our futuristic cities. (*SC*, pp. 23–4; *SW*, p. 33)

In his early works, Baudrillard generally takes a critical Marxian posture toward the consumer society, suggesting that consumption constitutes a total homogenization and organization of everyday life (*SC*, pp. 25ff.; *SW*, p. 34) which veils the material underpinnings and the social labor which produces the consumer society and its goods. 'One should never forget,' he warns, 'that these goods are *the product of a human activity* and that they are dominated not by natural ecological laws but by the laws of exchange value' (*SC*, p. 18; *SW*, p. 30). Then, signaling that he is writing under the sign of Marx, Baudrillard quotes a passage from Marx's *Contribution to a Critique of Political Economy* about the profusion of commodities in the London of his day (*SC*, p. 18). Yet Baudrillard adds a cultural dimension to the Marxian critique of political economy in his interpretation of the consumer society as a system of signs. In his analysis, consumption of commodities signifies happiness, well-being, affluence, success, prestige, eroticism, modernity and so on. He describes the consumer mentality as a form of '*magical thought* which reigns over consumption. It is a miraculous mentality which rules everyday life, a primitive mentality in the sense that it is defined as belief in the omnipotence of thoughts: in this case, belief in the omnipotence of signs' (*SC*, p. 27). For the consumer believes that possession and display of the signs of affluence, prestige and so on will bring real happiness and real social prestige.

In *La société de consommation* Baudrillard utilizes a much more explicit Marxian framework than in his previous and succeeding books. He criticizes ideologies of growth, progress and happiness through consumption, as well as ideological claims concerning the overcoming of class in the consumer society, and thus provides a neo-Marxian critique of the contemporary stage of capitalism. Moreover, contrary to his first and later books, he frequently conceptualizes the development of the consumer society in terms of the system of production, and thus assigns the logic of production an important role. Yet he argues that with the emergence of the consumer society, 'production is entangled with *an order of consumption*, which is an order of the manipulation of signs' (*SC*, pp. 29–30).

In developing his own theory, Baudrillard criticizes the standard, mainstream view which conceptualizes consumption in terms of a rational satisfaction of needs with the aim of maximizing utility. Against this view, Baudrillard posits a 'socio-cultural' approach which stresses the ways in which society produces needs through socialization and conditioning thereby managing consumer demand and consumption. Although he shares with American theorists such as Packard, Riesman and Galbraith a critique of the assumption of a free, rational, autonomous ego which satisfies 'natural' needs through consumption, he criticizes Galbraith's model of the production of artificial needs and management of consumer demand. Baudrillard's argument is that critics of the 'false,' or artificial, needs produced by the consumer society generally presuppose something like true human needs or a stabilizing principle in human nature that would maintain a harmonious balance and equilibrium were it not for the pernicious artificial needs produced by advertising and marketing. Yet, Baudrillard claims, there is no way to distinguish between true and false needs – at least from the standpoint of the pleasure or satisfaction received from various goods or activities of consumption. In addition, he maintains that

> Galbraith does not take into consideration the logic of social differentiation. Hence he is forced to represent the individual as a completely passive victim of the system. These processes of class and caste distinctions are basic to the social structure and are fully operational in 'democratic' society. In short, what is lacking is a socio-logic of difference, of status, etc., upon which needs are reorganized in accordance to the *objective* social demand of signs and differences. Thus consumption becomes, not a function of 'harmonious' individual satisfaction (hence limited according to the ideal rules of 'nature'), but rather an infinite social *activity*.' (*SC*, p. 102; *SW*, p. 4)

In this and his next book Baudrillard focuses on the 'logic of social differentiation' whereby individuals distinguish themselves and attain social prestige and standing through the purchase and use of consumer goods. He argues that the entire system of production produces a system of needs that are rationalized, homogenized, systematized and hierarchized. Rather than a consumer being seduced into purchase of a single commodity which Baudrillard equates with the primitive notion of mana, he or she is induced to buy into an entire system of objects and needs through which one differentiates oneself socially, yet integrates oneself into the consumer society. Baudrillard suggests that this activity can best be conceptualized by seeing the objects of consumption as signs and the consumer society as a system of signs: 'In this way a washing machine *serves* as equipment and *plays* as an element of comfort, or of prestige and so on. It is the latter that is specifically the field of consumption. . . . A need is not a need for a particular object as much as it is a "need" for difference (the *desire for social meaning*)' (*SC*, pp. 106–7; *SW*, pp. 44–5).

Baudrillard presents consumption as an unending activity of forward flight and unlimited renewal of needs, suggesting that the imperatives of an entire system of needs and objects require a vast labor to learn about the products, to master their use and to earn the money and leisure to purchase and use them. Consumption is thus productive activity which requires education and effort. Consequently, Baudrillard proposes that consumption is not to be interpreted primarily in relation to pleasure or the satisfaction of needs, but as a mode of social activity whereby one inserts oneself into the consumer society, conforming to socially normative behavior and signifying that one is a member of this society.

In this view,

> consumption is a system which assures the regulation of signs and the integration of the group: it is simultaneously a morality (a system of

ideological values) and a system of communication, a structure of exchange. . . . According to this hypothesis, as paradoxical as it may appear, consumption is defined as *exclusive of pleasure*. As a social logic, the system of consumption is established on the basis of the denial of pleasure. Pleasure no longer appears as an objective, as a rational end, but as the individual rationalization of a process whose objectives lay elsewhere. Pleasure would define consumption *for itself*, as autonomous and final. But consumption is never thus. Although we experience pleasure for ourselves, when we consume we never do it on our own (the isolated consumer is the carefully maintained illusion of the *ideological* discourse on consumption). Consumers are mutually implicated, despite themselves, in a general system of exchange and in the production of coded values. (*SC*, p. 109; *SW*, p. 46)

In the language of Lévi-Strauss, Baudrillard is suggesting that consumption is not derived primarily from the realm of nature but from the realm of culture, and that it should be interpreted as a system of signs organized by codes and rules, rather than on the basis of a 'natural' satisfaction of needs through goods. Thus, for Baudrillard, commodities and consumption constitute a 'global, arbitrary and coherent system of signs, a *cultural* system which substitutes a social order of values and classifications for a contingent world of needs and pleasures, the natural and biological order' (*SC*, p. 111; *SW*, p. 47). Thus, 'Marketing, purchasing, sales, the acquisition of differentiated commodities and object/signs – all of these presently constitute our language, a code with which our entire society *communicates* and speaks of and to itself' (*SC*, p. 112; *SW*, p. 48). The consumer, therefore, can not avoid the obligation to consume, because it is consumption that is the primary mode of social integration and the primary ethic and activity within the consumer society. The consumer ethic and 'fun morality' thus involve active labor, incessant curiosity and search for novelty, and conformity to the latest fads, products and demands to consume. Consequently,

We don't realize how much the current indoctrination into systematic and organized consumption is *the equivalent and the extension, in the twentieth century, of the great indoctrination of rural populations into industrial labor, which occurred throughout the nineteenth century.* The same process of rationalization of productive forces, which took place in the nineteenth century in the *production* sector, is accomplished, in the twentieth century, in the *consumption* sector. Having socialized the masses into a labor force, the industrial system had to go further in order to fulfill itself and to socialize the masses (that is, to control them) into a force of consumption. The small investors or the sporadic consumers of the pre-war era, who were free to consume or not, no longer have a place in the system. . . . Production and consumption are *one and the same grand logical process* of reproduction of the expanded forces of production and of their control. (*SC*, p. 115; *SW*, p. 50)

Thus, on this view, consumption is not the free activity of an autonomous subject; rather, it is constrained by the order of production, which gives rise to and manages a system of needs, and by the order of signification, which determines the relative social prestige and value of the system of goods. Yet the effects of organizing consumers politically could be tremendous, Baudrillard suggests, since consumer revolt could bring to a halt the dynamics of contemporary capitalism. However, such revolts have been manifested only

in a few strikes among American housewives and in the sporadic destruction of commodities (May 1968, the *No Bra Day* where American women publicly burned their bras). 'What does the consumer represent in the modern world? Nothing. What could he be? Everything, or almost everything. Because he stands alone next to millions of solitary individuals, he is at the mercy of all other interests.' . . . In general the consumers, as such, are unconscious and unorganized, just as workers may have been at the beginning of the nineteenth century. As such, consumers have been glorified, flattered and eulogized as 'public opinion,' that mystical, providential and '*sovereign*' reality. (*SC*, pp. 121–3; *SW*, pp. 54–5).

The consumer society also has its negative effects, such as 'anomie in the society of abundance,' subcultural and criminal violence, and fatigue with the demands of labor, leisure and consumption (*SC*, pp. 278ff.). Drawing on journalistic sources, Baudrillard points to contemporary manifestations of irrational violence erupting within the consumer society, which he interprets as a kind of social revolt. He also claims that the constant labor of production and consumption have led to a situation in which 'the heroes of consumption are fatigued.' Production and consumption are tiring, and the growing competition for more goods and services also wears out the heroic producers and consumers. Baudrillard describes fatigue itself as a

larval contestation, . . . a latent revolt, endemic and unconscious of itself. . . . Because it is a (latent) activity, it can suddenly reconvert itself into open revolt, as May '68 demonstrated everywhere. The spontaneous contagiousness . . . of the movement of May can only be understood on this hypothesis: what was usually perceived as lifelessness, disaffection and generalized passivity was in fact a potential of *active* forces in their very resignation, in their fatigue, in their ebb and therefore were immediately available. (*SC*, p. 294)

Baudrillard concludes by valorizing 'multiple forms of refusal,' which can be fused in a 'practice of radical change' (*SC*, p. 295); and he alludes to the expectation of 'brutal eruptions and sudden disaggregations' which, 'in a fashion as unforeseeable but certain, as in May '68, will come to shatter this white mass' (of consumption) (*SC*, p. 316). On the other hand, in the conclusion, Baudrillard also describes a situation in which alienation is so total that it cannot be surpassed, because 'it is the very structure of the consumer society' (*SC*, p. 307). His argument is that in a society in which everything is a commodity that can be bought and sold, alienation is total. Indeed, the term 'alienation' originally signified 'to sale,' and in a totally commodified society in which everything is a commodity, alienation is ubiquitous. Moreover, the conclusion describes 'the end of transcendence' a phrase borrowed from Marcuse, a state in which individuals can perceive neither their own true needs nor another way of life (*SC*, pp. 307ff.).

Consequently, Baudrillard distances himself from the Marxist theory of revolution and instead postulates only the possibility of revolt against the consumer society in an 'unforeseeable but certain' form. He thus has an ambivalent relation to classical Marxism at this point. On the one hand, he carries forward the Marxian critique of commodity production which delineates and criticizes various forms of alienation, reification, domination and exploitation produced by capitalism. At this stage, it appears that his critique comes from the standard neo-Marxian vantage point which sees capitalism as blameworthy because it homogenizes, controls and dominates social life while robbing individuals of their freedom, creativity, time and human potentialities. On the other hand, he cannot point to any revolutionary forces, and in particular does not discuss the situation and potential of the working class as an agent of change in the consumer society. Indeed, Baudrillard has no theory whatsoever of the subject as an active agent of social change (thus perhaps following the structuralist and poststructuralist critique of the subject popular at the time). Nor does he have a theory of class or group revolt, or any theory of political organization, struggle or strategy.

Baudrillard's problematic here is particularly close to that of the Frankfurt School, especially that of Marcuse, who had already developed some of the first Marxist critiques of the consumer society.[6] Like Lukács and the Frankfurt School, Baudrillard employs a mode of thought according to which commodification constitutes a totalizing social process that permeates social life. Following the general line of critical Marxism, Baudrillard argues that the combination of homogenization, alienation and exploitation constitutes a process of *reification* in which objects come to dominate subjects, thereby robbing them of their human qualities and capacities. For Lukács, the Frankfurt School and Baudrillard, this process of reification, whereby human beings become dominated by things and themselves become more thinglike, comes to dominate social life.[7]

In a sense, Baudrillard's work can be seen as rendering an account of a higher stage of reification and social domination than that described by the Frankfurt School. Baudrillard goes beyond the Frankfurt School by utilizing the semiological theory of the sign to describe the world of commodities, media and the consumer society, thus, in a sense what he does is to take the Frankfurt School theory of 'one-dimensional society' to a higher level. Eventually, his analysis of domination by signs and the system of objects leads him to even more pessimistic conclusions; for he sees the problematic of the 'end of the individual' sketched by the Frankfurt School as having reached its fruition in the total defeat of the subject by the object world (see chapter 6). Yet in his early writings Baudrillard has a somewhat more active theory of consumption than that of the Frankfurt School, which generally portrays consumption as a passive mode of social integration. By contrast, consumption in Baudrillard's early writings is itself a kind of labor, 'an active manipulation of signs,' a way of inserting oneself into the consumer society and working to differentiate oneself from others. Yet this active manipulation of signs does not imply an active subject who could resist, redefine, or produce his or her own signs and consumer practices; thus Baudrillard fails to develop a genuine theory of agency (see 1.4 for an alternative model of consumption and agency).

In the consumer society, consumption thus replaces production as the central mode of social behavior from which standpoint the society can be interpreted and critically analyzed. Baudrillard thus conceives consumption as a mode of being, a way of gaining identity, meaning and prestige in the contemporary society. In Baudrillard's later works, he further elaborates neo-Saussurean theories of signs and signification, which he then uses to analyze and critique the consumer society, thus adding a semiological dimension to previous neo-Marxian critiques of the consumer society. Building on his earlier work, he develops a much more elaborate and sophisticated theory of the life of signs in society, which he uses to criticize both establishment and Marxian political economy.

1.3   *FOR A CRITIQUE OF THE POLITICAL ECONOMY OF THE SIGN*

Baudrillard continued his exploration of the consumer society while beginning to criticize the Marxian critique of political economy during the early 1970s. Some articles from this period were subsequently collected in *For a Critique of the Political Economy of the Sign* (1972), in which he discusses problems with both standard bourgeois and Marxian analyses of commodities, consumption and needs, while arguing that a sociologically oriented semiology could help to develop more adequate perspectives. Though critical of classical Marxism, these studies are less dismissive than his later works, starting with *The Mirror of Production* (1973); indeed, they can be read as an attempt to strengthen and reconstruct the Marxian critique of political economy – even though, as I shall indicate, Baudrillard was already beginning to distance himself from Marxism in the *Critique*.

Consequently, while Baudrillard's problematic is always significantly different from classical Marxism and eventually was to break with Marxism altogether, I would argue that his first three books can be situated within a neo-Marxian framework which supplements and updates the Marxian critique of political economy. Baudrillard's analyses concentrate on phenomena which were either neglected by Marx or had not yet appeared during Marx's lifetime. For instance, since Marx's own work focuses primarily on the production process, Baudrillard's early analyses of consumption concretize and develop themes in ways that I believe can be assimilated to the Marxian critique of capitalism. Thus, while Baudrillard also makes some sharp criticisms of classical Marxism, much of his early work can be incorporated in the Marxian theory and critique of capitalism.

In view of Baudrillard's later rejection of Marxism, it is important to see that his vision in his early writings, that of the triumph of the market and commodification, is an important part of Marx's world view, and indeed, was sketched out by Marx himself. A passage in *The Poverty of Philosophy*, quoted by Baudrillard, allows us to grasp both his similarities and his differences with classical Marxism. Marx wrote:

> There was a time, as in the Middle Ages, when only the superfluous, the excess of production, was exchanged.
>
> There was again a time, when not only the superfluous, but all products, all industrial existence, had passed into commerce, when the whole of production depended upon exchange. . . .
>
> Finally, there came a time when everything that men had considered as inalienable became an object of exchange, of traffic and could be alienated. This is the time when the very things which till then had been communicated, but never exchanged; given but, never sold; acquired, but never bought – virtue, love, conviction, knowledge, conscience, etc. – when everything finally passed into commerce. It is the time of general corruption, of universal venality, or, to speak in terms of political economy, the time when everything, moral or physical, having become marketable value, is brought to the market to be assessed at its truest value.[8]

Baudrillard claims that Marx correctly perceived the radical discontinuity between stages one and two (that is, feudalism and early capitalism), but failed to see the fundamental cleavage between stages two and three) that is, early and later capitalism) (*MoP*, pp. 120ff.). For Marx, stage three is only a quantitative extension of market relations and commodification, whereas

Baudrillard claims that it is fundamentally different due to a new logic of *sign value and fetishism*. Under the reign of sign value, consumption and display become a central locus of value, and are as important as production in determining the logic, nature and direction of social processes.

Sign Value

Baudrillard's argument is that the 'conspicuous consumption' and display of commodities analyzed by Veblen in his *Theory of the Leisure Class* has been extended to everyone in the consumer society. Conspicuous consumption for Veblen is linked to expenditure, display and the establishing of style, taste and the social power of wealth. Whereas such display is confined to the upper classes in Veblen's book, Baudrillard sees the entire society as organized around consumption and display of commodities through which individuals gain prestige, identity and standing. In this system, the more prestigious one's commodities – houses, cars, clothes and so on – the higher one's standing in the realm of sign value. Thus, just as words take on meaning according to their status in a differential system of language, so sign values take on meaning according to their place in a differential system of prestige and status.

Baudrillard's early writings are thus characterized by the attempt to combine semiological theories of the sign with Marxist critiques of capitalism. For Baudrillard, the crucial feature of the consumer society is the proliferation of commodity signs through which commodities take on ever new and ever greater significance for those for whom consumption is a way of life. Whereas in his first two books Baudrillard resisted interpreting the consumer society as a linguistic system, as a language (see, for example, *SW*, pp. 14ff.), in his collection of essays *For a Critique of the Political Economy of the Sign*, he appropriates Saussure's semiological theory of language, which conceptualizes language as a differential system of signs, for his analysis of the system of commodities.

Baudrillard thus joined in the semiological revolution which was interpreting all aspects of social life as a system of signs. Commodities for Baudrillard, like language for Saussure, are both signifiers and signifieds, with the features of abstraction, equivalence and interchangeability which Saussure ascribed to the linguistic sign. That is, just as words for the semiologist are abstract concepts which can be bought together in linguistic structures according to specific rules of equivalence, exchange, substitutability and so forth, so commodities constitute a system in which exchange values – their prices, market value and so on – and commodity signs form systems of values in which one individual or good can be substituted for another. Thus, Baudrillard, building on his earlier analysis of the system of needs, suggests that commodities are structured into a system of sign values governed by rules, codes and a social logic.

To Marx's analysis of the commodity in terms of use value and exchange value,[9] Baudrillard thus proposes adding the further feature of sign value. His project of supplementing Marxist approaches is sketched out in 'The Ideological Genesis of Needs,' in which he calls for development of '1. A functional logic of use value; 2. An economic logic of exchange value; 3. A logic of symbolic exchange; 4. A logic of sign value. . . . Organized in accordance with one of the above groupings, the object assumes respectively the status of an *instrument, a commodity, a symbol, or a sign*' (*CPES*, p. 66). These distinctions allow Baudrillard to point to certain limitations in Marx's theory and the need for a semiological supplement. First he suggests that Marx's analysis of the commodity fails to address 'sign value' (*CPES*, pp. 66ff., *passim*). The commodity was analyzed by Marx primarily in terms of the relationships between exchange value and use value. Use value was defined by the use and enjoyment of a commodity in everyday life, whereas exchange value was defined by its worth in the marketplace. Capitalism produced commodities primarily for exchange value, and capitalists, Marx claimed, were more concerned with the profit extracted from production and exchange than with the actual uses of commodities.

For Marx, commodity fetishism referred to a mode of perception which perceived commodities simply as natural fulfilments of human needs and failed to see the social labor that produced them or the exploitation involved in this process.[10] Commodity fetishism thus projects values onto objects that are socially produced, mystifies them and fails to see their social-material underpinnings, just as in pre-capitalist societies individuals fetishized natural objects like trees or the moon as divine or supernatural, failing to see that they were simply products of nature.

Baudrillard believed that in contemporary capitalist society, fetishism had expanded, and that Marxian theories of value, commodities and fetishism must be further developed. Consumption in contemporary capitalist societies, Baudrillard argued, should be conceived of primarily as a process in which sign values are conspicuously consumed and the fetishism of commodities is not simply a projection and investment of values in certain privileged goods, but rather concerns fetishism of an entire system of social prestige and differentiation. Thus for Baudrillard fetishism involves entanglement in a whole system of (arbitrary, artificial) social differentiations organized and functionalized by the code of political economy social distinctions and prestige (*CPES*, pp. 88ff.).

In Baudrillard's theory, the capitalist mode of production thus produces a system of fetishized exchange values, use values *and* sign values through which commodities are displayed in consumption. Sign values are generated through hierarchical ordering among commodities, in which, for instance, certain types of cars or perfumes attain varying prestige through signifying the rank, social position and status of their owners or consumers. Sign values are thus characterized by differences and hierarchy, and are produced by what Baudrillard calls a 'sumptuary' operation connected to expenditure and social prestige. Sign values are thus linked to fashion and to what Veblen, one of Baudrillard's acknowledged influences, called 'conspicuous consumption.'

The analysis of sign values, Baudrillard believes, provides important insights, neglected by most Marxists, into the ways in which dominant sumptuary values are established, and thus into the ways in which the dominant class instils its tastes, values and privileges so as to achieve class domination (*CPES*, p. 115). He suggests that sign value is governed and organized by a code of political economy that marks the differences and establishes equivalences and a hierarchy of values. In Baudrillard's view, 'it is the code that is determinant: the rules of the interplay of signifiers and exchange value. Generalized in the system of political economy, it is the code which, in both cases reduces all symbolic *ambivalence* in order to ground the "rational" circulation of values and their play of exchange in the regulated equivalence of values' (*CPES*, pp. 146–7). It appears that by 'code,' Baudrillard is referring to the semiological structure of political economy – that is, to the rules which organize objects and meanings into a hierarchical system of prices, uses, values and prestige. The code manages the exchange of values just as language manages the interplay of signifier and signified (*CPES*, p. 146). That is, just as the rules and system of language determine meaning, reduce symbolic ambivalence and make possible communication, so the code of political economy determines the needs, uses and values possessed by various commodities and types of consumption. The code 'rationalizes and regulates exchange, makes things communicate, but only under the law of the code and through the control of meaning' (*CPES*, p. 147).

Baudrillard's key distinction is between the realm of value – produced and regulated by the code of political economy – and what he calls 'the symbolic' or 'symbolic exchange.' Whereas the latter is ineluctably ambivalent, thereby escaping regulation and control by any system or code, value is subject to a logic of equivalents, differentiation, substitution, order and control. In the next chapter (in 2.2), I shall further discuss the importance for Baudrillard of 'symbolic exchange,' which is opposed to all economic exchange governed by the 'the fundamental code of our society' that refers to the entire system of rules within political economy (*CPES*, p. 147).

Baudrillard's argument here is that the system of objects and signs produces homogenized, equivalent, rationalized and systematized needs for a world of objects that are the same for everyone. The result is a tautology of systemic power whereby the subject exhibits needs produced by the system, and the system satisfies these needs, reproducing them and thereby continuing the chain of consumption. Subjects are thus reduced to a socially produced system of needs, while objects are reduced to a homogenized system arranged in terms of sign values. Subjects, for Baudrillard, became mere 'productive forces.' His argument is that just as a subject is reduced to abstract labor power in production, carrying out social labor that any (exchangeable, equivalent) other person could do just as easily, so too the subject of consumption is reduced to a system of homogenized, rationalized and generalized needs. A 'logic of equivalence' thus rules the consumer society in which objects function equivalently as signs and have equivalent uses, values and purposes for all consumers, while all consumers have equivalent needs.

In this analysis, Baudrillard goes quite far with the structuralist critique of the subject as a mere product of the social system: 'The division of labor, the functional division of the terms of discourse, does not mystify people; it socializes them and informs their exchange according to a general abstract model. The very concept of the individual is the product of this general system of exchange' (*CPES*, p. 147). Individual needs – and the individual him or herself – are thus viewed as a product of the system of needs:

> Far from the individual expressing his needs in the economic system, it is the economic system that induces the individual function and the parallel functionality of objects and needs. The individual is an ideological structure, a historical form correlative with the commodity form (exchange value) and the object form (use value). The individual is nothing but the subject thought in economic terms, rethought, simplified and abstracted by the economy. The entire history of consciousness and ethics (all the categories of occidental psycho-metaphysics) is only the history of the political economy of the subject. (*CPES*, p. 133)

On Baudrillard's view, the analyses of sign values and fetishism will provide new insights into how social domination takes place. He suggests that neglect of these phenomena by most Marxists vitiates their understanding of how capitalism achieves power and control over individuals who allegedly fall prey to the values and practices of the consumer society and come to value objects according to that society's hierarchies and commodity sign values. Polemicizing against the alleged primacy of use value in the Marxian theory, Baudrillard writes that 'objects never exhaust themselves in the function they serve and in this excess of presence they take on their signification of prestige. They no longer "designate" the world, but rather the being and social rank of their possessor' (*CPES*, p. 32). Commodities are therefore not so much the locus of the satisfaction of needs, as classical political economy claims, but 'confer social meaning and prestige,' which serve as indices of social standing in the consumer society (*CPES*, p. 33).

Consequently, Baudrillard believes that, without a theory of sign value, political economy cannot explain *why* commodities become such objects of desire and fascination, why certain types of consumption take place (as, for example, conspicuous consumption), why certain commodities are preferred to others, and why consumption can take on such an important function in contemporary capitalist societies. The theory of sign value, Baudrillard argues, combined with what he calls a 'political economy of the sign,' explain these phenomena by pointing out that socially constructed prestige values (sign values) are appropriated and displayed in consumption. This theory implies that certain objects or brands are chosen over others because of their sign value – that is, their relative prestige over other brands or types of commodities – and because consumer societies are constituted by hierarchies of sign values in which one's social standing and prestige are determined by where one stands within the semiological system of consumption and sign values.

Baudrillard implies that members of the consumer society have some sense of the code, or system, of sign values, and thus can interpret other members' standing through the sign values they exhibit. Yet such a code of standing is somewhat indeterminate and ambiguous. In fact, Baudrillard is not as interested in sketching empirically the actual system of hierarchized consumer values in a given society as in investigating its social logic. Moreover, he admits the possibilities of some ambiguity within this system: 'A correct sociological analysis must be exercized in the concrete syntax of object ensembles . . . and in the lapses, incoherencies and contradictions of this discourse' (*CPES*, p. 37).

Toward a Semiology of Consumption and the Domestic Environment

In order to explore and map out the world and logic of consumption more fully, Baudrillard proposes a 'more subtle semiology of the environment and of everyday practices.' He believes that one can study the logic of consumption as a system, since

> objects, their syntax and their rhetoric refer to social objectives and to a social logic. They speak to us not so much of the user and of technical practices, as of social pretension and resignation, of social mobility and inertia, of acculturation and enculturation, of stratification and of social classification. Through objects, each individual and each group searches out her/his place in an order, all the while trying to jostle this order according to a personal trajectory. Through objects a stratified society speaks and, if like the mass media, objects seem to speak to everyone (there are no longer by right any caste objects), it is in order to keep everyone in a certain place. In short, under the rubric of objects, under the seal of private property, it is always a continual social process of value which leads the way. And everywhere and always, objects, in addition to utensils, are the terms and the avowal of the social process of value. (*CPES*, p. 38)

Baudrillard's most substantive sketch of this project is found in 'Sign Function and Class Logic.' He suggests here that a semiology of objects and consumption would analyze interiors and domestic spaces and the distribution of objects within them, as well as doing a 'vertical' analysis that would look at the hierarchical scale of each category of objects within the social universe (*CPES*, pp. 34ff.). Such a semiology of consumption would involve what he calls a 'rhetorical and syntactic analysis of the environment,' which would examine hierarchies of models and series of goods, as well as the organization and social use of objects.

This project is similar in some ways to Roland Barthes's analyses of fashion and food in *Système de la mode*.[11] Baudrillard suggests that after analyzing the structure of the system of objects in the consumer society, the social semiologist next move toward explicating the social logic of consumption by carrying out a 'strategic analysis of the practice of objects' (*CPES*, pp. 35ff.). Here objects are taken as 'indices of *social* membership' and 'as the scaffolding for a *global structure* of the environment, which is simultaneously an active structure of behavior' (*CPES*, p. 35). 'At bottom, individuals know themselves (if they do not feel themselves), to be judged by their objects, to be judged according to their objects and each at bottom submits to this judgment, though it be by disavowal' (*CPES*, p. 40). The middle classes in particular, he suggests, are forced to gain public recognition and legitimacy through consumption, precisely because of a deficit of prestige in their cultural, political and professional lives. But this fact in turn renders their prestige through commodities and consumption ambiguous, for 'behind their triumph as signs of social promotion they secretly proclaim (or avow) social defeat' (*CPES*, p. 40).

Demystifying what he calls the 'democratic alibi,' or 'universal,' of consumption, Baudrillard argues that, in fact, analysis of consumption provides indices of the extent to which the consumer society is stratified by class, as well as a sense of the immense differences between social classes in capitalist society. The analysis also suggests some of the ways in which class conflict is displaced as exploited classes succumb to the allures of consumption. Here Baudrillard sarcastically suggests that the consumer ethic among these subordinate classes functions as a new 'slave morality' whereby the frantic consumption of these classes is itself 'a sign of their social relegation,' which 'marks the limit of their social chances' (*CPES*, p. 61).

While 'Sign-Function and Class Logic' is one of Baudrillard's most stimulating articles, it also contains quite problematical perspectives on consumption which I shall criticize in the next section. Part of the problem is that in this and in his following works, Baudrillard carried out little phenomenological explication of his semiology of the environment and everyday life; thus his programmatic project set out in 'Sign-Function' is somewhat formal and abstract, and is not really carried through. One senses that Baudrillard is both fascinated and repelled, interested and then bored, by the object world that he confronts and describes in his early essays. Patience and immersion in the particular do not seem to be his particular virtues. Consequently, in his early essays – indeed throughout his work – he often opens interesting lines of thought and research and then jumps into something else – though, as we shall see, certain themes permeate his work and define its general contours.

Many other essays in *For a Critique of the Political Economy of the Sign* contain illuminating insights into the constitution and structure of everyday life in the consumer society. Most of the essays focus on the general logic of signification in political economy and especially on how consumption produces sign values. I shall discuss some of these essays in later chapters; but now I want to give a critical discussion of the contributions and limitations of the three books which mark the first stage of Baudrillard's work.

1.4   BAUDRILLARD AND POLITICAL ECONOMY

While Baudrillard's theory of sign value provides some important insights into the dynamics of consumption in the consumer society, it also provides a rather limited, one-sided theory of consumption. For Baudrillard, consumption consists more in the appropriation and display of sign values than in the use and enjoyment of objects as characterized by Marx.[12] Baudrillard, by contrast, argues that capitalism establishes social domination through the imposition of a system of sign values whereby individuals are situated within the consumer society and submit to its domination through the activity of consumption. This model rules out in advance, however, the possibility that consumption might be a sphere of self-activity, of self-valorization, of the use and enjoyment of objects for one's own ends, and instead conceptualizes it solely as a locus of class domination where individuals submit to the dictates of capital and assimilate its values and practices.

An alternative perspective on consumption is found in the work of Michel de Certeau.[13] In his book *The Practice of Everyday Life* and in other studies of oppositional practices, he shows various ways in which consumption can serve the interests of self-valorization and be used to promote the interests of individuals and oppositional groups against the hegemony of capital. Certeau points out that the French notion of *'usage'* can mean 'custom' in the sense of traditional, predefined, inherited patterns of use and behavior. Or it can signify 'the *manner* of employment,' the particular ways in which individuals use objects (as in the sense of 'customized' when individuals use, modify and perhaps transform objects to suit their needs and desires).[14]

Such a perspective is foreclosed in advance by Baudrillard, who assumes that all needs, use values and consumption are entirely produced and controlled by the system of the consumer society. Baudrillard denies all human agency and creativity, and fails to analyze any of the ways in which commodities can be integrated into our own projects and self-valorization. While people and societies have always organized their lives around objects, Baudrillard makes it appear that in the consumer society, objects organize people's lives and are demiurges of social domination that individuals cannot use for their own purposes, enjoyment or projects.

Certeau, on the contrary, suggests exploring the ways in which the 'consumer sphinx' produces its own practices, styles and uses of objects. This would involve drawing up *'the repertoire on which the users draw to make up their own performances. . . .* [which] form the lexicon for the users' practices.'[15] This project would then carry out such studies of how individuals watch, listen to and use films, television and popular music; how they decorate and structure their homes to serve their own needs and interests; and how inventiveness and creativity is possible in cooking and other consumer practices.

Now obviously the consumer industries have attempted to manage and control all the spheres of consumption and to control leisure activity to promote their aims and interests; but Certeau suggests that individuals can and do resist the objects and practices of the cultural and consumer industries. He proposes developing strategies and tactics for waging commodity struggle in ways such that individuals, and not corporations or corporate capital, primarily benefit. These tactics would range from 'borrowing' – a euphemism for ripping off objects from work for use at home – to producing one's own food, clothes and objects, thus circumventing commodification and the market.

For Baudrillard, by contrast, consumption is solely a mode of commodification, social integration and domination. To be sure, this is how the consumer society manages to assert its power over many individuals, and Baudrillard provides some valuable insights into how this takes place. But in a curious way he projects the fantasy of capitalists – what we might call *the capitalist imaginary* – as the governing principle of the consumer society.[16] In other words, Baudrillard describes precisely how capitalists would like the world to be. He assumes that the consumer society and consumption are managed and controlled by capital merely to ensure the maximization of profits and power by the capitalist class. Further, he sees consumption and sign values as the ways in which the capitalist class controls society. Baudrillard rules out the possibility of consumption being used in ways that would serve individual needs and interests or of it being structured by individuals as a sphere of opposition (to work, to exploitation, to repression, to production) which might actually create new problems of management for capital (as when workers' demands for higher wages for more consumption cut into profits and so on).[17]

Thus, as Harry Cleaver insists in *Reading Capital Politically*, all social phenomena should be analyzed both from the standpoint of the working class and from the standpoint of capital, or, using Antonio Negri's term, from the standpoint of self-valorization versus that of capital-valorization.[18] On this view, consumption – or any activity – can be directed toward self-valorization if the subject realizes his or her goals or receives self-gratification from the process and if the activity undermines capital realization rather than contributing to it. However, Baudrillard's analysis analyzes consumption solely from the standpoint of the capitalist class, by describing only how consumption serves to integrate individuals into the consumer society so that they may serve the interests of class domination. While this procedure provides valuable insights into some of the mechanisms of class domination, it is one-sided, and fails to conceptualize ways in which class conflict, resistance and oppositional practices are also bound up with the sphere of consumption. Thus he completely rules out oppositional practices or self-valorization in this sphere.

Moreover, a central theoretical problem emerges in Baudrillard's work from this period. For Baudrillard never clearly or systematically defines his central semiological categories of the 'code' which determines the hierarchy of sign value within what he calls 'general political economy.' Thus, although he constantly claims that sign values are determined by a 'code,' he neither clearly defines the code which determines the hierarchy of sign values in the system of commodity signification in the consumer society nor indicates how it is produced or who produces it.[19] There is no institutional analysis in (any of) Baudrillard's works; nor does he assign determination or control of the code to any specific class, groups or individuals. Moreover, he uses the term 'code' in a sometimes confusing multiplicity of ways. Usually it refers to the structure of the entire system of political economy in which all commodities are assigned certain sign values through the system as a whole, just as exchange value is determined in Marx's theory. In other places, where he claims that the 'commodity is a code,' Baudrillard uses the term to refer to the imposition of the code of the commodity on social life as a new model of social organization, and thus refers simply to what Marxists call 'commodification.' Still later in his work (see ch. 3), Baudrillard detaches code from the general system of political economy and uses it to refer to a variety of simulation models which are imposed upon and thus come to structure and organize social reality.

Yet in his first three books, Baudrillard generally seems to use the term 'code' in the singular to stand for the system of political economy as a whole and the rules and the hierarchies through which differences and sign values of commodities are produced and regulated. The analogy would then be to the semiological theory of language, which produces meaning through differences, rules of the interplay of signifiers, rules relating signifiers to the signified, and so on. Yet it is not clear that this linguistic analogy is particularly appropriate on a theoretical level; for it is difficult to imagine how we might detect and establish the rules of the production of sign values with the same rigor and accuracy with which we can analyze language. Instead, Baudrillard's linguistic analogy seems to call attention to the ways in which consumption communicates and signifies, rather than providing analytic tools for rigorous systematization and formalization of the 'laws' of consumption.

Moreover, there is no analysis in Baudrillard of contradictions, conflicts and shifts in sign value. Advertising wars in capitalist societies are predicated on the possibility of positioning one's car, soft drink or hamburger as more prestigious and valuable than those of one's competitors, and there is a conflicting and shifting contest among various commodities for their place in the hierarchy of sign value. Rather than equivalence and nonambivalence being the rule for sign value, careful investigation of the advertising and consumer world shows that different products take on different values and different positions in the hierarchy of the sign world as fashion, advertising campaigns and consumer habits shift and mutate, often deliriously. Baudrillard, by contrast, views the code as an overarching regulative principle or system that determines the relative prestige or sign value of commodities; but it is not clear who establishes the code or how, or how it functions in specific cases.

Thus, Baudrillard's theory does not seem to account for the role of advertising in the consumer society and the conflicts, ambiguities and waste it produces. Rather than advertising being subject to a code which reduces symbolic ambivalence in the production of sign values, specific ads are predicated on a practice which systematically produces ambiguities and competition in sign value through claims that its products are best; while its competitors make counterclaims in a war of position whose outcome is determined by amorphous market choices and not – recognizably at least – by a master code. Thus it is doubtful whether there is a pre-established code that produces rank and hierarchy of sign values, which are frequently rated quite differently in different societies, regions, subcultures, or even by different individuals. And even if there is, Baudrillard does not tell us where to look for it or much about it.

Furthermore, I believe that there are more useful semiological theories of code and production of meaning than Baudrillard's. For example, in Barthes's semiological theory of code in *S/Z*, there is an interplay of a multiplicity of codes in which meaning is overdetermined, open to a multiplicity of readings and constantly changing. This theory of code seems more appropriate to analysis of commodity sign values than Baudrillard's more monolithic code, which is analogous to language as a system which produces a homogenized, equivalent system of values.[20] Against Baudrillard's semiological model that assimilates cultural phenomena such as consumption to a model of language, one could argue that linguistic models are inappropriate to certain domains of everyday life, and that Baudrillard's semiological reduction is predicated on a false analogy between natural language and consumption, between the production of linguistic meaning and the production of sign value.

In Baudrillard's later writings, he abandons his attempts to develop semiological theories of the life of signs, codes and messages in the consumer society and no longer makes the consumer society per se a central focus of his analysis. In both his earlier and later writings, Baudrillard neither defines adequately or illustrates some of his basic semiological concepts, nor does he actually explicate a system of hierarchies and organizations of commodities in any given social field, as Barthes does with regard to fashion in *Système de la mode* or reading a text in *S/Z*, beyond some sketchy remarks in *La société de consommation* or *For a Critique of the Political Economy of the Sign*. Thus, while Baudrillard often presents some extremely interesting semiological analyses and programs of research, he often fails to define and illustrate his central semiological categories, and does not always systematically develop his theory. Consequently, he does not carry through some of his most interesting research programs, such as the ones set forth in the essays in *Critique*. Therefore, he ultimately fails both in elaborating a theory of the consumer society and in carrying out a sufficient number of concrete investigations of the commodity world to illustrate and substantiate his ideas.

In addition, for the most part, Baudrillard severs his analysis of consumption and signification from analysis of production and the logic of capital. He hardly ever analyzes the mode of production or the labor process, or the relations between the systems of production, distribution, exchange and consumption – though in *La société de consommation* he indicates that consumption should be analyzed in relation to the system of production. Although Baudrillard seems to imply, against Marx's emphasis on the primacy of production, that in the consumer society consumption and circulation are what primarily produce needs and values and thus are the primary determinants of social organization and behavior, he never really documents or substantiates this, and in fact does not discuss such salient features of a capitalist economy as profit, savings, investment, surplus, sectors of the economy or corporate advertising, marketing or packaging strategies.

The problem with Baudrillard's reconstruction of political economy is that in some instances he reacts so strongly against classical Marxian positions that the logic of production or capital realization completely disappears from view. Indeed, Baudrillard is never really clear concerning whether the consumerist logic of signification – that is, the production of sign-value – is independent of the logic of capital accumulation, or even determines it. He never analyzes their actual relations and interconnections, since the logic of capital is rarely a focus of his analysis. Thus, in reading Baudrillard's early works, it is impossible to determine whether he intends to reject classical and Marxian political economy altogether, or whether his enterprise – at least through 1973 – is intended to supplement or replace Marxian political economy with analyses of consumption and the role of signification in the consumer society.

The best way to make use of Baudrillard's analysis is, I believe, as a semiological supplement to Marx's theory of political economy. Since Marx focused his energies primarily on analysis of production and the labor process, Baudrillard's analysis of consumption provides a useful supplement to classical Marxism. Moreover, using semiological theories of sign value calls attention to how value is constructed socially in the consumer society and how commodities function in people's lives to provide a lure and fascination which constitute a significant aspect of the life world of contemporary capitalist societies. The limitations of Baudrillard's social theory, however, are that he tends to downplay or neglect the continuing importance of labor and production in contemporary social formations and to project a rather monolithic model of contemporary capitalist societies without contradictions, crises or apparent possibilities of radical social transformation.

This critique raises the thorny question of Baudrillard's relation to Marxism, an issue that I shall take up in the next chapter.

2

Beyond Marxism

Baudrillard's relation to Marxism is extremely complex and volatile. As I have argued, his first two books can be read as a supplement to and development of the Marxian critique of political economy which follow Marxian explorations of production into the mode of consumption and can be utilized to develop a neo-Marxian critical theory of capitalism. For in these books Baudrillard at least occasionally relates consumption to the mode of production, focuses on the commodity and its uses, and engages in class analysis and critical demystifications of dominant ideologies of consumption, leisure and so on. But his third book, *For a Critique of the Political Economy of the Sign*, begins to criticize certain Marxian notions more aggressively, and the later books, *The Mirror of Production* and *L'échange symbolique et la mort*, carry out a wholesale rejection of Marxism and thus constitute a break with Marxian theory.[1] Yet throughout this period, Baudrillard continues to situate his work within a problematic of 'critical' and 'revolutionary' social theory, in contrast to his later 'postmodern' works, which enter into a completely different theoretical universe and attempt to take radical social theory and politics into a new post-Marxian problematic.

In this chapter, I will sketch Baudrillard's critique of, then break with, classical Marxism, while pointing to his alternative social theory and politics. I will also examine the extent to which his criticisms are either justified and may thus be seen to constitute an advance beyond classical Marxism, or simply fall behind Marx and the other radical social theorists of the day. At stake in this chapter, therefore, is whether Baudrillard properly understands and legitimately criticizes Marx, or whether his critique applies more properly to bourgeois economics rather than Marxism; and whether Baudrillard does or does not provide an advance over previous theories of political economy, Marxian or non-Marxian.

2.1   MARX, NEEDS AND USE VALUES

In the last chapter, I argued that Baudrillard's major contributions to political economy and radical social theory include his notion of the political economy of the sign, which combines semiological analysis of sign value with the Marxian theory of the commodity and critique of capitalism. His semiological perspective also allows him to produce a provocative critique of the theories of needs, use values and commodities that he finds in both bourgeois political economy and Marxism. Baudrillard claims that there is no such thing as pure use value or a pure subject with essential needs for whom objects have essential uses. Rather, he argues that both needs and uses are socially constructed, through a system of political economy that produces sign values whereby objects acquire meaning or allure which seduce the consumer into purchasing commodities as objects of desire and prestige. From this position, Baudrillard attacks the strategy of Marxists who appeal to the primacy of use value over exchange value and the anthropology of basic human needs which is then used to critique false needs. Baudrillard argues instead that since both use value and needs are socially constructed, the concepts of human needs and use values cannot be used to attack their alleged distortions under capitalism.

Yet he also criticizes bourgeois notions of utility, rational preference and the ideology that consumption primarily aims at maximizing utility value through consumer choice, by arguing that utility, or use value, is a product of political economy, which itself produces the system of needs and use values that rationalize and functionalize an economic subject. Baudrillard claims that the system of political economy organizes and reduces hetrogeneous and complex desires into a rationalized system of needs and thus produces a rationalized subject. Baudrillard's argument is that just as commodities are conceived by Marx as embodiments of certain quantities of abstract labor, which he calls 'socially necessary labor time,' and just as exchange value is conceived by Marx as the embodiment of equivalents of determinate quantities of abstract labor time, so use values are determined by a logic of equivalence within the system of political economy. On this view, the socioeconomic system produces a system of objects with predefined uses which are as much a product of the system as the objects themselves; thus one 'uses' a car as a sign of belonging and of status, as well as for transportation. Likewise, the system produces *needs* for objects like luxury cars and fashionable clothes to manage consumer demand and to establish hierarchies of social differentiation. Thus, Baudrillard polemicizes against the notion of essential human needs and basic human use values for commodities by arguing that both needs and use values are socially constructed as part of a *system* of homogenized, rationalized and func-tionalized objects and needs (*CPES*, pp. 63ff., 130ff., *passim*).

Baudrillard's other key point is that the individual produced by political economy is rationalized and functionally integrated into a system of needs whose 'satisfaction' reproduces their own social domination. Baudrillard is thus suspicious of all Marxian attempts to appeal to use values or needs to criticize capitalism or to advocate more rational consumption or to distinguish between true and false needs or to advocate socialism on the grounds that it would lead to production according to use values for human needs rather than exchange values for capitalist profits. Yet I would argue that Baudrillard sets up something of a straw-man Marx, and greatly exaggerates the alleged naturalism in Marx's theory of needs and use value. I will also suggest that Baudrillard's theory of sign value is compatible with a historical materialist approach to use values, needs and consumption.

Baudrillard claims that Marx assumes that use values exist prior to commodity production and exchange and that they stand in direct relation to pre-existing natural human needs which they are supposed to satisfy (*CPES*, pp. 130ff., and *MoP*, pp. 22ff.). Although there may be some passages in Marx that might suggest such a reading – and there may be some Marxists who indeed read Marx this way – it can be shown that this naturalism is inconsistent with Marx's historical materialism, and that other passages in Marx suggest a much closer link with Baudrillard's own historicist position.

Robert D'Amico points out that when in *Capital* Marx seems to speak of natural and immediate universal human needs, 'The terms *natural* and *immediate* do not refer to a fixed need . . . but to the form of appearance of objects.'[2] Marx indeed speaks of commodities having a *double form*, by which he means both a natural form and a value form. His point is that while commodities appear in their natural form as the direct expression of human needs, they are in fact socially produced – which is precisely Baudrillard's point. Moreover, I would add that it is the bourgeois political economy which claims that commodities satisfy pre-existing natural needs and contain inherent use values against which Marx is constantly polemicizing. Against the position, maintained by capitalists and their ideological supporters to this day, that they are just giving people what they want and are just satisfying people's pre-existing needs, Marx consistently argues that commodity production and exchange constitute a social and historical process which produces needs, use values and ideologies to assure class domination (see citations below). But whereas Baudrillard claims that all needs and use values are completely socially constructed and merely serve as an 'alibi' for capitalist domination (that is, that they are giving people what they need), Marx argues that needs and use values are merely socially *mediated*, shaped and channelled by sociohistorical practices and conditions, and thus allows the formulation – which I shall soon take up – of needs and use values that can be directed against the existing social system.

Indeed, Baudrillard glosses over or ignores key passages that set out Marx's and Engels's historical materialist position, as in *The German*

Ideology, where they write that 'the satisfaction of the first need, the action of satisfying and the instrument of satisfaction which has been acquired, leads to new needs; and this creation of new needs is the first historical act.' There are also passages in Marx's *Grundrisse* which argue that human needs, objects and uses are sociohistorically constructed. And in 'Wage Labor and Capital,' Marx writes that 'Our desires and pleasures spring from society. We measure them, therefore, by society and not by the objects which serve for their satisfaction. Because they are of a social nature, they are of a relative nature.' Finally, in *Capital*, Marx writes: 'The coat is a use-value that satisfies a particular want. Its existence is the result of a special sort of productive activity, the nature of which is determined by its aim, mode of operation, subject, means and result.' This argument refers equally well to Marx's perspective on commodities like a coat, the uses to which people put coats and the needs that they satisfy. In addition, in the chapter on machinery in *Capital*, Marx continually points out how machines and technologies produce use values and themselves represent a form of socially constructed use value that is variable in different societies at different periods of history.[3] These arguments and many other passages in Marx could be marshaled against a view of natural, pregiven needs or use values and in support of a theory of needs and use values as historically and socially mediated. Indeed, such a position is central to Marx's historical materialist theory, for which all phenomena are socially mediated and products of history.

Thus, I believe that Baudrillard's polemic against Marx's theory of use value and needs, – albeit much celebrated by his followers, – is clearly predicated on a one-sided reading of Marx, and downplays the extent to which his own position builds on a more historicized version of Marxism. For although Marx occasionally seems to naturalize use values and needs, at other points he stresses that they are socially constructed and specific to given social formations. Indeed, I believe that Baudrillard fails to indicate how some of his own reflections on commodities, needs and consumption were anticipated by Marx, as early as the *Economic and Philosophical Manuscripts of 1844*, in which Marx analyzed the production of needs, advertising, huckstering and the power of money in capitalist society.[4]

Yet in some ways Baudrillard's analysis provides a substantial advance over classical Marxism. Although Marx stressed the sociohistorical production of needs, he never analyzed how needs were produced, ordered and systematized by signs – that is, by the working of semiology. Since advertising, fashion, mass media, and so on were not as well developed in his day as in ours, Marx failed to perceive the important role of sign value and social differentiation in structuring needs and value. Moreover, he never really conceptualized how a system of needs would provide a logic of social differentiation which would be increasingly functionalized, rationalized and systematized.

Yet, Baudrillard goes much further than Marx when he claims that *all* needs and use values are socially created and so cannot be used as concepts to criticize specifically alienating uses or false needs. By presenting the concepts of needs and use value as solely the product of capitalism and political economy, Baudrillard is unable to articulate standpoints from which one can criticize capitalist society or present oppositional consumer practices or politics, since in his view all consumption serves simply to integrate individuals into the system of needs and objects.[5] Against this monolithic postulation of needs and use values as purely a means of social integration and control, I would argue that Baudrillard's perspectives on needs, commodities and consumption are one-sided and incomplete. For he is theorizing use values and needs strictly from the standpoint of how they are perceived by capital and how capitalists might fantasize that they are actually producing use values and needs. From a two-class or multi-perspectival standpoint, however, one can see that commodities have various uses, some defined by the system of political economy and some created by consumers or users.[6] The system of political economy attempts to produce needs and specific utilities for objects, but individuals may in fact use objects in quite different ways from those and may exert much more autonomy and creativity within the sphere of consumption than Baudrillard allows. For him, however, use values and needs – and even the individual (see 1.3) – are completely a function and effect of the system of needs and commodities which govern and control all consumption and other activity in the consumer society.

Thus, for example, although capital produces cars and computers not only to realize profit but also to impose a social system or way of life on individuals, these commodities can be customized, used and circulated for a variety of purposes and goals with a corresponding variety of effects. Computers can be used to produce and circulate revolutionary theory, as well as to integrate workers into a new cybernetic/information society. In general, use values have two aspects: those designed and reproduced by capital and those produced and developed by independent producers and consumers.[7] Music, for example, can be seen as the outcome of needs for self-expression, social communication and bonding. Capital, by contrast, can commodify music and use it to sell records and concerts, whereas individuals may use it to circulate subversive messages, thereby giving rise to new values and visions of life which may be antithetical to existing capitalist societies.

In discriminating between various types and objects of production and consumption in various social systems, I believe that concepts of needs and use value are useful and even necessary, and thus that Baudrillard's suggestion that we eliminate these concepts from the discourse of social critique should be resisted. Although it would be a conceptual mistake to think that there are essential human needs and/or use values which we could use to measure the value of commodities or consumer practices, I believe that we can specify what needs and use values of various commodities serve our own purposes and self-defined needs (that is, what furthers the goals of self-valorization in opposition to capital-valorization); and that we can establish hierarchies of needs and use values that will enable us to measure the extent to which varying commodities are useful and valuable to us. Further, social theorists can also calculate the extent to which a given society is or is not fulfilling the needs of its citizens at a certain level of social development concerning which there is a consensus (that is, that an individual requires a certain standard of living, health care, education and so on). Here, however, one should be clear that one's concepts of needs and use value are normative constructs that are variable, plural and subject to constant scrutiny and revision.

In fact, I would suggest that most individuals and societies *do* prioritize needs and the use values of commodities in everyday consumer practices and social policies, although individuals and societies may not always be clear as to what they actually need or what is useful. Here processes of experimentation and inquiry can help determine whether commodities, practices, ideas and so forth are really useful and valuable. Then processes of dialogue or struggle can help build a consensus as to what a given society needs at a certain stage of its development. But I would see it as more useful to be clear and discriminating about the hierarchy of one's needs and the use values of different products than simply to expel altogether, as Baudrillard does, the concepts of needs and use values as part of the capitalist system of domination which have no relative autonomy or autonomous value for the individual.

Rather, I believe that we can discover what will fill our various needs and develop our various potentials through critical scrutiny of our experience with commodities and consumption, combined with observation of other consumer practices. With effort, we can discern what we need to be healthy, happy and creative (or whatever we take our ultimate values to be) and what products or activities neither provide genuine satisfaction and well-being nor fulfil whatever goals and values we posit. One can always be mistaken or deluded, but in at least some degree one can generally determine one's needs and create one's own use values, and thus evaluate commodities according to their uses for specific ends and projects. Likewise I believe that societies can also determine a hierarchy of goods and services which will satisfy certain needs and promote certain values. Thus, against Baudrillard, I would argue that concepts of needs and use values can continue to be useful in social theory and practice as long as one is aware of the provisional, conventional and normative nature of what one determines as needs and use values, and hence that the challenge of constructing a socialist, or any noncapitalist, society requires defining and prioritizing needs and use values.

For Baudrillard, on the contrary, consumption follows a 'logic of signification' in which sign value is determined by the relative standing in the system of hierarchies concerning the commodity bought and used. Thus, under the rule of 'the logic of signification' 'needs lose all their autonomy; they are coded. Consumption no longer has a value of enjoyment per se; it is placed under the constraint of an absolute finality which is that of production' (*MoP*, p. 128). Baudrillard is thus claiming that within the consumer society there are no longer independent needs; all needs are socially coded and serve to induce consumers to buy products by which to socially position themselves and thus submit to domination by the logic of corporate capital. As I have already suggested, this position projects the imaginary of the capitalist class, thereby ruling out other perspectives on needs and consumptions.

There is one passage, however, in *Critique* which suggests the perspective on needs that I am presenting. In a footnote, almost as an afterthought, Baudrillard writes: 'Nonetheless, this emergence of needs, however formal and subdued, is never without danger for the social order – as is the liberation of any productive forces. Apart from being the dimension of exploitation, it is also the origin of the most violent social contradictions, of class struggle. Who can say what historical contradictions the emergence and exploitation of this new productive force – that of needs – holds in store for us?' (*CPES*, p. 84). Baudrillard does not illustrate or pursue this line of thought, however, and in general I would argue that while he provides powerful insights into how capital attempts to rationalize, organize and systematize needs and use values, he ignores or downplays analysis of how individuals can engage in struggle, resistance and alternative cultural practices, and soon he will abandon a posture of radical opposition altogether. Thus to the extent that capital does not control the totality of our needs and uses of commodities and consumption, Baudrillard's perspective is limited and flawed – although his analysis *does* provide insight into the mechanisms and extent to which needs and use values are actually constructed in existing productivist societies.

Consequently, there are problems with Baudrillard's much celebrated polemic against needs and use values, even if his theory of sign value provides important new dimensions to radical critique of neo-capitalist societies and his critiques of some of the concepts of bourgeois and Marxian political economy are valuable. Yet in texts after *Critique* Baudrillard accelerates his criticism of classical Marxism, and eventually breaks with Marxism altogether. It is to this crucial development that we will next turn.

2.2 MARX AND *THE MIRROR OF PRODUCTION*

Baudrillard began to criticize certain Marxian theories and terminology in *Critique*; there he distanced himself from Marxian dialectical categories, rejecting the distinctions between base and superstructure and hence between economics and ideology, 'along with the desperate contortions ("superstructure," "dialectic," "structure in dominance") that this entails' (*CPES*, pp. 143–4). Baudrillard also polemicized against the Marxian categories of alienation, ideology, and so forth, yet proposed a new synthesis of Marxism and semiology which would preserve at least certain aspects of the Marxian theory. Rejecting a one-sided Marxian economism that refuses or is unable to perceive the roles of signs and culture, as well as a one-sided semiology which focuses only on signs, Baudrillard writes: 'The object of this political economy, that is, its simplest component, its nuclear element – that which precisely the commodity was for Marx – is no longer today properly either commodity or sign, but indissolubly both' (*CPES*, p. 148).

Against classical Marxism, Baudrillard argues that the object of political economy must be conceptualized as a sign as well as a commodity, at the same time suggesting to semiologists that objects be regarded as commodities as well as signs. In addition, he criticizes Marx's failure to adequately conceptualize communications, and rejects attempts to develop a Marxian theory of the media (*CPES*, pp. 164ff.; see my discussion in 3.2). Nonetheless, he continued to use many Marxist categories and theories, while attempting to supplement or reconstruct the Marxist critique of political economy in his analyses of the consumer society, the media and so on in *Critique* before abandoning Marxism altogether in *The Mirror of Production*.

In *Mirror*, Baudrillard argues that Marx's categories and theory are too conservative to be useful to revolutionary theory, because they are too deeply embedded in political economy to be of use in constructing a new social order free from the imperatives of production and political economy. Baudrillard thus rejects Marxism both as a 'mirror,' or reflection, of a 'productivist' capitalism and as a 'classical' mode of representation that purports to mirror 'the real.' He thus participates in the poststructuralist critique of representational thought, and utilizes Jacques Lacan's notion of 'the mirror stage' and the 'imaginary,' arguing that in 'the mirror of production' – that is, political economy and Marxism – individuals come to an 'imaginary' understanding of production, labor, value, their place in the world, human nature and the rest (*MoP*, pp. 19ff.).[8] This Marxian imaginary speaks to what is wrong with life under capitalism – alienated labor, exploitation and so on – and provides a fantasy of a nonalienated life – development of productive forces for human use, autonomous, worker-controlled, self-fulfilling labor, and dictatorship of the proletariat whereby workers control society and so forth. Yet the Marxian imaginary, Baudrillard maintains, simply reproduces the primacy of production, which is itself a product of capitalism and closes off what Baudrillard takes as more radical possibilities for liberation.

Baudrillard's critique parallels to some extent critiques by Habermas and others who see Marx's 'productivist' logic as too reductive, because it reduces everything to labor and the mode of production and so cannot account for many social phenomena like communication.[9] Baudrillard's critique goes beyond this position, however, and is more dismissive of Marx than Habermas, who implies that Marx's theory is of some use in that it adequately conceptualizes the logic of production and thus can be used to analyze this sphere, while Baudrillard rejects Marxism entirely, arguing that Marx's theory of production is itself flawed and problematic.

In *The Mirror of Production* Baudrillard gives his critique in five separate studies which are linked in critical strategy. In each he shows how Marxism is inadequate when it comes to describing 'primitive,' 'archaic' and feudal societies, and must be abandoned to clear the way for more adequate perspectives on the respective phenomena under investigation. But the main point behind his critique emerges in the fifth study, where he argues that Marxian theory provides inadequate perspectives not only on contemporary capitalist societies, but on a revolutionary alternative as well, and thus must be abandoned by contemporary revolutionary theory. I shall briefly recapitulate here some of Baudrillard's most striking criticisms of classical Marxism, and attempt to show that his critique of Marxism at this point is motivated by both theoretical and political concerns that are themselves open to question.

In his study of 'The Concept of Labor' (*MoP*, pp. 21ff.), Baudrillard polemicizes against what he calls the 'anthropology' and 'ethic' of labor which he sees as characterizing most versions of Marxism. For Marx, labor is the primary human activity through which basic human needs are satisfied and human potentialities are developed. He saw labor as alienated under capitalism to the extent that it precluded full development of human potentialities. For Marxism, overcoming alienated labor would thus involve constructing another mode of labor and another system of production whereby individuals themselves controlled the labor process and the fruits of their labor, while at the same time engaging in a wealth of activities to fully develop their many-sided being.

Against the anthropology and ethic of labor, Baudrillard suggests that this view of human nature and value is precisely the capitalist view of human beings as production machines, a view which in fact presupposes capitalist values of unchained and unlimited productivity as the goal of life. 'Historical materialism, dialectics, modes of production, labor power – through these concepts Marxist theory has sought to shatter the abstract universality of the concepts of bourgeois thought (Nature and Progress, Man and Reason, formal Logic, Work, Exchange, etc.). Yet Marxism in turn universalizes them with a "critical" imperialism as ferocious as the other's' (*MoP*, p. 47).

Once again, Baudrillard is setting up a straw-man Marx and ignoring the many passages in which Marx presents his goal as achieving a 'realm of freedom' beyond labor, a new society which he describes as a 'free association,' and a vision of social life, based on his analysis of the Paris Commune, in which social activity would supplant labor and production as the organizing principle of society.[10] Some Marxists, Baudrillard admits, supplement the ethic of labor with what he calls an aesthetic of play (for example, Marcuse); but Baudrillard proposes what he considers (at this point) a more radical alternative. In place of the domination of all human activity in capitalist society by exchange value or use value (that is, the idea that what is valuable is that which is useful or has monetary worth), Baudrillard proposes valorization of precisely what has no value (in capitalist terms), but only symbolic value. Thus he is proposing a new concept, that of symbolic exchange. Since this is a key theoretical and political concept for Baudrillard at this point, we will now discuss his alternative framework and politics in some detail.

Bataille and Symbolic Exchange

While one finds references to symbolic exchange in his earlier writings (_CPES_, pp. 30, 64ff., 97ff., 123ff., 206ff.), starting with _Mirror_, Baudrillard sharply contrasts 'symbolic exchange' to consumption, production and all realization of either use values, sign values or exchange values. The term was deeply influenced by Georges Bataille's notion of a 'general economy,' in which expenditure, waste, sacrifice and destruction were claimed to be more fundamental than economies of production and utility. Bataille took as his model the sun, which freely expends its energy without asking anything in return. He argued that if individuals want to be truly sovereign – that is, free from the imperatives of capitalism – they should pursue a 'general economy' of expenditure, giving, sacrifice and destruction so as to escape determination by existing imperatives of utility.

Bataille saw human beings as creatures of _excess_, with excessive energy, fantasies, drives, needs and so on. From this point on, Baudrillard presupposes the truth of Bataille's anthropology and general economy. In a 1976 review of a volume of Bataille's _Complete Works_, Baudrillard wrote: 'The central idea is that the economy which governs our societies results from a misappropriation of the fundamental human principle, which is a solar principle of expenditure.'[11] In the early 1970s, Baudrillard took over Bataille's anthropological position and what he calls Bataille's 'aristocratic critique' of capitalism, which is allegedly grounded in the crass notions of utility and savings rather than the more sublime 'aristocratic' notion of excess and expenditure. Bataille and Baudrillard presuppose here a contradiction between human nature and capitalism. They maintain that humans 'by nature' gain pleasure from such things as expenditure, waste, festivities, sacrifices and suchlike, in which they are sovereign, and are free to expend their energy excess and thus follow their 'real nature'. The capitalist imperatives of labor, utility, savings and so on are by implication 'unnatural,' and go against human nature.

Baudrillard argues that the Marxian critique of capitalism, by contrast, merely attacks exchange value, while exalting use value and hence utility, instrumental rationality and so forth, thereby

> seeking a *good use* of the economy. Marxism is therefore only a limited petit bourgeois critique, one more step in the banalization of life toward the 'good use' of the social! Bataille, to the contrary, sweeps away all this slave dialectic from an aristocratic point of view, that of the master struggling with his death. One can accuse this perspective of being pre- or post-Marxist. At any rate, Marxism is only the disenchanted horizon of capital – all that precedes or follows it is more radical than it is (p. 60).

This passage is highly revealing, and marks Baudrillard's switch to an 'aristocratic critique' of political economy, one that is deeply influenced by Bataille and Nietzsche (see 3.5 where I discuss the Nietzschean turn and elements in Baudrillard). For Bataille and Baudrillard are presenting a version of Nietzsche's 'aristocratic,' 'master morality,' in which value articulates an excess, an overflow and an intensification of life energies. Baudrillard would continue to attack the bourgeoisie, capital, political economy and so forth, but from a point of view which valorizes 'aristocratic' expenditure and sumptuary, aesthetic and symbolic values. The dark side of his switch in political allegiance is a valorization of sacrifice and death; this informs his succeeding work *L'échange symbolique et la mort*, which I will discuss in both 3.1 and chapter 4. Here, however, I will note a major departure from Bataille that Baudrillard highlights in his review.

Although Bataille founds his general economy on a 'solar economy' without reciprocal exchange, an economy in which the sun unilaterally bestows its energy and warmth on the earth, thereby providing a model of unilateral gift giving and free bestowing of excess, Baudrillard claims that Bataille has misunderstood Marcel Mauss's concept of the gift.[12] He argues that

> the unilateral gift does not exist. This is not the law of the universe. He who has so well explored the human sacrifice of the Aztecs should have known as they did that the sun gives nothing, it is necessary to nourish it continually with human blood in order that it shine. It is necessary to challenge [*défier*] the gods through sacrifice in order that they respond with profusion. In other words, the root of sacrifice and of general economy is never pure and simple expenditure – or whatever drive [*pulsion*] of excess that supposedly comes to us from nature – but is an incessant process of challenge [*défi*] (p. 61).

Hereafter the notion of *challenge* becomes a critical anthropological key to Baudrillard's theory, which is rooted in a metaphysical view of the world which emerges full-blown only in his later works (see chapter 6). Yet we see that he was already extricating himself from the familiar Marxian universe of production and class struggle into a quite different neo-aristocratic, metaphysical world view. Baudrillard seems to assume at this point that pre-capitalist societies are governed by forms of symbolic exchange similar to Bataille's notion of a general economy, supplemented by Mauss's theory of the gift and countergift, rather than by production and utility. Thus Baudrillard presupposes a fundamental dividing line in history between symbolic societies – that is, societies fundamentally organized around symbolic exchange – and productivist societies – (that is, societies organized around production). He thus rejects the Marxian philosophy of history which posits the primacy of production in all societies, and rejects the Marxian concept of socialism, arguing that it does not break radically enough with capitalist productivism, but offers itself merely as a more efficient and equitable organization of production rather than as a completely different sort of society with a different logic, values and life activities.

Thus, in effect, Baudrillard is positing – or dreaming of – another break in history as radical as the rupture between symbolic societies and capitalism, a break which would constitute a return to symbolic societies as his 'revolutionary' alternative. Henceforth, he will oppose – in one way or another – his ideal of symbolic exchange to the logic of production, utility and instrumental rationality which governs capitalist (and existing socialist) societies. 'Symbolic exchange' thus emerges as Baudrillard's 'revolutionary' alternative to the values and practices of capitalist society, and stands for a variety of heterogeneous activities in his writings of the 1970s. For instance, he writes in *Critique*: 'The exchange of looks, the present which comes and goes, are like the air people breathe in and out. This is the metabolism of exchange, prodigality, festival – and also of destruction (which returns to non-value what production has erected, valorized). In this domain, value isn't even recognized' (*CPES*, p. 207). A more systematic discussion of symbolic exchange, however, is found in *The Mirror of Production*, where he writes: 'The symbolic social relation is the uninterrupted cycle of giving and receiving, which, in primitive exchange, includes the consumption of the "surplus" and deliberate anti-production' (*MoP*, p. 143). The term therefore refers to symbolic or cultural activities which do not contribute to capitalist production and accumulation, and which therefore constitute the 'radical negation' of productivist society.

Baudrillard contrasts the abstraction, reduction and rationalization in productivist societies with 'the richness of symbolic exchange,' and valorizes the latter over the former (*MoP*, p. 45). In these and other passages, there is a nostalgia for the 'primitive,' the pre-capitalist; and at least part of

Baudrillard's theory of symbolic exchange derives from anthropological studies of exchange in 'primitive societies.'[13] One might interpret his political position at this point as a nostalgia for primitive communism, for a communal, ritualistic social order organized around symbolic exchange (and not production and the rest). In other passages, however, symbolic exchange becomes even more diverse and heterogeneous, as when, against Marx's anthropological emphasis on the primacy of labor and production in human life, Baudrillard valorizes 'a discharge with a pure waste, a symbolic discharge in Bataille's sense (pulsating, libidinal). . . . a gratuitous and festive energizing of the body's powers, a game with death, or the acting out of a desire' (*MoP*, pp. 43–4). This would suggest that nonreproductive, 'pulsating' sex, exhibitionism, nonutilitarian waste and gratuitous violence serve as paradigms of 'symbolic exchange.' In fact, as with 'code,' Baudrillard never clearly or consistently defines this central concept; it thus stands as a negative antithesis to 'productive' activity or to any activity that follows the logic of capitalist societies. Yet in this he appears to be presupposing Bataille's anthropology, by assuming that symbolic exchange flows from an excess of human energy and desire, thereby providing the energy for transgression and rebellion (which Bataille, in Nietzschean fashion, also celebrated).[14]

Baudrillard seems to be arguing that by engaging in symbolic exchange, which is caught up in neither use values nor exchange values, one escapes domination by the logic of political economy, and is able to subvert the logic of a system which demands that all activity have specific uses, values and purposes. Instead, he suggests that activities of symbolic exchange like gratuitous gift giving, festivities, destruction, sacrifice and waste provide a mode of activity that is more radically subversive of the values and logic of capitalism than the sort of practices advocated by Marxists, which he claims fail to escape the logic of the system and are thus but a reflex of the 'mirror of production' – for example, workers' control, socialization of the means of means of production and so forth. Further, in accepting Bataille's anthropology, Baudrillard also seems to be arguing that expenditure and all forms of symbolic exchange are more deeply rooted in human nature than production, for which human beings need training and discipline. Thus, despite his critique of Marxian essentialism, something of an essentialist anthropology underlies his celebration of symbolic exchange, which emerges as a distinctive and privileged form of human activity.

Micropolitics and Cultural Revolution

Against the values and practices of capitalist society, Baudrillard is searching for a form of life in radical opposition to the dominant types of exchange, use and sign value in productivist societies. For Baudrillard, symbolic exchange is precisely that mode of exchange which is ambivalent, non-equivalent, nonreductive and polysemic. That is, whereas sign value and exchange value are both determined by capitalist codes which reduce commodities and consumption to things such as prices, social prestige and so forth, symbolic exchange has the opposite features. Baudrillard seems to assume here that activities such as gratuitous gift giving, sacrifice, festive play and destruction stand outside and oppose the logic of capital which tries to control and profit from every aspect of life. For symbolic exchange seems to involve activity that puts one outside of and beyond the logic of capital and its value system since it involves the giving of gifts or goods for no particular reason, the expenditure of time and energy for no particular purpose, and engagement in activities – festive, destructive or whatever – from which one gains no benefits or profits and which have no discernible uses. For Baudrillard at this point in this theory, to engage in symbolic exchange would thus seem to be to engage in activities that are not determined by the logic of bourgeois semiotics or capital, activities that are potentially subversive and oppositional.

In *The Mirror of Production*, Baudrillard locates his cultural revolutionary project in the revolt of 'marginal groups' like blacks, women, homosexuals and others who supposedly subvert the 'code' of racial or sexual difference, and hence are more 'radical' and 'subversive' than, say, socialists who operate within the code of political economy. At this juncture, Baudrillard thus seems to advocate a politics of difference and of margins, whereby those groups which affirm their own values and needs over and against those of the dominant society are seen as more radical than groups which operate within the codes and logic of contemporary societies.[15] This politics of margins and difference is also related to the micropolitics of desire advocated by Lyotard, Deleuze and Guattari and others in France at the time.[16] Micropolitics would focus on the practices of everyday life, and would involve revolution in life-style, discourse, sexuality, communication and so on that would provide the preconditions for a new society and would emancipate individuals from social repression and domination. Baudrillard never went as far as Lyotard or Deleuze and Guattari in advocating a liberation and unleashing of desire as the basis of radical politics. Indeed, later he would explicitly criticize and frequently mock this position. But he was nevertheless close to their position of locating political change and radical politics in the microspheres of everyday life, culture, semiotics and so forth, rather than in class struggle, the work place or the state.

At the time, Baudrillard was calling for a 'cultural revolution' and a 'total revolution' (*MoP*, pp. 130ff.); but it is not clear how this revolution was to be carried out or what it could accomplish in view of the hegemony of dominant codes which he described. In fact, there seems to be great tension at this point between his advocacy of cultural revolution and his description of the system's ability to absorb all oppositional practices. For it would seem that a 'cultural revolution' would give rise to new practices, institutions, signs, codes, values and the rest, whereas in Baudrillard's theory all practices, signs and so on are controlled by and absorbed into the almighty 'code.' Thus, the only practice that he can really recommend is total refusal, total negativity and the utopia of radical otherness (*MoP*, pp. 130ff., *passim*).

Baudrillard's politics at this time thus circulate in the trajectory of ultra-leftist '*gauchiste*' political ideas which purport to be more 'radical' and 'revolutionary' than traditional Marxism. He and other French thinkers of the period, deeply influenced by the heterogeneous uprisings of May 1968, decisively broke with Marxian working-class politics and sought alternative perspectives for revolutionary politics. I will criticize Baudrillard's politics or anti-politics throughout this and the following chapters. First, however, I want to discuss the extent to which Baudrillard's analysis constitutes a devastating critique of the premises of Marx's critique of political economy and theory of revolution and socialism. Is Marxism as reductive and petit bourgeois as Baudrillard claims? And do its concepts and the alternative it offers simply mirror the capitalist mode of production, thereby failing to provide a truly revolutionary alternative? And does Baudrillard offer a viable counter-alternative?

It must be admitted that some of Baudrillard's polemics are convincing and strike at the heart of at least some reductivist and orthodox interpretations of Marx and Marxism. I find especially convincing the arguments in his studies of so-called primitive, feudal, archaic and noncapitalist societies that the classical Marxist theory of stages of historical development and the primacy of production and the economic cannot provide an adequate account of these societies, and that it is imperialistic and reductive to fit these societies into rigid Marxist categories and schema. Utilizing traditional and contemporary anthropology against French versions of Marxist anthropology (in particular Maurice Godelier's structural Marxism), Baudrillard continues his critique of Marxism in the studies in *The Mirror of Production*, these entitled 'Marxist Anthropology and the Domination of Nature' (chapter 2), 'Historical Materialism and Primitive Societies' (chapter 3), 'On the Archaic and Feudal Mode' (chapter 4) and 'Marxism and the System of Political Economy' (chapter 5).

His general argument in these studies is that Marxism cannot provide an adequate account of modes of production other than capitalism because its categories are too deeply implicated in bourgeois political economy and the capitalist mode of production (and thus mirror this social order). Baudrillard's references to symbolic societies organized around cultural rituals and symbolic exchange of various sorts indicate why he does not believe that Marxian productivist models apply to these societies and why, therefore, he can conclude that Marxism is ethnocentric and even imperialistic. At this point I will pass over his specific criticisms of the use of Marxism in anthropology so as to advance our discussion. In any case, his critique should be answered within anthropology by Marxist anthropologists, although, as far as I have been able to determine, Marxist anthropologists have never answered Baudrillard's criticisms in any published writings; thus there has been no productive debate following his critique.

I would suggest, however, that Baudrillard's critique is more damning for a specific version of structuralist Marxian anthropology than for Marxism *tout court*. That is, just as his critique of Marxian theories of use value and needs was more devastating for a naturalistic version of Marxism than for more historical materialist versions, so his critiques here apply more to the especially reductive and economistic versions of Marxism that characterize some versions of structuralist Marxism than to other more dialectical and historicist versions.[17] In fact, Baudrillard often picks out the weakest and most reductive version of Marxism as the target of his polemics, which he then generalizes to Marxism as such – a procedure that I would see as unfair and unacceptable both theoretically and politically. For while some versions of Marxism are as ethnocentric, reductive, economistic and epistemologically dubious as the Marxism that Baudrillard attacks, other versions are less subject to these drawbacks.

Baudrillard's strongest challenge to classical Marxism is perhaps the fifth study in *The Mirror of Production*, in which he argues that Marxism's premises are inadequate even for correctly analyzing and providing an alternative to contemporary capitalist societies. He begins with some criticisms of Marxist pretensions to inscribe a universal science of history and nature (*MoP*, pp. 111ff.). Although he makes many telling points against scientific Marxism, he ignores another tradition of dialectical Marxism which has quite different theoretical presuppositions, methodology and aims (see note 17). Baudrillard's claims that *no* version of Marxism can adequately conceptualize contemporary social development and provide a revolutionary alternative (*MoP*, pp. 119ff.) are much more challenging for versions of critical Marxism which attempt to develop Marxism as a historically specific critique of contemporary capitalist society (rather than as a universal science). What are Baudrillard's claims concerning the obsolescence of Marxism, and how convincing are they?

In *Mirror*, Baudrillard makes a definite break with Marxism for the first time, – though one can read his earlier works in retrospect as leading up to this break – and presents his own theory as providing superior perspectives on contemporary society. He claims that there is as decisive and revolutionary a mutation between the classical capitalism characterized by Marx and contemporary capitalism as between capitalism and feudalism. In short, he declares that the era of production is over, and that we have entered a new era in which radical semiurgy – that is, the production and proliferation of signs – has replaced production of objects as the center of social life and as a new mode of social control. Baudrillard thus concludes that the entire Marxian analysis is no longer adequate to contemporary conditions, which now require passage to '*the political economy of the sign*' (*MoP*, p. 121).

In this radically new situation, 'The super-ideology of the sign and the general operationalization of the signifier – everywhere sanctioned today by the new master disciplines of structural linguistics, semiology, information theory and cybernetics – has replaced good old political economy as the theoretical basis of the system' (*MoP*, p. 122). Consequently Baudrillard believes that it is old-fashioned and romantic to criticize the corruption of art, the media, sexuality, nature and so on by capitalist market relations, when it is the code of sign value – and not exchange value or the market – that controls these spheres. He claims that '*control of the code*' and the proliferation of sign values are of more significance than control of labor and the sphere of production (*MoP*, pp. 122ff.).

This analysis suggests that 'code' now refers to the rules, laws and structures of the political economy of the sign. Marxism, by contrast, mirrors the code of political economy, that of the imperatives, laws and structures of the capitalist system of production. On this analysis, Marxism can be seen as a reflex of a previous code, belonging to an earlier stage of history. In this context, Baudrillard's position can be read as a Left variant of theories of the post-industrial society, the information society, the cybernetic society or postmodern society in which it is claimed that socioeconomic development has moved beyond the previous stage of development and has entered a new stage in which the theories and categories of the previous stage are no longer adequate or relevant to the new social conditions (see further development of this position in chapter 3 and 4). At stake is whether the transformation and differences are as radical as Baudrillard suggests, whether the older theories, like Marxism, are completely obsolescent, and whether we need entirely new theories and categories to make sense of the new developments.

Baudrillard argues that 'This new ideological structure, that plays on the hieroglyphs of the code, is much more illegible than that which played on productive energy. This manipulation, that plays on the faculty of producing meaning and difference, is more radical than that which plays on labor power' (*MoP*, p. 122). Presumably, while capitalism previously channeled labor power into production and exploited productive energies of workers for profit, today signs and codes channel consciousness and behavior into certain predetermined paths like consumption, conformity, fascination with media spectacles, representative democracy and so on. What I will call 'sign control' articulates differences (in class, sex, race, political affiliation and so on) and channels individuals into some predefined mode of thought and behavior or another, closing off more radical alternatives (symbolic exchange, as it turns out once again).

Sign control is especially efficacious because 'The form-sign applies to the whole social process and it is largely unconscious' (*MoP*, p. 123). Sign control for Baudrillard is therefore unconscious, illegible and thus hard to combat. Presumably we are not aware how we are channeled into certain forms of class behavior, consumer behavior, conformity, sex role behavior, ethnic behavior and the like which are being controlled by the code (never defined, but always hegemonic and totalitarian in Baudrillard's theory). For in 'the planned cycle of consumer demand, the new strategic forces, the new structural elements – needs, knowledge, culture, information, sexuality – have all their explosive force defused' (*MoP*, p. 126). All phenomena are functionally integrated into a new 'mode of strategic control' which eliminates all contradictions, potential threats to order and social crises.

Baudrillard argues that what appears to be new, different, oppositional or subversive is merely part of a differential play of signs in a semiotic system which itself regulates and controls all signification and meaning. To the Marxian claims for the primacy of production and the mode of production, Baudrillard counters a concept of 'the mode of signification,' which he claims is now prior to and more determinant than the mode of production and its laws, logic and exigencies. In order words, he claims that semiotic control takes place through the proliferation and dissemination of signs. Signification now operates according to its own logic and laws, and absorbs everything back into its system. No behavior can refer back to a particular use value or meaning for an individual, because all meaning and use value are prescribed in advance and circumscribed by the code. Consequently 'the sign no longer designates anything at all. It approaches its true structural limit which is to refer back only to other signs. All reality then becomes the place of a semiurgical manipulation, of a structural simulation' (*MoP*, p. 128). The entirety of Baudrillard's subsequent work to the present explores this situation, and draws out its implications. It rests henceforth on the proposition that we have entered a new stage in history, in which sign control is almost complete and totalitarian. Signs, simulations and codes have become the primary social determinants, and supposedly follow their own logic and order of signification. Consequently previous theories predicated on the logic of production, like Marxism, are no longer useful or relevant to the new social situation.

Because Marxism is rooted in the logic of production, it is not able to conceptualize sign control, and thus rise to the level of a general theory of contemporary society (*MoP*, pp. 123ff.). For in theorizing about contemporary society 'one goes from a system of productive forces, exploitation and profit, as in the competitive system dominated in its logic by social labor time, to a gigantic operational game of question and answer, to a gigantic combinatory where all values commutate and are exchanged according to their operational sign' (*MoP*, p. 127). Baudrillard will pursue this logic and move completely beyond classical Marxism and political economy. In the next section, I will point to some of the reasons why I do not accept Baudrillard's claims that Marxian categories can provide neither an adequate critique of contemporary capitalist societies or emancipatory perspectives on an alternative (socialist) society.

For Marx

Contra Baudrillard, I believe that there are good reasons to maintain that we still live in a society in which the mode of production dominates much of our cultural and social life. Thus I am skeptical as to whether we can make sense out of our current social order without using the categories of Marxian political economy. For if one grants that 'the mirror of production' is Marx's imaginary, his conceptual vision of society and history, with inevitable omissions, distortions, illusions and so on, then, by the same token, one can conceive of 'the mirror of signification,' or what I have called 'sign control,' or the semiological imaginary, as Baudrillard's imaginary. With regard to the previous discussion, one could argue that, just as Baudrillard's first three works on the consumer society can be read in retrospect as projections of a capitalist imaginary, as the articulations of capitalist dreams to totally control society through consumption and the management of consumer demand, so Baudrillard now projects what might be called a cybernetic imaginary. This imaginary consists in the fantasy of a certain technocratic stratum that society can be controlled through steering mechanisms, through the imposition of codes and rules whereby cybernetic organization and management successfully achieves total social control and domination. (Baudrillard differs from more banal cyberneticists in believing that signs and signification by themselves – without human intervention – will become the controlling force, thereby advancing perhaps the first theory of semiological determinism; but this position will not become clear until the works that I shall discuss in the next chapter.)

From this cybernetic-technocratic standpoint, Baudrillard is proposing a new perspective on society and history which provides some useful insights, but also contains its own omissions, distortions and illusions. In particular, Baudrillard will progressively erase materiality – that is, political economy, capital, the body, human suffering and so on – from his theory, a move anticipated by his severing of his now radically semiological theory from political economy in *Mirror*. The theoretical problem with Baudrillard's position, on this level, is that he is simply proposing the substitution of one imaginary, his, for another, Marx's. Against such monocular perspectives I would argue that to make sense of the social processes and transformations going on, we need many theories, of which theories of production and signification would *both* seem to be important. Thus I am proposing precisely what the later Baudrillard resists most stubbornly: conceptual mediation and synthesis and a multiperspectival vision. While in *Critique* Baudrillard explicitly calls for a synthesis of political economy and semiology, and in his first three books assumes – correctly I believe – that the logics of production and signification are intertwined in contemporary capitalist societies, from *Mirror* to the present he argues that information, media and the other constituents of postindustrial societies are severed from the logic of production. I will argue in various contexts throughout this book that this rupture is too absolute, and that the dynamics of labor, production and political economy continue to often determine, or act upon, signification and the production of signs and meaning, at the same time admitting that the logic of signification likewise affects production and consumption and can play a relatively autonomous role in social reproduction. Instead of such a dialectical view (which was to become anathema to him), Baudrillard ascribes a new role to signification as a primary mode of social determination. (In the next chapter we will see that simulation is eventually assigned this role.) But does signification escape the logic of production so easily? Is it an autonomous social force with its own ends, goals, purposes and interests?

I think not. We are still in a society where the imperatives of capital and production play a crucial structuring role in politics, culture, and social and economic life through capitalist control of the media, advertising, packaging, design, architecture, urbanization, computerization and so forth.[18] Against Baudrillard's position, I would argue that some of the most useful work in contemporary cultural and social theory has combined economic, political and cultural approaches, and that it would be perverse to dismiss political economy, production and Marxism completely from contemporary social theory. For, even minimally, such perspectives can provide illuminating approaches and concepts in dealing with a wide range of phenomena.

Baudrillard might argue against this proposal that it is impossible to combine radically different logics of production and signification, and that Marxism is intrinsically reductionistic, imperialistic and terroristic and refuses to be combined with any theories that oppose in any way its categories and logic. But just as I argued in 2.1 that Baudrillard's critiques of Marx's theories of use value and needs were unfair to Marx who himself anticipated many of Baudrillard's points in his critique of bourgeois political economy, so I would also argue that Marxism is not as economistic or reductive as Baudrillard claims, and that Marxists like Henri Lefebvre, Guy Debord and the Critical Theorists of the Frankfurt School anticipated many of Baudrillard's positions – though admittedly not in such an extreme, anti-Marxist form.

In general, it seems to me that Baudrillard, especially in his middle and later periods, is so intent on demolishing Marxism that he fails to appreciate to what extent all theories of neo-capitalist societies, including his own, build on Marx's work. Marx arguably established the conceptual framework for the sort of analysis of consumption and the consumer society, as well as the critical perspectives on capitalist society, which characterize Baudrillard's early and middle works at least. Moreover, I believe that readings of Marx which claim that he reduces all social phenomena to epiphenomena of the mode of production, and that he uses a logic of production to explain all social phenomena are themselves reductionistic readings.

Walter Adamson, for example, has shown that Marx utilizes four different models of the relation between production, culture and society in his various works and conceptualizes production in at least four different ways.[19] Whereas an analytic philosopher might take this as an indication of conceptual confusion on Marx's part, I prefer to see it as a Marxian recognition that concepts have different uses in different contexts, and that meaning is therefore relative to context and use. In some contexts, therefore, one might well characterize production in rather narrow economic terms, as Marx sometimes does. In other contexts – and one finds Marx doing this as well – one might employ the term 'production' to include cultural, symbolic and communicative interaction.

Thus, while there are reductionistic and economistic passages in Marx which seem to reduce cultural superstructures and all social processes to their economic base, there are more historical and less reductive passages as well (just as I earlier argued that there were naturalistic passages, although Marxism was predominantly historicist). Consequently, I would argue that while Baudrillard provides a strong polemic against reductionist, naturalistic and economistic readings of Marx, his broadside attack and dismissal of Marxism *tout court* is unfair and unwarranted. Part of Baudrillard's problem with Marx is symptomatic of his approach to many of the theories and thinkers he polemicizes against. In general, Baudrillard does not go in for careful, patient, detailed textual readings of his polemical targets. Instead, he takes positions out of context and gives the impression that his goal is destruction rather than dialogue and conceptual appropriation, mediation and synthesis. Baudrillard thus seems to be engaging in a particular type of capitalist activity – rising above, even attempting to destroy, one's competitors – that itself, as I will suggest below, is determined by the logic of the cultural market in France (see 5.4). Adopting a Baudrillardian notion and style, we might refer to his mode of criticism as *hypercriticism* which is – to use a Baudrillardian trope – 'more critical than critical' and reminiscent of the 'critical criticism' of the Young Hegelians attacked by Marx.[20]

Indeed, Baudrillard's hypercriticism is completely undialectical, and attempts to destroy the object of critique rather than to appropriate valid or useful insights or positions. In particular, Baudrillard seems to reject concepts of mediation and *Aufhebung* which would attempt to raise positions, or stages of history, into a higher synthesis. Thus criticism for him is primarily negative. (Later we will see that he explicitly assigns precisely this role to the intellectual and to intellectual critique.) Nonetheless, some of his criticisms are provocative and useful, though perhaps less devastating than the critical critic and some of his bedazzled disciples seem to think.

2.3   BAUDRILLARD'S POLITICS AND THE CRITIQUE OF
FRENCH COMMUNISM

In his writings prior to the late 1970s, Baudrillard situated his thought in the tradition of revolutionary theory and politics. The aim of revolutionary theory was to promote revolutionary politics, and the problematic of revolution was central to his thought and writing. In the 1960s, it appears that Baudrillard pursued rather conventional lines of radical politics. In the 1960s, he seemed to subscribe to a Left-revolutionary position. In 1968, he published a translation of Peter Weiss's *Discourse on Vietnam*, subtitled 'discourse on the genesis and the unfolding of a very long war of the liberation of Vietnam which illustrates the necessity of armed struggle of the oppressed against their oppressors.'[21] This notion has a certain ironic – even surrealist – ring to it in light of Baudrillard's later texts; but one can imagine that in 1968 he was serious in his identification with armed struggle and revolutionary violence. This was a popular position in Paris and elsewhere at the time, and we will see that Baudrillard is not afraid to defend various forms of violence at different junctures in his political trajectory.

It is one thing to celebrate the armed struggle of the Vietnamese or other national liberation movements, of course; it is something else to call for armed struggle in advanced capitalist countries. In his first few published books, Baudrillard tended to support cultural revolution in a micropolitics of the transformation of everyday life. Since the life of signs was playing such a central role in the reproduction of capitalist societies, it made sense to locate the center of radical politics in cultural practices which attack the dominant codes signifying practices and signs and to oppose capitalist semiology with alternative signs, cultural practices and discourses. Thus Baudrillard posited 'symbolic exchange' against the manifold forms of exchange in contemporary capitalist societies, and called for radical refusal of dominant modes of thought, discourse and behavior.

Yet a tension evolved between his ultra-Left politics and his emphasis on radical activism in view of his analyses of the ability of the system to absorb and contain all oppositional activity, and eventually he collapsed this tension by rejecting the whole notion of micropolitics and cultural revolution. When asked by the editorial collective of the radical French journal *Dérive* in 1976 whether he still believed in a micropolitics of desire, he answered: 'Pufff . . . . I no longer believe in it. Indeed, I confess that I was propagandizing this [politics] a bit.'[22] Hereafter Baudrillard would never affirm any specific position within the existing spectrum of radical politics. One might conclude that he had in effect surrendered to the power and fascination of the semiotic-cybernetic system whose hegemony appeared to be so complete that revolution or radical politics seemed no more than an illusion and trap. Consequently, in his post-1976 publications, Baudrillard gave up –

consistently with his theory – his 'ultra-radical' political gestures and rhetoric, though some moments of the old critical-revolutionary impulse keep surfacing.

Throughout this period, Baudrillard carried out polemics against the Left. In *Le P.C. ou les paradis artificiels du politique* he attacked the Communist Party and the Union of the Left.[23] Presumably he began this enterprise in March 1977, when it appeared that a union between the French Communist and Socialist parties which had been in effect since 1972 would win the upcoming 1978 election.[24] This possibility incited Baudrillard to write a series of stinging attacks on the French Communists, beginning with a polemic against 'The Calvary of the Union of the Left,' which is cutely titled 'La lutte enchantée ou la flûte finale' ('The Enchanted Struggle or the Final Flute') which played on the chorus of 'The Internationale' celebrating the 'final struggle' (*lutte finale*) as well as on the title of Mozart's *Magic Flute*. The use of religious metaphors to describe the Communists is reminiscent of Marx's satires on Saint Max (Stirner) and 'the Holy Family' in some of his early polemics.

Baudrillard begins with a satire on the beginning of 'The Communist Manifesto': 'A specter haunts the spheres of power: communism. But a specter haunts the communists themselves: power' (*GD*, p. 13). He then carries out an analysis which he will repeat in other writings concerning the alleged fear of taking power in today's Euro-Communist parties:

> Everything is fraudulent in the contemporary political scenario, ruled by a simulacra of revolutionary tension and of a taking of power by the communists (and the Left in general). In fact, behind this *mise en scène* where the communists continue to dedicate themselves to confronting the Right and thus to preserve the whole political edifice, it is the negative obsession with power which works over them. . . . They are not alone in this case, for politics escapes everybody and the Right itself is without real energy. But it so happens that the communists have always appeared historically in the Leninist perspective to which they all adhere (and to which they believe themselves to be faithful) as *political*, indeed as professionals in the taking of power. It is therefore in their camp that the political weakness and decay is the most flagrant. (*GD*, p. 13)

Baudrillard argues that a strong Communist Party is needed to create the illusion of a bipolar political system and of real electoral contests between the Right and the Left when differences between the political poles are in fact imploding in a media-saturated society in which such differences become mere simulations.

> Right and Left taken globally play *together* in the work of establishing differences, work *together* to preserve the model of political simulation

and this collusion dominates completely their respective strategies. There is besides no longer any strategy anywhere in this system of simulated dissension, in this system of deterrence (which is also that of peaceful coexistence on the world level), but a sort of destiny which absorbs us all, a destiny of ineluctable production of the social and *deterrence* through the social. (*GD*, p. 28).

Baudrillard thus claims that the Communists are playing an essential role in simulating real political differences and choices within the electoral system, thereby helping to keep alive a moribund system of political representation which needs large doses of controversy and opposition to maintain it. Furthermore, he claims that the 'revolutionary' politics of the French Communist Party is merely a simulation, and that in reality the party does not want power, because it is more comfortable in its role as a loyal opposition (*GD*, pp. 13ff., 27ff.). In addition, he claims that the Communists suffer from the *moral* illusion that it is possible to manage society rationally, and to create a more just and more equitable society. It has consequently 'lost that which is immoral and beyond measure in the idea of revolution which had defied capital on the terrain of its virulence (and not on that of its pretended rationality).'

In a long footnote Baudrillard explains that in his view capital is fundamentally immoral, and thus can only be confronted effectively on the terrain of violent confrontation and struggle, an ultra-Left position typical of the period. He praises episodes in the nineteenth century in which the proletariat 'frontally challenged power while risking their lives in crushed rebellions, and especially in the [Paris] Commune' (*GD*, p. 18). Thus he envisages revolution as a violent confrontation between two ruthless, immoral and implacable enemies in a life-and-death struggle, and rejects as idealist the view that socialism is guaranteed by a rational dialectic of historical progress. This position fleshes out his celebration of sacrifice and death in symbolic exchange, and in effect glorifies challenges to power in which participants risk their lives.

Baudrillard presents capital itself as 'a demented enterprise, without limits, to abolish the symbolic universe in an indifference that is always greater and in a circulation of values always accelerated' (*GD*, p. 19). Capital is described as 'the reign without limits of exchange value'; and thus he denies that capital is based on a rational order of interests, profit, production and labor. Rather, 'it imposes a disconnection, a deterritorialization of everything, an unmeasurable extension of [the law of] value and thus an irrational order of investment *at all costs* (the contrary to rational calculation according to Weber's theory)' (*GD*, pp. 19–20). Notions that capital is rational are nonsensical, Baudrillard insists on the contrary, 'capital is a challenge to the natural order of value which knows no limits and which aims at the triumph of exchange value at all costs' (*GD*, p. 20).

Consequently, its 'axiom is investment and not production' (*GD*, p. 20).[25]

Marxism in turn, according to Baudrillard, moralizes production by projecting the standard of use value, of a rational organization of the economy and a good use of the social, which will allegedly be the principle of social organization opposed to capitalist exchange value. Here he repeats his polemic against the category of use value, claiming that it merely provides the alibi for political economy – capitalist or socialist – which justifies its system of domination on the grounds that it is fulfilling needs and producing objects for use (*GD*, pp. 20–1). Baudrillard claims that the Communists maintain a religious belief in the use value of labor, the social, matter and history, believing in the reality of the social, of classes, of class struggle and the rest: 'They believe everything, they want to believe everything, that is their profound morality. It is that which saps them of all political capacity' (*GD*, p. 22).

While the Communists believe in a deep morality and rationality in history, Baudrillard complains that they 'do not believe any longer in the sacred horizon of appearances' (ibid.). Instead they believe in a rational teleology of history, a rational administration of things: 'Everything escapes them of what is unlimited and immoral and of the simulation and seduction which constitutes politics' (ibid.). We see here that Baudrillard is developing a completely different notion of politics which eventually will lead him beyond conventional politics altogether (see 7.1). He claims that at best the Communists help administer capitalist society and provide one pole of a bipolar French electoral system which is itself a deterrent to revolutionary upheaval and that therefore 'the great Marxist promise [of revolution] is over' (*GD*, p. 23).

In effect, he is again claiming that Marxism is not radical enough in its opposition to capital and does not provide a significantly different alternative. Baudrillard claims that when the bourgeoisie put an end to the feudal order, 'they truly subverted an order and a code of social relations (birth, honor, hierarchy) in order to substitute another order (production, economy, rationality, progress)' (ibid.). Moreover, the bourgeoisie replaced the feudal society of estates with a class society, whereas Marxism, it is claimed does not break with the logic of class society and replace it with something completely different; it merely offers the possibility of one class (the proletariat) replacing another (the bourgeoisie). Thus the Communists can do no more than simulate revolution, because they do not have a radical alternative to offer.

This presentation is not at all fair to Marx's conception of a classless society, though it is true that if the French Communist Party were to gain power through elections, it would hardly be in a position to produce a classless society, and would probably be limited to managing class conflict and capitalist crises. In any case, Baudrillard's distance from Marxism is now clear: he is moving toward a totally different theoretical and political universe, one that will become increasingly hermetic and idiosyncratic.

In the rest of his studies of the collapse of the Union of the Left, Baudrillard does not really offer any new critiques of Marxism or new ideas of his own. His second study, 'Castrated on the Night of His Marriage,' alludes to the collapse of the Union of the Left in September 1977, on the eve of the election, when the French Communist Party and Socialist Party could not agree on a common program for the election. Rather than providing an analysis of the complex set of political reasons for the rupture, Baudrillard merely continues his increasingly ill-tempered attack on the Left and in particular the French Communist Party. The key idea is that socialism in today's context involves the injection of homeopathic doses of the social and the political into a body in which the previous vestiges are dying (*GD*, pp. 27ff.).

Baudrillard concludes with a 'Ballad for a Defunct Left' written at the time of the 1978 elections, which all the polls and most commentators had expected the Left to win. The first part, 'What Makes Marchais Smile,' repeats his analysis of why the Communists really did not want power and are happier and better off in the role of opposition, while the second, 'What Makes Althusser Write,' takes issue with the criticisms of the French Communist Party strategy published by the French Marxist Louis Althusser in *Le Monde*.[26] Baudrillard writes in regard to Althusser's critique:

> That which cannot continue any longer [according to Althusser] is simply that which has been going on for fifty years and whose ritual denunciation marks the annals of the party. It aims as always at the restitution of a transparency of the party, of a dialectic of the base and of the summit (which has never occured historically), of a dialectic of practice and of theory (which has not even occurred philosophically). Nothing new: the anti-Stalinist incantation is even more mystifying than the Stalinist party apparatus. (*GD*, pp. 56–7)

Althusser's sort of 'critical' discourse, he suggests, merely inserts homeopathic doses of democracy into an apparatus which is itself moribund, just as the party itself functions to administer small doses of the illusion of democratic opposition and choice in a polity that is likewise moribund.

Baudrillard then claims that there is an interesting structural parallel between Althusser's critique of Stalinism and the critiques of Marxism by the so-called new philosophers:[27]

> It's the same obscurantism which rules over the new philosophers and their vision of the Gulag and Althusser, even if he diverges from our master dissidents, Althusser presents to us the same regressive form of

analysis: neo-humanism opposed to a retrospective totalitarianism, the reactivation of an old idea of the state and its powers founded upon a conception still panoptic of political space (the state of surveillance and the Gulag). A recycling of freedom, of rights, of responsibility, of autonomy, of dissidence. . . . This is exactly the scenario of the deceptive offensive of Althusser against the party. The eternal phantasm of the great manipulative subject, the state, the apparatus, power and of the powerless, oppressed subject, who will become great: civil society, the militant, the dissident. (*GD*, pp. 63–4)

The crux of Baudrillard's critique of the Left in France, as well as of its Rightist 'new philosopher' critics, is that they fail to grasp the profound changes going on in society and politics and the growing role of the media, simulations, information and massification and the corresponding decline and death of the very domains of the social and the political. It is in other texts of the same period that Baudrillard elaborates these new theoretical perspectives which constitute a dramatic break with his earlier writings and with the theoretical and political positions of his generation. It is to this new phase in Baudrillard's trajectory that we now turn.

3

Media, Simulations and the End of the Social

During the 1980s Jean Baudrillard has been promoted in certain circles as the most advanced theorist of the media and society in the so-called postmodern era. His theory of a new, postmodern society rests on a key assumption that the media, simulations and what he calls 'cyberblitz' constitute a new realm of experience and a new stage of history and type of society. To a large extent Baudrillard's work consists in rethinking radical social theory and politics in the light of developments in the consumer, media, information and technological society. Baudrillard's earlier works focus on the construction of the consumer society and how it provides a new world of values, meaning and activity, and thus inhabit the terrain of Marxism and political economy. From the mid-1970s on, however, reflections on political economy and the consumer society disappear almost completely from his texts, and thereafter simulations and simulacra, media and information, science and new technologies together produce what Baudrillard calls 'implosion' and 'hyperreality.' These novel phenomena become the constituents of a new postmodern world which – in Baudrillard's theorizing – obliterate all the boundaries, categories and values of the previous forms of industrial society, while establishing new forms of social organization, thought and experience.

In this chapter I will first discuss the general outlines of Baudrillard's new postmodern social theory as it was presented in *L'échange symbolique et la mort* (3.1), and then focus in more detail on his analyses of the media (3.2), his theories of simulation, hyperreality and implosion (3.3), and his discussion of how these developments constitute an 'end of the social' and hence the obsolescence of previous social theory (3.4). I conclude by raising questions of the relationships between Baudrillard's new social theory, Nietzsche and poststructuralism (3.5).

3.1   ON THE WAY TO POSTMODERNITY

The Mirror of Production marked Baudrillard's break with Marxism, and in his next book, *L'échange symbolique et la mort* (1976), he moves beyond his early critique of political economy and his first sketch of an alternative social theory into a more systematic development of his new theory of simulations.[1] Indeed, he moves beyond political economy altogether, into the brave new world of radical semiurgy, of the incessant proliferation and dissemination of signs, by means of mesmerizing media, ever changing fashion and the other manifestations of what I shall call the 'postmodern carnival' (chapter 4). Baudrillard now not only claims that the era of political economy is over; he also announces the end of the previous world in characteristically dramatic form:

> The end of labor. The end of production. The end of political economy.
> The end of the dialectic signifier/signified which permitted the accumulation of knowledge and of meaning, the linear syntagm of cumulative discourse. The end simultaneously of the dialectic of exchange value/use value, the only one to make possible capital accumulation and social production. The end of the linear dimension of discourse. The end of the linear dimension of merchandise. The end of the classic era of the sign. The end of the era of production. (*ES*, p. 20; *SW*, pp. 127–8)

We are instead, Baudrillard claims, in a new era in which new technologies – media, cybernetic models and steering systems, computers, information processing, entertainment and knowledge industries and so forth – replace industrial production and political economy as the organizing principle of society. In this era, labor is no longer a force of production, but is itself a 'sign among signs' (*ES*, p. 23) – that is, a sign of one's social position, one's servitude and how one is integrated into the social apparatus: 'the important thing is that every one be the terminal of the whole network, a tiny terminal, but a term nevertheless. . . . The choice of occupation, the utopia of an occupation custom-made for everyone means that *the die is cast*, that the system of socialization is complete. Labor power is no longer violently bought and sold; it is designed, it is marketed, it is merchandised. Production thus joins the consumerist system of signs' (*ES*, pp. 28–9; *SW*, p. 134).

Baudrillard describes this situation as a shift from a society in which the *mode of production* is primary to a society in which the *code of production* becomes the primary social determinant: 'To analyze production as a code is to transcend the material presence of machines, industry, labor time, products, wages, money and those that are more formal, yet just as objective, such as surplus value, the market, capital, in order to identify the rules of the game and to destroy the logical connections in the determinations of capital, even in the critical connections of Marxist categories that analyze it' (*SW*, p. 132). Baudrillard thus breaks here with the Marxian materialist theory of production, and offers a theory in which *codes* come to constitute the primary organizing principles of social life.

While Baudrillard does not define 'code' with any precision here, he will soon equate the concept with a series of 'simulation' models, and will increasingly move to what I would call a *semiological idealism*, whereby signs and codes becomes the primary constituents of social life. In this new situation a person's labor power, body, sexuality, unconscious, and so on are not primarily productive forces, but are to be seen as 'operational variables,' 'the code's chess pieces,' which are to be mobilized in social institutions and practices. Wages too bear no rational relation to a person's work and what he or she produces; rather they signify that the person is playing the game, fitting into the system (*ES*, pp. 36ff.). And money is a 'cool medium' which allows participation and involvement in the system, and itself volatizes into an international system of 'floating' speculative capital (*ES*, pp. 39ff.). But, crucially, political economy is no longer the foundation, the social determinant, or even a structural 'reality' in which other phenomena can be interpreted and explained (*ES*, pp. 53ff.). Instead, we live in a 'hyperreality' of simulations in which images, spectacles and the play of signs replace the logic of production and class conflict as key constituents of contemporary capitalist societies.

Modernity for Baudrillard is thus the era of production governed by the industrial bourgeoisie. The era of simulations by contrast is an era of information and signs governed by models, codes and a system of 'general economy.' Baudrillard never specifies the economic forces or social groups behind this process; rather, he advances a sort of technological determinism whereby models and codes become the primary determinants of social reality (see 3.3 for more details). Yet he can still describe the new stage of society as 'the brothel of capital' (*ES*, p. 21; *SW*, p. 128), and write that it is *capital* which 'abolishes social determination through the mode of production. It is capital which substitutes the structural form of value for the commodity form. And it is this [that is, the structural law of value] that determines the current strategy of the system' (*ES*, p. 20; *SW*, p. 128). Thus Baudrillard is presumably describing an entirely new form of capitalist society. However, he never specifies what specific sectors or types of capital are the major players; nor does he discuss any specific strategies of capital realization, thus severing 'capital' from the mode of production and political economy. Indeed, strictly speaking, from now on he erases political economy completely from his social theory.

Baudrillard also argues that social *domination* is a more overarching goal

than profitability or exploitation of the older sort, and claims th
of the 'general system' is of a higher level than the previous 'comr
of value' in the industrial era of production (*ES*, pp. 23, 11). I
postindustrial, postmodern era, the model or code structures soc
and erodes distinctions between the model and the real. Using N
cybernetic concept of *implosion*, Baudrillard claims that in the contemporary
world the boundary between representation and reality implodes, and that,
as a result, the very experience and ground of 'the real' disappears.[2]
Baudrillard is thus taking certain semiological theories of the sign and
cybernetic theories of the code to their ultimate limits by describing a
society that is governed primarily by signs and codes. In a section on 'The
Structural Revolution of Value,' he suggests some of the implications of this
new way of seeing, which will henceforth guide his thought and constitute
the core of his semiological imaginary. Whereas in a previous stage of the
philosophy of language and metaphysics, words referred to objects and
things, and representations were believed to refer to a 'real,' this era of
thought and discourse has now come to an end:

> The structural dimension gains autonomy, to the exclusion of the
> referential dimension, establishing itself on the death of the latter.
> Gone are the referentials of production, signification, affect, substance,
> history, i.e. the whole equation of real contents that still gave the sign
> weight by anchoring it with a kind of carrying capacity, of gravity – in
> short, its form as representative equivalent. All this is surpassed by the
> other stage of value, that of total relativity, of generalized com-
> mutation, which is combinatory and simulatory. This means simulation
> in the sense that from now on signs will exchange among themselves
> exclusively, without interacting with the real (and they only exchange
> themselves among themselves smoothly, they only exchange them-
> selves perfectly *on the condition* that they no longer exchange
> themselves with the real). The emancipation of the sign: released from
> that 'archaic' obligation that it might have to designate something, the
> sign is at last free for a structural or combinatory play according to
> indifference and a total indetermination which succeeds the previous
> role of determinate equivalence. (*ES*, p. 18; *SW*, p. 125)

On this semiological view, signs and modes of representation come to
constitute 'reality', and signs gain autonomy and, in interaction with other
signs, come to constitute a new type of social order in which it is signs and
codes that constitute 'the real.' Baudrillard is arguing that commodity signs,
for instance, refer to and gain their significance in relation to other
commodity signs within the code of a 'structural law of value,' rather than to
any external referents or ground of value, just as media representations refer
primarily to other media representations rather than to any outside world.

Likewise, on this analysis, contemporary theories refer intertextually primarily to other theories rather than to a 'real' outside – or they just float in a free-flowing space of their own (*ES*, pp. 19–21). Furthermore, Baudrillard seems to suggest that individuals are so caught up in a world of commodity signs, media spectacles, representations and simulations that there is no longer any access to a 'real' which is itself presented as an effect of the code or system. We thus now live in a radically relativistic, idealist and imaginary universe:

> Determination is dead, indeterminism reigns. We have witnessed the ex-termination (in the literal sense of the word) of the reals of production and of the real of signification. . . . This historical and social mutation is readable at every level. The era of simulation is henceforth opened everywhere through the commutability of terms once contradictory or dialectically opposed. The same 'genesis of simulacra' is apparent everywhere: commutability of the beautiful and the ugly in fashion, of the Left and the Right in politics, of the true and the false in every message from the media, of the useful and the useless in objects, of nature and culture at every level of signification. All the grand humanist criteria of value, those of an entire civilization of moral, aesthetic and practical judgment, are wiped out in our system of images and signs. Everything becomes undecidable – this is the characteristic effect of the domination of the code which is based everywhere on the principle of neutralization and indifference. This is what the generalized brothel (*bordel*) of capital is, not a brothel of prostitution, but a brothel of substitution and commutation. (*ES*, pp. 19, 20–1; *SW*, pp. 127–8)

In this universe of radical indeterminacy, it becomes increasingly difficult to distinguish true from false, good from bad, for in the society of simulations it is impossible to gain access to a real or to perceive what is determining or constituting various events and processes. Not only is the Marxian theory of political economy obsolescent in this situation, but Marx's concepts have a completely opposite valence and sense (we shall see that the category of reversal will henceforth play a more important role in Baudrillard's mode of thought):

> Labor is no longer exploitation, it is a gift provided by capital; – wages are no longer extracted but are also a gift to the worker; moreover, wages no longer purchase labor power but redeem the power of capital;
> – the slow death of work is no longer submitted to, but is a desperate act, a defiance in the face of the unilateral gift of labor by capital;

– the sole efficacious response to power is to give it back what it gives you and that is only possible symbolically through death. (*ES*, p. 72)

It is clear that Baudrillard's discourse has now moved completely beyond and against Marxian theory. He develops the above 'theses' in discussions of labor, wages, money, strikes, unions, the working class and production (*ES*, pp. 26ff.) which attack Marxian uses of these categories. Although he still uses the category of 'capital,' it functions simply as a sign among signs within the system of simulations, rather than the master category which structures social relations and produces a social system, as for Marx. Baudrillard's general case against Marxism thus rests on the postulate that we have entered an entirely new era in which the categories of the previous era no longer have any relevance or application. The possibility of automation, for example, supposedly renders manual labor superfluous, and makes machines, computers and other technologies the main forces of production. In this situation, Baudrillard rather sardonically suggests that the capitalist who continues to employ workers should be seen as a benefactor, and that the Marxian concept of exploitation is therefore historically obsolete.

Since production is no longer of interest for contemporary social trends and developments, Baudrillard now turns his attention to the realm of culture and leisure (in fact, it is not clear that he ever had any interest in the realm of production). Henceforth Baudrillard's books explore this new era of simulations, and leave political economy and Marxism behind. The organization of *L'échange symbolique et la mort* recapitulates the new trajectory of Baudrillard's thought. The opening studies of 'The End of Production' are followed by studies of 'The Orders of Simulacra' (see 3.3), a discussion of fashion in terms of his new theory of simulations (rather than in terms of its function within the consumer society), followed by studies of 'The Body or the Display of Signs,' 'Political Economy and Death,' and language and the unconscious (see my discussion of these themes in chapter 4).

Throughout the book, Baudrillard contrasts economic exchange and utility under capitalism with symbolic exchange, now explicated in terms of challenge, or defiance – *le defi*, his favorite new concept – and sacrifice. He claims that the only 'catastrophic' – that is, genuinely revolutionary – strategy is one that pushes a system to its end point, and thus its point of radical collapse and reversal. Since it is symbolic exchange which represents the antithesis to value and utility under capitalism, the logic of exchange and value must ultimately be pushed to its limit and reversed, which would presumably lead to a return to symbolic exchange as a dominant organizing principle of society. In fact, however, Baudrillard does not delineate any specific strategies of reversal. All he does is to make some cryptic references to Mauss's notion of the countergift, Saussure's anagrams and Freud's death instinct. And while he uses radical rhetoric alluding to the desire to 'catch up with the hyperreal and strike it dead' and calls for 'subversive theory and practice,' it appears that he is opting out at this point of conventional politics: 'Can we fight DNA? Certainly not with the blows of class struggle. Can we invent simulacra of an even higher logical (or illogical?) order, beyond the current order . . . perhaps only death, the reversibility of death, is of a higher order than the code. Only symbolic disorder can breach the code' (*ES*, p. 12; *SW*, p. 122).

Henceforth, Baudrillard will focus his attention on the new configurations of media, simulations, new technologies and cybernetics. It is to his analyses of these phenomena that we shall now turn.

3.2 McLUHAN, MEDIA AND INFORMATION

Among Baudrillard's most provocative theses are his reflections on the role of the media in constituting the postmodern world. Indeed, he provides paradigmatic models of the media as all-powerful and autonomous social forces which produce a wide range of effects.[3] To explicate the development and contours of his theory of the media, I will follow his reflections from the late 1960s to the present, and then assess his contributions and limitations.

In 1967 Baudrillard wrote a review of Marshall McLuhan's *Understanding Media* in which he claimed that McLuhan's dictum that the 'medium is the message' is 'the very formula of alienation in a technical society,' and he criticized McLuhan for naturalizing that alienation.[4] At this time, he shared the neo-Marxian critique of McLuhan as a technological reductionist and determinist. Soon, however, McLuhan's formula had become the guiding principle of his own thought.

Baudrillard began developing his own theory of the media in an article entitled 'Requiem for the Media' in *Toward a Critique of the Political Economy of the Sign* (1972). The title is somewhat ironic, for Baudrillard is in fact only just beginning to develop a social theory in which the media play crucial roles in constituting a new postmodernity. What he is really writing is a requiem for a *Marxist* theory of the media, arguing: 'McLuhan has said, with his usual Canadian-Texan brutalness, that Marx, the spiritual contemporary of the steam engine and railroads, was already obsolete in his lifetime with the appearance of the telegraph. In his candid fashion, he is saying that Marx, in his materialist analysis of production, had virtually circumscribed productive forces as a privileged domain from which language, signs and communication in general found themselves excluded' (*CPES*, p. 164).

Baudrillard begins distancing himself from Marxism here, and in particular attacks Marx's alleged economic reductionism, or 'productivism,' and the alleged inability of the Marxian theory to conceptualize language, signs and communication (Habermas at the time was developing a parallel position within Critical Theory).[5] As an example of the failure of Marxian categories to provide an adequate theory of the media, Baudrillard criticizes the German activist and writer Hans-Magnus Enzensberger's media theory and his attempts to develop a socialist strategy for the media.[6] Baudrillard dismisses this effort as a typical Marxian attempt to liberate productive forces from the fetters of productive relations, one that fails to see that *in their very form* the mass media of communication

> are anti-mediatory and intransitive. They fabricate non-communication – this is what characterizes them, if one agrees to define communication as an exchange, as a reciprocal space of a speech and a response and thus of a *responsibility* (not a psychological or moral responsibility, but a personal, mutual correlation in exchange) . . . *they are what always prevents response*, making all processes of exchange impossible (except in the various forms of response *simulation*, themselves integrated in the transmission process, thus leaving the unilateral nature of the communication intact). This is the real abstraction of the media. And the system of social control and power is rooted in it. (*CPES*, pp. 169–70)

It is curious that Baudrillard, interpreted by many of his followers as an avant-garde, postmodern media theorist, reveals in this passage both technophobia and a nostalgia for face-to-face conversation which he privileges (as authentic communication) over debased and abstract media communication. Such a position creates a binary dichotomy between 'good' face-to-face communication and 'bad' media communication, and thus occludes the fact that interpersonal communication can be just as manipulative, distorted, reified and the rest as media communication (of which Ionesco and Habermas, among others, were aware). It also rules out in advance the possibility of 'responsible' or 'emancipatory' media communication, a point to which I will return in the conclusion to this section.

Media and Postmodernity

In another study in *Critique*, Baudrillard noted how the 'TV Object' was becoming the center of the household, and was serving an essential 'proof function' that the owner was a genuine member of the consumer society (*CPES*, pp. 53ff.). The escalating role of the media in contemporary society is for Baudrillard equivalent to THE FALL into the postmodern society of simulations from the modern universe of production. Whereas modernity centered on the production of things, commodities and products, postmodernity is characterized by radical semiurgy, by a proliferation of signs.

Furthermore, following McLuhan, Baudrillard interprets modernity as a process of explosion of commodification, mechanization, technology and market relations, in contrast to postmodern society, which is the site of an *implosion* of all boundaries, regions and distinctions between high and low culture, appearance and reality, and just about every other binary opposition maintained by traditional philosophy and social theory. Furthermore, while modernity could be characterized as a process of increasing differentiation of spheres of life (Max Weber as interpreted by Habermas), postmodernity could be interpreted as a process of *de-differentiation* and attendant implosion.[7]

The rise of the broadcast media, especially television, is an important constituent of postmodernity for Baudrillard, along with the rapid dissemination of signs and simulacra in every realm of social and everyday life. By the late 1970s, Baudrillard was interpreting the media as key simulation machines which reproduce images, signs and codes which in turn come to constitute an autonomous realm of (hyper)reality and also to play a key role in everyday life and the obliteration of the social. This process constitutes a significant reversal of the relation between representation and reality. Previously the media were believed to mirror, reflect or represent reality, whereas now they are coming to constitute a (hyper)reality, a new media reality, 'more real than real,' where 'the real' is subordinate to representation thus leading ultimately to a dissolving of the real (see the further discussion of this point in 3.3 and 3.4).

In 'The Implosion of Meaning in the Media,'[8] Baudrillard claims that the proliferation of signs and information in the media obliterates meaning through neutralizing and dissolving all content, a process which leads to both a collapse of meaning and the destruction of distinctions between media and reality. In a society supposedly saturated with media messages, information and meaning 'implode,' into meaningless 'noise,' pure effect without content or meaning. Thus, Baudrillard claims, 'information is directly destructive of meaning and signification, or neutralizes it. The loss of meaning is directly linked to the dissolving and dissuasive action of information, the media and the mass media. . . . Information devours its own contents; it devours communication and the social. . . . information dissolves meaning and the social into a sort of nebulous state leading not at all to a surfeit of innovation but to the very contrary, to total entropy' (*SSM*, pp. 96–100).

Baudrillard uses here a model of the media as a black hole of signs and information that absorbs all contents into cybernetic noise which no longer communicates meaningful messages in a process in which all content implodes into form. We thus see how Baudrillard eventually adopts McLuhan's media theory as his own, claiming that:

> the medium is the message signifies not only the end of the message, but also the end of the medium. There are no longer media in the literal

sense of the term (I am talking above all about the electronic mass media) – that is to say, a power mediating between one reality and another, between one state of the real and another – neither in content nor in form. Strictly speaking this is what implosion signifies: the absorption of one pole into another, the short-circuit between poles of every differential system of meaning, the effacement of terms and of distinct oppositions and thus that of the medium and the real. . . . This critical – but original – situation must be thought through to the very end; it is the only one we are left with. It is useless to dream of a revolution through content or through form, since the medium and the real are now in a single nebulous state whose truth is undecipherable. (*SSM*, pp. 102–3)

Baudrillard also suggests that the media intensify massification by producing mass audiences and homogenized ideas and experience. On the other hand, he claims that the masses absorb all media content, neutralize, or even resist, meaning, and demand and obtain more spectacle and entertainment, thus further eroding the boundary between media and 'the real.' In this sense, the media implode into the masses to such an extent that we no longer know what effects the media have on the masses and how the masses process the media. Consequently, on this view, the media pander to the masses, reproducing their taste, their interest in spectacle and entertainment, their fantasies and way of life, thereby giving rise to an implosion between mass consciousness and media phantasmagoria. In this way Baudrillard short-circuits the manipulation theory which sees media manipulation imposed from above producing mass consciousness. Yet he seems to share the contempt for the masses that characterizes standard manipulation theory, claiming that the masses want nothing more than spectacle, diversion, entertainment and escape, and are incapable of, or uninterested in, meaning.

In *De la séduction* (1979) Baudrillard utilizes McLuhan's distinction between 'hot' and 'cool' media to describe the ways in which the media devour information and exterminate meaning.[9] According to Baudrillard, the media take 'hot' events like sports, wars, political turmoil, catastrophes and so forth, and transform them into 'cool' media events, which he interprets as altogether different. Concerning the difference between a televised and a live sports event, Baudrillard writes: 'Do not believe that it is a matter of the same game: one is hot, the other is cool – one is a contest where affect, challenge, *mise en scène* and spectacle are present, whereas the other is tactile, modulated (visions in flash-back, replays, close-ups or overhead views, various angles, etc.): a televised sports event is above all a televised event, just as *Holocaust* or the Vietnam War are televised events of which one can hardly make distinctions' (*SED*, p. 217).

For Baudrillard, all the dominant media become 'cool', eventually

lematical) distinction between hot and cool media is
for Baudrillard all the media of information and com-
alize meaning, and involve the audience in a flat, one-
lia experience, which he defines in terms of a passive
images or resistance to meaning, rather than an active
production of meaning. On this account, therefore the
a have nothing to do with myth, image, history or the
construction of meaning (or ideology). Television is viewed instead as a
media 'which suggests nothing, which magnetises, which is only a screen, or
is rather a miniaturized terminal which in fact is found immediately in your
head – you are the screen and the television is watching you. Television
transistorizes all neurons and operates as a magnetic tape – a tape not an
image' (*SED*, p. 220).

We see here how Baudrillard out-McLuhans McLuhan in interpreting
television and all other media simply as technological forms, as machines
which produce primarily technological effects in which content and
messages or social uses are deemed irrelevant and unimportant. We also see
how, like McLuhan, he anthropomorphizes the media ('the television is
watching you'), a form of technological mysticism (or to be more nasty,
mystification) as extreme as that of McLuhan. Like McLuhan, Baudrillard
also globalizes media effects, thereby making the media demiurges of a new
type of society and new type of experience.

He also practices McLuhan's method of probes and mosaic constellations
of images and concepts, which here take on an experimental and provisional
nature. Consequently, whereas Baudrillard sets forth theoretically articulated
theses about the media in 'Requiem,' in his studies of simulations (see 3.3
below) and later writings he tends to cluster images, concepts and descriptive
analyses within which the media often play a key role, rather than articulate
systematically a well-defined theoretical position, thus adopting a key
McLuhanite literary strategy.

Yet we might contrast here McLuhan's ecumenical Catholicism with
Baudrillard's somewhat puritanical Protestantism.[10] McLuhan fantasized a
new type of global community and even a new universal (media)
consciousness and experience through the dissemination of a global media
system, the global village. He also believed that the media could overcome
the alienati~ produced by the abstract rationality of book culture, which
w~~ ~ d by a new synaesthesia and harmonization of mind and
d technologies. Baudrillard, by contrast, sees the media as
– or idols of the mind, to continue the Protestant
duce and fascinate the subject and enter subjectivity to
ciousness and privatized, serialized life-style (Sartre's
McLuhan ascribes a generally benign social destiny to
sees the function of television and mass media as
by isolating and privatizing individuals, trapping

them in a universe of simulacra in which it is impossible to distinguish between the spectacle and the real and in which individuals come to prefer spectacle to 'reality' (which then loses both interest for the masses and its privileged status in philosophy and social theory).

Baudrillard thus views the mass media as instruments of a 'cold seduction' whose narcissistic charm consists in a manipulative self-seduction, in which we enjoy the play of lights, shadows, dots and events in our own mind as we change channels or media and plug into the variety of networks – media, computer, information – that surround us and allow us to become modulators and controllers of an infinitely variable panoply of sights, sounds, information and events. In this sense, media have a chilling effect – which is why Baudrillard allows McLuhan's 'cool' to become downright 'cold' – which freezes individuals into functioning as terminals of media and communication networks who become involved as part and parcel of the very apparatus of communication. The subject, then, becomes transformed into an object as part of a nexus of information and communication networks.

The interiorization of media transmissions within the screen of our mind obliterates, he claims, the distinction between public and private, interior and exterior space, both of which are replaced by media space. Here Baudrillard inverts McLuhan's thesis concerning the media as extensions of the human, as exteriorizations of human powers, and argues instead that people internalize the media and thus become terminals within media systems – a new theoretical anti-humanism. On this model the eye and the brain replace the sense organs and the hand as primary instruments of human practice, just as information processing replaces production, techné and poèsis as fundamental forms of human activity.[11]

Once again Baudrillard projects a cybernetic imaginary which sees people as becoming more and more like machines, like information processing, in which the body and the senses are devalued and excluded from analysis. In 'The Ecstasy of Communication' Baudrillard describes the media as instruments of obscenity, transparency and ecstasy – in his special sense of these terms.[12] He claims that in the postmodern mediascape, the domestic scene – or the private sphere per se – with its rules, rituals and privacy is exteriorized, or made explicit and transparent,

in a sort of *obscenity* where the most intimate processes of our life become the virtual feeding ground of the media '
United States, the innumerable slices of peasar
French television). Inversely, the entire univ
arbitrarily on your domestic screen (all the us
comes to you from the entire world, like a mic
of the universe, useless, excessive, just like the
porno film): all this explodes the scene forme

minimal separation of public and private, the scene that was played out
in a restricted space. (p. 130)

Further, the spectacles of the consumer society and the dramas of the
public sphere are being replaced by media events which replace public life
and scenes with a screen that shows us everything instantaneously and
without scruple or hesitation. The ecstasy of communication: everything is
explicit, ecstatic – out of or beyond itself – and obscene in its transparency,
detail and visibility: 'It is no longer the traditional obscenity of what is
hidden, repressed, forbidden or obscure; on the contrary, it is the obscenity
of the visible, of the all-too-visible, of the more-visible-than-visible. It is the
obscenity of what no longer has any secret, of what dissolves completely in
information and communication' (p. 131). One thinks here of such 1987–88
media revelations as those concerning the intimate details of the sexual
escapades of Gary Hart and Donna Rice or Jim Bakker and Jimmy
Swaggart, of Ronald and Nancy Reagan's cancer operations and predilections
for astrology, of the dirty business deals of Reagan's associates and the dirty
political deals of Iran/Contra, all of which have been exposed to the glaring
scrutiny of the media in such a way that what used to be private, hidden and
invisible suddenly becomes (almost) fully explicit and visible.

In the ecstasy of communication, a promiscuity of information and
communication is circulated and disseminated by a teeming network of cool,
seductive and fascinating sights and sounds which are played on one's own
screen and terminal. With the disappearance of exciting scenes (in the home,
in the public sphere), passion evaporates in personal and social relations; yet
a new fascination emerges ('the scene excites us, the obscene fascinates us')
with the very universe of media and communication. In this universe we
enter a new form of subjectivity, in which we become saturated with
information, images, events and ecstasies. Without defense or distance, we
become 'a pure screen, a switching center for all the networks of influence'
(p. 133). In the media society, the era of interiority, subjectivity, meaning,
privacy and the inner life is over; a new era of obscenity, fascination, vertigo,
instantaneity, transparency and overexposure begins: Welcome to the
postmodern world!

In his more recent, 1980 writings, which I shall examine in later chapters –
and which tend to recycle his earlier positions – Baudrillard continues to call
attention to McLuhan as the great media theorist of our epoch and to
subscribe to the positions that I have explicated above. He also suggests that
one should go even further than McLuhan in denying that the media are
producers of meaning and that media content or apparatus is important – a
position that I shall now critically engage.

Three Subordinations

Undoubtedly the media are playing an ever greater role in our personal and social lives, and have dramatically transformed our economy, polity and society, in ways that we are only now becoming aware of. Living within a great transformation, perhaps as significant as the transformation from feudalism to industrial capitalism, we are engaged in a process of dramatic mutation, a process we are barely beginning to understand, as we enter a new world of media saturation, computerization, new technologies and new discourses. Baudrillard's contribution lies in his calling attention to these novelties and transformations and providing new concepts and theories to understand them.

Yet doubts remain as to whether the media are having quite the impact that Baudrillard says they are and whether his theory provides adequate concepts for analyzing the complex interactions between media, culture and society today. In this section I will suggest that Baudrillard's media theory is vitiated by three subordinations which undermine its theoretical and political usefulness and also raise questions about the status of postmodern social theory. I will suggest that the limitations in Baudrillard's theory can be related to his uncritical acceptance of certain positions within McLuhan's media theory, and therefore that earlier critiques of McLuhan can accurately and usefully be applied to Baudrillard. This critique will suggest that Baudrillard can be seen as a 'new McLuhan' who has repackaged McLuhan into new postmodern cultural capital.

First it should be noted that Baudrillard, like McLuhan, privileges the *form* of media technology over its content, meaning and the use of media, reducing the media to their purely formal structure and effects, and thus to what might be called a *formalist subordination*. Baudrillard – much more than McLuhan, who at least gives some media history and analysis of the media environment – tends to abstract the form and effects of the media from their sociohistorical environment, thereby erasing political economy, media production and media environment – that is, society at large – from his theory. Against this, I would argue that the use and effects of the media should be carefully examined and evaluated in terms of specific contexts. Context and use, form and content, media and reality, all dissolve, however, in Baudrillard's one-dimensional theory, in which global theses and glib pronouncements replace careful analysis and critique.

Baudrillard might retort that it is the media themselves which abstract from the concreteness of everyday, social and political life and provide abstract simulacra of actual events which themselves become more real than 'the real' which they supposedly represent. Yet even if this is so, media analysis should attempt to recontextualize media images and simulacra, rather than simply focusing on the surface of media form. Baudrillard thus offers a rather flat, one-dimensional picture of the media world, one that replaces what might be called a 'dialectics of the media' by reducing the media to determinate (formal) effects. That is, it is media form not content, media images not institutions, media codes and not apparatuses, which are the key terms for Baudrillard's media theory. He thus occludes key constituents within media production, distribution and reception by abstracting media from social systems so that they appear as mere epiphenomena of technology and semiurgy – just like McLuhan.

Against Baudrillard and McLuhan, one could argue that the forces and imperatives of capitalism continue to be a primary determinant of media form and content in neo-capitalist societies, just as state socialism helps determine the form, nature and effects of technologies in certain state socialist societies. Moreover, I would argue that, rather than simply operating with a model of (formal) media effects, it is preferable to operate with a dialectic of form and content, media and society, and to posit multiple roles and functions for television and other media. This brings us to a second subordination in Baudrillard's theory, one in which a more dialectical position is subordinated to *media essentialism and technological determinism*. For – according to Baudrillard at least – it is the technology of television, for instance, that determines its effects (one-way transmission, semiurgy, implosion, extermination of meaning and the social, obscenity and so on) rather than any particular content or message (the media is the message) or its construction or use within specific social systems. For Baudrillard, media technology and semiurgy are the demiurges of media practices and effects, separated from their uses by specific economic and political interests, individuals and groups, and the social systems within which they function.

Baudrillard, like McLuhan, often makes essentializing distinctions between media like television or film, ascribing one essence to one and an opposed essence to the other.[13] Yet it seems highly problematical to reduce apparatuses as complex, contradictory and many-sided as television (or film or any mass medium) to its formal properties and effects and its technological essence. Thirdly, there is a subordination of cultural interpretation and politics to what might very loosely be called 'theory,' thus constituting a *theoricist subordination* in Baudrillard. In other words, just as Althusser subordinated concrete empirical and historical analysis to what he called 'theoretical practice' – and thus was criticized for his 'theoreticism' – so Baudrillard rarely engages in close analysis or readings of media texts, and instead simply engages in rather abstract theoretical ruminations. Here his armchair or television-screen theorizing might be compared with Foucault's archival research or to more detailed and systematic media theory and critique, to Baudrillard's detriment.

Consequently, there is no real theory or practice of cultural interpretation in Baudrillard's media (increasingly anti-) theory, which also reflects an anti-hermeneutical bias which denies the importance of content and is against interpretation.[14] Furthermore, for the most part, Baudrillard rigorously avoids the messy but important terrain of cultural politics. His theorizing has nothing concerning alternative media practices, for instance; indeed, he seems to rule them out in advance, because on his view *all* media are mere producers of noise, noncommunication, the extermination of meaning, implosion and so on. In 'Requiem for the Media,' Baudrillard explicitly argues that all mass media communication falls prey to 'mass mediatization' – that is, 'the imposition of models.' 'In fact, the essential Medium is the Model. What is mediatized is not what comes off the daily press, out of the tube, or on the radio: it is what is reinterpreted by the sign form, articulated into models and administered by the code (just as the commodity is not what is produced industrially, but what is mediatized by the exchange value system of abstraction)' (*CPES*, pp. 175–6).

For Baudrillard, then, all 'subversive communication' has to circumvent the codes and models of media communication – and thus of the mass media themselves, which invariably translate all contents and messages into their codes. Consequently not only general elections, but general strikes, have 'become a schematic reducing agent' (*CPES*, p. 176). In this (original) situation:

> The real revolutionary media during May [1968] were the walls and their speech, the silk-screen posters and the hand-painted notices, the street where speech began and was exchanged – everything that was an *immediate* inscription, given and returned, spoken and answered, mobile in the same space and time, reciprocal and antagonistic. The street is, in this sense, the alternative and subversive form of the mass media, since it isn't, like the latter, an objectified support for answerless messages, a transmission system at a distance. It is the frayed space of the symbolic exchange of speech – ephemeral, mortal: a speech that is not reflected on the Platonic screen of the media. Institutionalized by reproduction, reduced to a spectacle, this speech is expiring'. (*CPES*, pp. 176–7)[15]

Baudrillard here displays once again a nostalgia for direct, unmediated and reciprocal speech (symbolic exchange), which is denied in the media society. Haunted by a disappearing metaphysics of presence, Baudrillard valorizes immediate communication over mediated communication, forgetting that all communication is mediated (through language, signs, and so on). Furthermore, he romanticizes a certain form of communication (speech in the streets, graffiti) as the only genuinely subversive or revolutionary communication and media. Consistently with this theory, he calls for a (neo-Luddite) 'deconstruction' of the media 'as systems of non-communication,' and thus for the 'liquidation of the existing functional and technical structure of the media' (*CPES*, p. 177).

Against Baudrillard's utopia of immediate speech, I would defend the project of structural and technical refunctioning of the media, as suggested earlier by Brecht, Benjamin and Enzensberger.[16] Baudrillard, by contrast, not only attacks all form of media communication as nonrevolutionary, but by the late 1970s has completely surrendered his commitment to revolutionary theory and dropped the notion of revolutionary communication or subversive cultural practices altogether. This political development is related to his turn to a more extreme postmodern social theory.

3.3   SIMULATION, HYPERREALITY AND IMPLOSION

Baudrillard began elaborating his new model of society in a discussion of cybernetics contained in an important early 1970s study entitled 'Design and Environment or How Political Economy Escalates into Cyberblitz,' collected in *Critique*. Anticipating his later theory of simulations, he points to the importance of 'the passage out of a *metallurgic* into a *semiurgic* society' (*CPES*, p. 185). In this passage, the object takes on a life of its own, as an embodiment and functional part of a system of signs, independent of its status as a commodity. This situation is first evident, Baudrillard believes, in the German Bauhaus movement, in which objects function as pure signs, pure functionality, rather than as products or commodities. 'It is the Bauhaus that institutes this universal semantization of the environment in which everything becomes the object of a calculus of function and of signification. Total functionality, total semiurgy. It is a "revolution" in relation to the traditional mode, in which objects (for lack of a better word) are bound together and not liberated, have no status of their own and do not form a system among themselves on the basis of a rational finality (functionality)' (*CPES*, pp. 185–6).

Here Baudrillard sees the same systematization of objects on the level of design and architecture that he analyzed on the level of commodities and needs in his theory of the consumer society. Now, however, cybernetic systematization and control take place on a higher level of abstraction, and connect more obviously with social control, homogenization and design than do attempts to manage society on the level of consumption, where one could argue that the anarchy of competing corporations and advertisers is more salient than any centralized efforts at control and management.

The Bauhaus synthesis 'of form and function, of "beauty and utility," of art and technology,' in Baudrillard's view, anticipates technocratic and cybernetic projects of developing a whole system of objects controlled from above that would produce a functionalized universe in which the meaning and function of every object would be determined by its place and role in the functionalized system. The result would be a 'universal semiotic of technological experience' – Baudrillard uses Jeremy Shapiro's phrase here – which comes to characterize the totality of experience in contemporary society, in which 'the whole environment becomes a signifier, objectified as an element of signification' (*CPES*, pp. 186–7).[17]

In a sense, this would involve a higher level of social organization and control than that theorized by Marcuse and the Frankfurt School in the notion of a one-dimensional society.[18] It is of course questionable whether our entire environment is already organized and administered through such design and cybernetic projects; but it is clear that such projects are attempted in at least some areas of social life (city planning, architecture, political planning and steering mechanisms, shopping malls and so on). Baudrillard goes on to describe the role of style, aesthetics and functionalism in these enterprises which he designates as the triumph of signifying culture over nature that produces a new artificial environment and evacuates the aesthetic dimension of any oppositional potential. The cyberneticization of society also signifies the triumph of functionalization in a society of total control and total organization in which functionalized aesthetics are incorporated in the very organization of society. Consequently Baudrillard concludes that the Bauhaus's functionalizing of aesthetics allegedly reaches completion in the structural organization of contemporary society.

For the next few years Baudrillard's main focus would be what he called 'cyberblitz,' whereby individuals, objects and society are subjected to the effects of cybernetic codes, models, modulations and the steering systems of a society which aims at perfecting its instruments of social control. In Baudrillard's later writings, political economy, the media and cybernetics coalesce to produce a new social order beyond the stage of capitalism described by Marxism, the new postmodern society. The new forms of technological determinism become central themes in his mid- to late 1970s writings, some of which have been translated and collected in *Simulations* and *In The Shadow of the Silent Majorities*. In these texts, the masses, the silent majorities, passively consume commodities, television, sports, politics, information and so on to such an extent that traditional politics and class struggle become obsolete. In Baudrillard's universe, simulacra and simulation play such a key role in social life that previous boundaries and categories of social theory dissolve altogether. All dichotomies between appearance and reality, surface and depth, life and art, subject and object, collapse into a functionalized, integrated and self-reproducing universe of 'simulacra' controlled by 'simulation' models and codes.

The Orders of Simulacra

The initial sketch of this new social situation is found in 'The Orders of Simulacra,' first published in French in *L'échange symbolique et la mort* (1976) and collected in *Simulations* (1983).[19] This study contains a historical sketch of various orders of simulacra, culminating in the society of simulations; while a later study, 'The Precession of Simulacra' (also collected in *Simulations*) contains a series of analyses of some of the ways in which simulations have come to dominate contemporary society and have produced a new kind of social order.

For Baudrillard, 'simulacra' are reproductions of objects or events, while the 'orders of simulacra' form various stages or 'orders of appearance' in the relationships between simulacra and 'the real.' Baudrillard presents a theory of how simulacra came to dominate social life, both historically and phenomenologically. In a historical sketch of the orders of simulacra, heavily influenced by Foucault's archaelogies of knowledge in *The Order of Things*,[20] Baudrillard claims that modernity broke with the fixed feudal-medieval hierarchy of signs and social position by introducing an artificial, democratized world of signs which valorized artifice (stucco, theater, fashion, baroque art, political democracy) over natural signs, thereby exploding fixed medieval hierarchies and order (*SIM*, pp. 83–92).

In the feudal era, according to Baudrillard, a fixed social order established a hierarchy of signs of class, rank and social position. Signs at this stage were fixed, restricted and perfectly clear and transparent – in a word, 'obligatory.' During this era one could readily read from an individual's clothes and appearance his or her social rank and status. In the succeeeding modern order however, the 'counterfeit' is the paradigmatic mode of representation, and a new order of simulacra begins. Haunted by the loss of the divine sanction and fixed value of the medieval era, the now arbitrary sign is 'liberated' by the bourgeoisie from the fixed medieval hierarchy, but seeks to imitate nature and to ground its signs in nature. Thus the art of the period attempts to imitate life, and representative democracy grounds its ideology in 'natural rights.' During this era, signs proliferate, and the new rising class, the bourgeoisie, dreams of creating a world in its own image. For Baudrillard, the new substance of stucco – the first prototype of semiurgic control – represents the potential for re-creating the world, on account of its suitability to creating simulacra of natural building materials, objects or art (as in the architecture of stucco churches and buildings).

In Baudrillard's terminology, a 'natural law of value' dominated this stage of early modernity, in which simulacra (from art to political representation) were held to represent nature or to embody 'natural' rights or laws. On Baudrillard's account, 'simulacra are not only a game played with signs; they imply social relations and social power' (*SIM*, p. 88). He finds examples of the new desire to control and remake the world in the Jesuits' political ambitions and in a French sculptor's attempts to produce a counterfeit world out of reinforced concrete (*SIM*, pp. 88ff.). Indeed, Baudrillard suggests that the inherent goal of the order of simulacra is to produce a flexible and controllable universal *system* of order and power: 'The counterfeit is working, so far, only on substance and form, not yet on relations and structures. But it is aiming already, on this level, at the control of a pacified society, ground up into a synthetic deathless substance: an indestructible artifact that will guarantee an eternity of power. . . . It is a project of political and cultural hegemony' (*SIM*, p. 91).

The 'second order' of simulacra appeared during the industrial revolution, when infinite reproducibility was introduced into the world in the form of the industrial simulacrum or series (*SIM*, pp. 96ff.). Production then became mechanized, and turned out series of mass objects: exact replicas, infinitely produced and reproduced by assembly-line processes and eventually automation. Baudrillard illustrates the difference between the first and second orders of simulacra by a comparison between an automaton, a mechanical imitation of humans, and a robot:

> The automaton plays the part of courtier and good company; it participates in the pre-Revolutionary French theatrical and social games. The robot, on the other hand, as his name indicates, is a worker: the theatre is over and done with, the reign of mechanical man commences. The automaton is the *analogy* of man and remains his interlocutor (they play chess together!). The machine is man's *equivalent* and annexes him to itself in the unity of its operational process. This is the difference between a simulacrum of the first order and one of the second. (*SIM*, pp. 92–3)

With the introduction of photography and then film, as Walter Benjamin saw, even art was taken over by mechanical reproduction, losing its aura and thus being forced to relinquish its claims to represent a higher dimension offering alternative and allegedly superior values and representations. In this order of simulacra, there is no longer nostalgia for a natural order: nature becomes the object of domination, and reproduction itself becomes a dominant social principle governed by the laws of the market. Baudrillard sees the industrial order as ruled by the 'commercial law of value,' equivalent exchange, and no longer by the 'natural law of value.' All serial objects of production are equivalent, and their worth is marked by their market value, which makes possible the change of equivalents, while reproducibility now becomes the fundamental logic and code of the society.

Yet today, Baudrillard claims, 'we are in the third-order simulacra; no longer that of the counterfeit of an original as in the first-order, nor that of the pure series as in the second' (*SIM*, pp. 100–1). This is the stage of 'simulation proper,' the end result of a long historical process of simulation, in which simulation models come to constitute the world, and overtake and finally 'devour' representation. Now 'the structural law of value' reigns, and models take precedence over things, while 'serial production yields to generation by means of models. . . . Digitality is its metaphysical principle . . . and DNA its prophet. It is in effect in the genetic code that the "genesis of simulacra" today finds its most accomplished form' (*SIM*, pp. 103–4).

Society thus moves from 'a capitalist-productivist society to a neo-capitalist cybernetic order that aims now at total control' (*SIM*, p. 111).

Baudrillard presents this theory in terms of suggestive analogies between language, genetics and social organization. Just as language contains codes or models that structure how we communicate, and just as our cells contain genetic codes, DNA, that structure how we experience and behave, so too society contains codes and models of social organization and control which structure the environment and human life. That is, urban, architectural and transportation models structure within certain limits how cities, houses and transportation systems are organized and used, and these in turn are governed by the logic of the simulation model or code. For example, within the track suburban houses, interior design manuals, exercise video-cassettes, child-care books, sexual manuals, cookbooks and magazines, newspapers and broadcast media all provide models that structure various activities within everyday life.

At this point in his development, the code of political economy, or production, which seemed to rule his earlier vision of society, has been pluralized into a variety of different simulation codes governing such widely diverse areas of social life as media, fashion, architecture, sexuality, design and consumerism. The constitution of society by codes is radically indeterministic, as it is often not clear which codes are constituting a given domain of social life. At this point his model of the code seems to be the DNA which programs various directions and constraints on behavior in an individual, but which itself is not perceived and which is subject to aleatory combinations and permutations in interaction with other social and environmental phenomena.

In the society of coded simulation, urban planners, for example, modulate codes of city planning and architecture in creating urban systems, in much the same way that television producers modulate television codes to produce programs. Models and codes thus come to constitute everyday life, and modulation of the code comes to structure a system of differences and social relations in the society of simulations. The codes send signals and continually test individuals, inscribing them into the simulated order. Responses are structured in a binary system of affirmation or negation: every ad, fashion, commodity, television program, political candidate and poll presents a test to which one is to respond. Is one for or against? Do we want it or not? Will we choose X or Y? In this way, one is inserted in a coded system of similarities and dissimilarities, of identities and programmed differences.

The society of simulations thus comes to control an individual's range of responses and options for choice and behavior. As opposed to previous determinist social theories, as well as conspiracy theories which postulate individuals or groups manipulating the public for certain ends, Baudrillard's model appears to be radically indeterminist, and offers a new model of social control in which codes and programming become the principle of social organization, and individuals are forced to respond to pre-coded messages and models in the realm of economics, politics, culture and everyday life (*SIM*, pp. 111ff.). Although one is allowed a range of choices – indeed such choice is constantly demanded – the options are predetermined and pre-coded (*SIM*, p. 117).

Michel Foucault's 'disciplinary society' with its modes of surveillance and punishment thus becomes for Baudrillard a society of simulated 'tests' and programmed differences.[21] Polling, elections, consumer purchases, fashions, media and so forth are all part of a system of binary regulation stabilized by two political parties, two opposing classes, two hostile superpowers, two (or more) choices at every moment. The matrix 'remains binary,' however, and from 'the smallest disjunctive unity (question/answer particle) up to the great alternating systems that control the economy, politics, world co-existence, the matrix does not change: it is always the 0/1, the binary scansion that is affirmed as the metastable or homeostatic form of the current systems. This is the nucleus of the simulation processes which dominate us' (*SIM*, pp. 134–5).

For Baudrillard, this binary system constitutes a 'deterrence model' in which all radical change is ruled out, since the very fact of an option between different political parties, products, life-styles and so forth acts as a deterrent against demands for radical social change. As a symbol of the homeostatic, stabilized society of simulations, Baudrillard points to the two towers of the New York World Trade Center which peacefully coexist in a noncompetitive harmony and stability: 'The two towers of the W. T. C. are the visible sign of the closure of the system in a vertigo of duplication, while the other skyscrapers are each of them the original moment of a system constantly transcending itself in a perpetual crisis and self-challenge' (*SIM*, pp. 136–7).

Likewise, Baudrillard interprets the nuclear weapons race as part of a worldwide deterrence system which stabilizes the world political system externally through a 'balance of terror,' while internally helping to perfect systems of social control: 'It isn't that the direct menace of atomic destruction paralyses our lives. It is rather that deterrence leukemises us. And this deterrence comes from the very situation which *excludes the real atomic clash*. . . . Deterrence excludes war – the antiquated violence of expanding systems. Deterrence is the neutral, implosive violence of metastable or involving systems. . . . The balance of terror is the terror of balance' (*SIM*, pp. 59–60).

The triumph of cybernetics is that everything is reduced to a binary system whose two supposedly dominant poles – political parties, world superpowers, seemingly opposing forces or principles and so on – cancel out their differences, and serve to maintain a self-regulating, selfsame, self-reproducing system. In his writings from the mid-1970s to the present, Baudrillard provides example after example to support these hypotheses.

The political upshot of his analysis seems to be that everything in the system is subject to cybernetic control, and that what appear to be oppositional, outside, or threatening to the system are really functional parts of a society of simulations, mere 'alibis' which only further enhance social control.

Cybernetics, Hyperreality and Baudrillard's High-Tech Social Theory

Baudrillard's vision of the society of simulations is symptomatic of a cybernetic imaginary which sees contemporary society as providing an elaborate system of deterrence – against such things as instability, revolutionary change and so on – in everything, from its weapons policy to its media, its educational system to its representational democracy. In Baudrillard's analysis, the Watergate affair exhibited the political scandals and illegal acts of the Nixon administration so as to create the illusion that the system in fact respected and embodied law and morality (*SIM*, pp. 26ff.). The scandal thus served to mask the perception that the system itself is fundamentally a scandal: cruel, immoral and unscrupulous. Hence revelations of wrongdoing in Watergate (or in Reagan's arms-for-Iran/cash-for-Contras scandal) provide systems of deterrence which strengthen the functionality and legitimacy of the system.

In a similar manner, Baudrillard claims that Disneyland presents itself as an imaginary space so as

> to conceal the fact that it is the 'real' country, all of 'real' America, which *is* Disneyland (just as prisons are there to conceal the fact that it is the social in its entirety, in its banal omnipresence, which is carceral). Disneyland is presented as imaginary in order to make us believe that the rest is real, when in fact all of Los Angeles and the America surrounding it are no longer real, but of the order of the hyperreal and of simulation. . . . It is meant to be an infantile world, in order to make us believe that the adults are elsewhere, in the 'real' world and to conceal the fact that real childishness is everywhere, particularly amongst those adults who go there to act the child in order to foster illusions as to their real childishness. (*SIM*, p. 25)

Disneyland provides an example of Baudrillard's difficult and crucial concept of hyperreality. For Baudrillard, the hyperreal is not the unreal but the more than real, the realler than real, as when models of the United States in Disneyland appear more real than their instantiations in the social world, as the United States becomes more and more like Disneyland (*SIM*, pp. 23ff.). On this theory, 'the very definition of the real has become *that of which it is possible to give an equivalent reproduction*,' and the 'hyperreal' is '*that which is always already reproduced*' (*SIM*, p. 146), that which perfectly instantiates its model: 'The real is produced from miniaturized units, from matrices, memory banks and command models – and with these it can be reproduced an infinite number of times' (*SIM*, p. X).

In a hyperreal world, 'the model comes first,' and its constitutive role is invisible, because all one sees are instantiations of models (while one reproduces models of thought and behavior oneself). For Baudrillard, the entire facade and ecosphere of neo-capitalist societies are hyperreal, in that more and more areas of social life are reproductions of models organized into a system of models and codes. Such a hyperreal society of simulations includes such things as interstate highway and urban freeway transportation systems, fashion, media, architecture and housing developments, shopping malls and products which are reproductions of models, instantiations of codes: 'Today it is quotidian reality in its entirety – political, social, historical and economic – that from now on incorporates the simulatory dimension of hyperrealism' (*SIM*, p. 147).

Everyday life thus becomes more and more hyperreal as hair, teeth, fingernails, food, flowers, grass and houses constitute a new hyperreality that is 'more real than real.' Thought and behavior are likewise determined by codes and models which are reproduced in everyday social interactions and the presentation of the self in everyday life. In such a universe there can be no explosive contradictions, crises or even opposition, because everything is designed and controlled. There is no 'reality,' or even potentiality, in the name of which oppressive phenomena can be criticized and transformed, because there is nothing behind the flow of codes, signs and simulacra. In this hyperreal universe, not even social critique or critical art are possible: 'The cool universe of digitality has absorbed the world of metaphor and metonymy. The principle of simulation wins out over the reality principle just as over the principle of pleasure' (*SIM*, p. 152).

Throughout the analysis, Baudrillard uses various scientific concepts as metaphors for social processes. For example, the Moebius strip is used as a metaphor for the proliferation of models and simulations. Just as a Moebius strip, when cut in half, produces a more complex spiralled structure, so simulations form a spiralling, circular system with no beginning or end, a system which becomes increasingly complex and entangled in itself the more it multiplies: 'If the entire cycle of any act or event is envisaged in a system where linear continuity and dialectical polarity no longer exist, in a field *unhinged by simulation*, then all determination evaporates, every act terminates at the end of the cycle' (*SIM*, p. 31).

Baudrillard seems to be paradoxically suggesting that determination is both total and totally indeterminate; for, while the system consists of its models and codes, which determine all action and possibilities, it is (generally? always?) impossible to determine in a causal model which codes are determining which action at a given moment, due to what Baudrillard calls 'implosion.' He rejects the model of media effects and models of the media as manipulation, claiming instead that the media should be conceived in terms of a DNA model in which

> in the process of molecular control, which 'goes' from the DNA nucleus to the 'substance' it 'informs,' there is no more traversing of an effect, of an energy, of a determination, of any message. . . . [Rather] nothing separates one pole from the other, the initial from the terminal: there is just a sort of contraction into each other, a fantastic telescoping, a collapsing of the two traditional poles into one another: an IMPLOSION – an absorption of the radiating model of causality, of the differential mode of determination, with its positive and negative electricity – an implosion of meaning. *This is where simulation begins.* (*SIM*, pp. 56–7)

Such (typical) passages are highly obscure; indeed, one of the more frustrating features of Baudrillard's method is his use of scientific, or pseudo-scientific metaphors and concepts to illustrate his theories. Baudrillard's writings are full of references to black holes, entropy, DNA and genetics, digital codes and information theory, satellites and cybernetics.[22] These writings constitute perhaps the first radical high-tech, new wave social theory. They also involve what is perhaps the first self-consciously produced science fiction social theory to project futuristic anticipations of the world to come, the world right around the corner. Baudrillard's writing makes use of the familiar associations and prestige of science, as well as familiarity with the media and shared social and political events. As we discuss these texts in the following chapters, we will be asking whether Baudrillard himself partakes of and reproduces the features and limitations of the social order he describes and sometimes attacks. In other words, are Baudrillard's texts mere simulations of social processes which are implicated in the object of critique so much that radical critique dissolves in the reproduction of its object? Or do these texts actually illuminate the transition to a new type of postmodern society, and provide perspectives that might be of use for critical social theory and for projects of political transformation?

3.4   THE END OF THE SOCIAL?

In his 1978 text 'In the Shadow of the Silent Majorities' (hereafter *SSM*), Baudrillard puts in question previous theories of the social and of related theories of class, social relations, socialism and so on, arguing that these concepts have imploded in the society of simulations.[23] Consequently, traditional theories of politics, the social, class conflict, social change and so forth are obsolete if they posit individuals, classes or masses as capable of social action. Instead, in an era of 'hyperconformity' the masses concern themselves solely with spectacle: 'Messages are given to them, they only want some sign, they idolize the play of signs and stereotypes, they idolize any content so long as it resolves itself into a spectacular sequence' (*SSM*, p. 10).

Baudrillard proliferates a series of metaphors to capture the nature of the masses, who he describes as that 'spongy referent, that opaque but equally translucent reality, that nothingness'; 'a statistical crystal ball . . . "swirling with currents and flows," in the image of matter and the natural elements'; an 'inertia,' 'silence,' 'figure of implosion,' 'social void,' and – what is probably his favorite metaphor – an 'opaque nebula whose growing density absorbs all the surrounding energy and light rays, to collapse finally under its own weight. A black hole which engulfs the social' (*SSM*, pp. 1–4). This 'black hole' absorbs all meaning, information, communication, messages and so on, thereby rendering them meaningless.

Baudrillard thus argues that 'the social' – with all its idealized resonances of human interaction, communication, civility and the rest – has imploded into 'the masses.' As 'evidence,' he poses the example of the refusal of the French to demonstrate against the extradition of a German lawyer when an important soccer match was on television (*SSM*, p. 12). This 'indifference' is presented as 'an explicit and positive counter-strategy – the task of absorbing and annihilating culture, knowledge, power, the social' (*SSM*, p. 11). Solicited to appreciate the culture in the Beaubourg cultural center in Paris, Baudrillard claims that the masses who go there instead look at each other rather than appreciating the cultural meanings proffered to them.[24] Refusing to participate in social and political events, the masses sullenly go their own ways, ignoring attempts to manipulate them. From these examples, he concludes that 'power manipulates nothing, the masses are neither misled nor mystified. . . . this indifference of the masses is their true, their only practice, . . . there is no other ideal of them to imagine, nothing in this to deplore, but everything to analyse as the brute fact of a collective retaliation and of a refusal to participate in the recommended ideals, however enlightened' (*SSM*, p. 14).

After describing the indifference of these 'silent majorities,' the masses,' Baudrillard concludes that the era of 'the social' is over. 'The energy of the social is reversed, its specificity is lost, its historical quality and its ideality vanish in favour of a configuration where not only the political becomes volatilised, but where the social itself no longer has any name' (*SSM*, pp. 18–19). This 'silent majority' does not signify that the masses no longer exist. Rather, it means

> that *their representation is no longer possible*. The masses are no longer
> a referent because they no longer belong to the order of representation.
> They don't express themselves, they are surveyed. They don't reflect
> upon themselves, they are tested. The referendum (and the media are a

constant referendum of directed questions and answers) has been substituted for the political referent. Now polls, tests, the referendum, media are devices which no longer belong to a dimension of representations, but to one of simulation'. (*SSM*, p. 20)

Baudrillard's argument seems to be that polling, testing, voting and so on pit individuals against simulation models rather than social forces or each other. It provides a quantitative abstraction of the social, a dead simulation. This simulation of the social, however, kills genuine sociality, and renders the masses more passive, apathetic and inertial. Yet in Baudrillard's view, this very inertia represents a form of resistance, and disturbs a power structure which wants at least some limited form of participation, response and activity. Consequently the system is desperately driven to try to produce 'the social.'

The main force in rendering the masses an apathetic silent majority seems to be the proliferation of information and media. Baudrillard claims that:

> Instead of transforming the mass into energy, information produces even more mass. Instead of informing as it claims, instead of giving form and structure, information neutralises even further the 'social field'; more and more it creates an inert mass impermeable to the classical institutions of the social and to the very contents of information. Today, replacing the fission of symbolic structures by the social and its rational violence, is the fission of the social itself by the 'irrational' violence of media and information – the final result being precisely an atomised, nuclearised, molecularised masses, the result of two centuries of accelerated socialisation and which brings it irremediably to an end. (*SSM*, pp. 25–6)

On this analysis, the social – taken as interpersonal relations, as a specific sphere mediating between the public and private spheres – is literally 'electified' in media and computer networks which relate and organize individuals through electronic circuits rather than libidinal or face-to-face social relations. Baudrillard thus opposes theories of the media and information which see the mass media as manipulating and information as socializing the masses, maintaining instead that the proliferation of information and media neutralizes the masses, bores and emulsifies them, thereby destroying the social. Consequently,

> From that point of view, it could be said that the social regresses to the same degree as its institutions develop. The process accelerates and reaches its maximal extent with mass media and information. Media, *all* media, information, *all* information, act in two directions: outwardly they produce more of the social, inwardly they neutralize

social relations and the social itself. But then, if the social is both destroyed by what produces it (the media, information) and reabsorbed by what it produces (the masses), it follows that its definition is empty and that this term which serves as a universal alibi for every discourse, no longer analyses anything, no longer designates anything. Not only is it superfluous and useless – wherever it appears it conceals something else: defiance, death, seduction, ritual, repetition – it conceals that it is only abstraction and residue, or even simply an *effect* of the social, a simulation and an illusion. (*SSM*, p. 66)

Without specifying what is at stake, Baudrillard is implicitly contrasting a (normative-metaphysical) concept of the social with what he sees as its demise in the contemporary situation. As the passage just cited indicates, Baudrillard assumes that the (genuine) social resides in (no surprise here) symbolic exchange – 'defiance, death, seduction, ritual, repetition'. The elimination of symbolic societies by productivist societies thus eliminates the (genuine) social and replaces it with a simulated social, with the social as residue and effect (of the system of production, first, and then simulation), as excremental remains of a now dead sociality, of a 'functional ventilation of remainders' (*SSM*, pp. 72ff.).[25] On this analysis, 'the social' consists of the reprocessing of dead remainders of labor, power, meaning and so on. Thus, as unemployment, disease, insanity, meaninglessness and other disruptive phenomena occur, 'the social' appears as attempts to reclaim and recycle its remnants through unemployment insurance, social security, hospitals and mental institutions, and media which try to rekindle meaning and reinstitute social relations.

In short and to conclude, Baudrillard claims that the social has imploded into the masses, and no longer exists as a self-sufficient domain of reality. Probably Baudrillard's most interesting claim is that the masses are reacting with increased ambivalence, disaffection and indifference to attempts to revivify the social through the proliferation of media communication. Too many messages, advertisements, ideological discourses, signs and meanings eventually lead to an oversaturation which makes audiences suspicious of – or bored with – manipulation and media hype. Yet he posits the possibility that the masses are stronger than any socializing force such as the media, and that rather than the media overpowering and absorbing the masses, it is the masses which 'envelop and absorb the latter – or at least there is no priority of one over the other. The mass and the media are one single process. Mass(age) is the message' (*SSM*, p. 44).

Against traditional manipulation theory, Baudrillard makes the startling suggestion that the masses might always have been stronger than any media, and that *they* are responsible for diverting cinema from the social and the documentary to entertainment and the imaginary, forcing science and techno-logy to produce moon shots and other spectacles for mass entertainment, pushing medicine to deliver a proliferating variety of medical services, pressuring the state to provide welfare, and forcing an increase in the level of consumption to satisfy their own needs and purposes:

> They know that there is no liberation and that a system is abolished only by pushing it into hyperlogic, by forcing it into an excessive practice which is equivalent to a brutal amortization. 'You want us to consume – O.K., let's consume always more and anything whatsoever; for any useless and absurd purpose.' . . . A parody and a paradox: it is by their very inertia in the ways of the social laid out for them that the masses go beyond its logic and its limits and destroy its whole edifice. A destructive hypersimulation, a destructive hyperconformity (as in the case of Beaubourg . . .) that has all the appearance of a victorious challenge – no one can measure the strength of this challenge, of the reversion exerted on the whole system. There lies the genuine stake today, in this underhand, inescapable confrontation between the silent majority and the social imposed on them, in this hypersimulation, reduplicating simulation and exterminating it according to its own logic – not in any class struggle nor in the molecular hodge-podge of desire-breaching minorities. (*SSM*, pp. 47–8)

Baudrillard is arguing that not only have a series of implosions taken place – between politics and entertainment, capital and labor, high and low culture, and so on – but that society overall is imploding into the masses, and thus lost its power over them. While this 'hyperreal conformity which is the extreme form of non-participation' is a 'calamity' for a society that seeks participation and allegiance, it is also a 'calamity of revolution' and socialism which wants an intensification and development of the social. 'Now,' however, 'the masses *aren't* the social, they are the reversion of any social and of any socialism. . . . This revolution by involution is not theirs; it is not critical-explosive, it is implosive and blind. It proceeds by inertia and not from a new and joyous negativity. It is silent and involutive – exactly the reverse of all speech making and consciousness raising. It has no meaning. It has nothing to say to us' (*SSM*, p. 49).

As a result of the implosion of meaning, the masses supposedly become more cynical and more apathetic, and at one and the same time silent and defiant (*SSM*, pp. 104ff.). This paradoxical situation can be interpreted either as a sign of the conformity and submissiveness of the masses or as a sign that they are so cynical and bored with media simulation and the artificial existence of advanced capitalism that they no longer allow themselves to be manipulated and dominated, no longer believe in the system, and that therefore they resist manipulation.[26] But if this is so, then the system is facing a new sort of legitimation crisis. On this view, the system no longer commands the loyalty of the masses, and no longer has an ideological hold

over them. Thus the question arises: 'Are the mass media on the side of
power in the manipulation of the masses, or are they on the side of the
masses in the liquidation of meaning, in the violence done to meaning and in
the fascination that results? Is it the media which induce fascination in the
masses, or is it the masses which divert the media into spectacle?'
(*SSM*, p. 105).

Baudrillard fittingly concludes on a paradoxical note by suggesting that
the seeming silence and apathy of the masses can be seen as a 'strategic
resistance' that is a 'refusal of meaning and a refusal of the word'
(*SSM*, p. 108). A 'positive' political reading of this position – which is not
Baudrillard's – could suggest that the apathy and cynicism of the masses
create the space for new meaning, and thus for the intervention of radical
cultural texts and politics aiming at the production of new systems of
meaning and a new society, thereby providing an opening for radical political
movements to attempt to produce new forms of struggle and politics – as
with Guy Debord and the situationists. On the other hand, one could
conclude that efforts at producing alternative means of communication,
alternative messages, only aid in the 'regeneration of meaning and speech'
which either will also be resisted by the silent majorities or which may even
serve the interests of a system which, to regain legitimacy, must regenerate a
belief in meaning.

This latter view is Baudrillard's preferred position (see his contemptuous
remarks about falling into 'the ecstasy of radio' in his reference to alternative
radio programming),[27] and parallels the 'theory' of artificial negativity
produced by some of Baudrillard's intellectual co-conspirators associated
with the journal *Telos*.[28] On this view, any reform whatsoever – economic,
environmental, political and so on – strengthens the system of domination,
and should thus be denounced by the critical critic who is truly 'radical.'
Baudrillard's own abstention from politics (except to attack the Left) might
suggest that he believes that a project of positive politics will only help the
existing system and will not change anything anyway and is thus a waste of
time.[29] Here Baudrillard reflects the widespread feeling of political apathy,
alienation and cynicism which followed the dashing of the utopian hopes of
1960s radical politics. This transformation in the French intellectual scene
was brought about in part by the increasingly important influence of
Nietzsche on New French Theory; so to conclude this chapter, I will discuss
the relations between Baudrillard, Nietzsche and poststructuralism.

3.5   BAUDRILLARD, POSTSTRUCTURALISM AND NIETZSCHE

At this point, it might be useful to discuss the ways in which Baudrillard's
theories of simulations, the end of the social and so forth manifest the move
from structuralism to poststructuralism in New French Theory, and how

Baudrillard takes certain poststructuralist positions to rather idiosyncratic extremes. Baudrillard's earlier works can be assimilated in some ways to the structuralist moment in French thought – for example, in texts in which he attempts to sketch out the system of objects, commodities, needs, design and so on that he believes is coming to structure and dominate contemporary capitalist society. Like those of most structuralists, Baudrillard's analyses tended to be at least somewhat abstract, formal, 'scientific' and systematic – though they were more phenomenological and less 'rigorous' and 'scientific' than those of more pure structuralists like Lévi-Strauss and Althusser (see chapters 1 and 2 below).

Critiques began to emerge in the late 1960s and early 1970s in France precisely of tendencies in structuralism toward abstraction, (pseudo-) scientificity and an absence of historical and empirical contextualization and grounding.[30] Moreover, new theories of language, signification, meaning and reference began to emerge, which put in question the fundamental premises of structuralist thought. Rather than signifying a priori or universal structures of society or meaning, systems of representation were said to refer only to other systems. For Derrida, 'there is nothing outside of the text,' and texts primarily refer, in one reading of this view, to other texts ad infinitum, never coming to rest in the presence of a secure 'real' or in any stable structures, grounds or foundation.

Baudrillard's theory of simulations is parallel in some ways to post-structuralist critiques of referentiality, in that for Baudrillard there is nothing outside the play of simulations, no 'real' in which theory can be grounded or radical politics reconstructed[31] – even though Baudrillard seems to be making 'realist' claims himself concerning certain social trends and developments (a point to which I will return in 7.2). His problematic exhibits a taking to the extreme of certain poststructuralist positions about language, reference and the absence of 'the real.' Henceforth the Baudrillardian universe will be one without stable boundaries, fixed points of reference or determinate structures. This denial of all the 'finalities' of contemporary theory – political economy, sexuality, the real and so on – will enable him to radically critique opposing positions and to affirm his own form of extreme skepticism and nihilism. The remainder of this study will, in fact, take place in the universe of discourse just alluded to – although we will encounter some surprising developments in Baudrillard's trajectory (see chapters 6 and 7).

It should be pointed out, however, that Baudrillard's work constitutes merely a variant of poststructuralism, one that can be opposed within the field of contemporary critical and social theory to other poststructuralist positions. Although some deconstructionists – Rorty's 'strong textualists' – seem to take literally Derrida's *bon mot* that 'there is nothing outside of the text,' and thus deny the possibility of reference altogether, other post-structuralists read Derrida and deconstruction as problematizing questions of meaning and reference but not necessarily obliterating these domains. On this view, it is possible to combine deconstruction with contemporary social and ideology critique and radical politics.[32]

Baudrillard, on the contrary, uses poststructuralist positions to dissolve the concepts and problematic of social theory and radical politics altogether. His method in his post-1976 texts is to take a central theme, such as the masses as silent majority, simulations and simulacra, seduction or whatever and to illustrate the theme with a wide range of contemporary examples. Though he criticizes and parodies Deleuze, Derrida, Foucault, Lacan, feminism and, indirectly, his own earlier work, with the exception of a pamphlet on Foucault (see 5.2), he rarely engages other poststructuralist positions systematically – although he frequently borrows their ideas and language. Yet I believe that Baudrillard – at least his work of the 1970s – is best read within the context of certain poststructuralist debates and the replacement of Marx and structuralism by Nietzsche as the master discourse of New French Theory.

The influence of Nietzsche on French poststructuralism is well documented and has been sharply criticized.[33] Baudrillard too has admitted his affection for Zarathrustra's *alter ego*, and quotations from Nietzsche and Nietzschean rhetoric and style as well. Much of *Simulations* and *In the Shadow of the Silent Majorities* has a certain revelatory aura, as if perspectivism, his attacks on the concept of truth, knowledge and the subject, his critiques of bourgeois society, his nihilism and his call for a transvaluation of values.[35] Baudrillard's texts often have the flavor of Nietzschean rhetoric and style as well. Much of *Simulations* and *In the Shadows of the Silent Majorities* has a certain revelatory aura, as if Baudrillard had descended from the mountain top with important new revelations for his contemporaries, reminiscent of the style of Nietzsche's Zarathustra. Many of his post-1976 texts are organized into short, essayistic and aphoristic forms, similar to Nietzsche's middle and later texts. Baudrillard seems also to aspire to be a Nietzschean 'destiny,' to be a fatal attraction for his contemporaries; moreover, eventually, as we will see in chapter 6, Baudrillard turns from social theory to a mutant variety of Nietzschean metaphysics.

All Baudrillard's post-1976 texts have a sharply prophetic ring; they contrast the voice of the theoretical prophet to the murmuring and sullen resentment of the masses and the banal wisdom of the society's official spokespeople. Baudrillard also posits an aristocratic form of duel, challenge, seduction and ritual to the banal strategies of the bourgeoisie and the societies of production and simulation. Like Nietzsche, this theoretical gladiator celebrates violence and a warrior ethos in an increasingly agonistic view of the universe.[36] Baudrillard thus increasingly aligns himself with what Habermas calls the 'dark writers of the bourgeoisie' and a specifically French Bohemian and Nietzschean tradition which extends from

Baudelaire through Bataille, is sometimes heard in Gide and Sartre, and appears in Blanchot, Klossowski, Foucault, Derrida, Deleuze, Lyotard and others.

In particular, Baudrillard's thought comes to orbit in the theoretical discourse inaugurated by Nietzsche's diagnosis of nihilism and the trajectory of the will to power (see 4.4). Baudrillard also follows Nietzsche in recurrently indulging in polemics against his contemporaries. It is to these provocations that we shall turn in chapter 5, once we have examined in more detail Baudrillard's excursions into what has become known as 'post-modernity,' that epoch which follows modernity.[37]

4

The Postmodern Carnival

Baudrillard's fifth book, *L'échange symbolique et la mort*, is the site of his entrance into what I will call 'the postmodern carnival.'[1] His first four books are well-organized theoretical treatises which focus on a central theme and develop his positions in a rather standard, sustained, linear fashion. *L'échange symbolique*, by contrast, contains six studies which open the way to a new universe of thought and discourse. The first study of 'the end of production' (see 3.1) and the second study of 'the order of simulacra' (see 3.3) delineate the differences between the era of production and what Baudrillard sees as the new era of simulation, the onset of which marks a rupture in history, which could be interpreted as a break from modernity to postmodernity. Baudrillard also carries out studies of 'fashion, or the enchanted fairy land of the code,' 'the body as the charnel house of signs,' 'political economy and death,' and 'the extermination of the name of god' which contains his critique of, and break with, Freud (see 5.1). In this text, Baudrillard thus begins exploring the set of phenomena which would become central to his work for much of the next decade.

This chapter will focus on Baudrillard's analyses of 'Fashion, the Body and Sexuality' (4.1), 'Life, Death, and Sign Fetishism' (4.2), 'Postmodern Art, Architecture, and Sign Culture' (4.3), and 'Nihilism and Postmodernity' (4.4). I refer here to 'the postmodern carnival' because the new phenomena of the postmodern scene give rise to a carnivalesque situation (in Bakhtin's sense) in which dominant norms are transgressed and a fundamentally different situation erupts.[2] Like Bakhtin's 'carnival king' – and this is no doubt a Baudrillardian imaginary – Baudrillard laughs at the pretensions of modernity and its (now obsolete) political economy, philosophy, politics, sexuality, fashion and culture, while mocking its exhibitions and discourses. Reveling in deconstruction, reversal and inversion, Baudrillard carries out the Bakhtinian carnivalesque 'logic of the turnabout' and 'the inside-out,' parodying modernity's rules of the game, codes, conventions and hierarchies and pointing to their conventionality, arbitrariness and frequent ludicrousness. Celebrating a 'gay relativity' (Bakhtin via Nietzsche), Baudrillard defies the 'last judgment' and collapses hierarchical distinctions, while emptying modernity's highest values of their significance and validity.

L'échange symbolique et la mort is Baudrillard's most deconstructive text, as well as the first delineation of what might be regarded as a new postmodern theory. Baudrillard's texts are also carnivalesque in that they break down the usual academic boundaries and transgress the limits of academic discourse, engaging in a different kind of textual practice and play. In *L'échange symbolique* – and this was to become typical of all Baudrillard's books henceforth – he mixes topics and subject matter that are usually separated, and explodes the generic conventions of social theory. He plays with new ideas and ritualistically replays old ones, while attempting to provoke the reader and scandalize established 'wisdom' and academic propriety. Without inhibitions, he irreverently and promiscuously moves from one tabooed, usually neglected topic to another, celebrating the demise of the previous universe (and mode of theorizing) while playfully entering a new universe as he produces novel theories and discourses.

But, while the postmodern carnival has its joys, it also has its melancholy and depressing aspects. Like all carnivals, it soon becomes repetitive and boring, and its novel attractions wear thin – the reveler becomes 'bored but hyper' as Andy Warhol once put it. Still, for a time, it provides some novel amusements, as well as some rather frightening horror shows. So let us leave behind the concerns of traditional social theory and explore the postmodern carnival.

4.1 FASHION, THE BODY AND SEXUALITY

Although discussions of postmodernism in the arts originated in the United States, the first works to designate themselves as 'postmodern' social theories originated in France in the late 1970s, and drew upon earlier French cultural and social theory. Anticipations of the later postmodern social theories associated with Baudrillard, Lyotard, Deleuze and Guattari and others are found in Roland Barthes's explorations of mythologies and popular culture, in the rediscovery of Ferdinand de Saussure, which led to intense explorations of language and signs in the 1960s and 1970s, in Henri Lefebvre's explorations of everyday life, in Guy Debord's critiques of 'the society of the spectacle,' and in the powerful criticisms of established philosophy and the 'human sciences' by those associated with 'post-structuralism' (Derrida, Foucault, *Tel Quel*, the later Barthes and so on).[3]

Baudrillard was perhaps the first to develop these studies of the contemporary scene into what might be viewed as a postmodern social theory, a theory of the end of modernity and the transition to a new stage of society and history beyond modernity. Although Baudrillard did not adopt the term 'postmodernity' until the 1980s, by which time it had become *the* fashion in some circles (see 4.4), his work of the late 1960s and early 1970s contained many proto-postmodernist themes such as the consumer society and its proliferation of signs, the media and its messages, environmental design and cybernetic steering systems, and contemporary art and sign culture. His work from the mid-1970s to the present, beginning with *L'échange symbolique* and continuing with *In the Shadow of the Silent Majorities*, *Simulacres et simulation* and related texts, contains many themes associated with postmodernism, and can be read as a proto-postmodernist social theory.

Fashion Show

Both modern and postmodern French theory have focused much attention on the appearances and activities of the body. In the 1940s French existential phenomenologists like Sartre and Merleau-Ponty discussed the body and its experiences and modes of being as a reaction against the previous mentalist/ spiritualist tradition in philosophy.[4] Later French theorists – Barthes, Foucault, Derrida and others – rejected the tradition of Cartesian mind– body dualism, and focused attention on bodily experiences and modes of dressing, fashion, pleasure and suffering. These theorists also promoted the rights and pleasures of the body as against their repression.[5] In Baudrillard's words, 'the body, beauty and sexuality are imposed as new universals in the name of the rights of the new man, emancipated by abundance and the cybernetic revolution' (*CPES*, p. 97). Yet against celebrations of the rights and pleasures of the body in modernity and attendant philosophies of liberation, Baudrillard, like Foucault, describes the down side of this alleged emancipation, focusing on the body's modes of subjugation, control, normalization and death.[6]

In his earlier work, Baudrillard sketched the framework for his later theory of the body pointing to ways in which design and the consumer society were transforming the body. 'Everything belongs to design, everything springs from it, whether it says so or not: the body is designed, sexuality is designed, political, social, human relations are designed . . . this "designed universe" is what properly constitutes the environment' (*CPES*, pp. 200–1). In a study entitled 'Fashion or the Enchanted Fairy Land of the Code' in *L'échange symbolique* Baudrillard applies his concepts of simulation and the code to an analysis of fashion and the fashioning of the body as a characteristic feature of modernity:

> Fashion only exists in the framework of modernity. That is, in a framework of rupture, of progress and of innovation. In any cultural context, the ancient and the 'modern' alternate in their significations. Yet there only exists for us, since the Engightenment and the industrial revolution, a historical and polemical structure of change

and of crisis. It seems that modernity puts in place simultaneously a linear time – that of technical progress, of production and of history – and a cyclical time, that of fashion. This is only an apparent contradiction, for in fact modernity is never a radical rupture. . . . A dialectic of rupture, modernity becomes very quickly a dynamism of amalgamation and recycling. In politics, in technology, in art, in culture, modernity defines itself by the rate of change tolerated by the system without really changing anything in the essential order. Thus fashion does not contradict at all: it enunciates simultaneously and very clearly the *myth* of change . . . and the structural *law* of change. . . . modernity is not the transmutation of all values, but is the commutation of all values, it is their mode of combination (*combinatoire*) and their ambiguity. Modernity is a code and fashion is its emblem. (*ES*, p. 135)

We see that at this point, Baudrillard is interpreting 'modernity' as the privileged code for his investigations of the contemporary scene. The intensification of modernity, a hypermodernity, which produced the dramatic rupture in history, would later lead Baudrillard to adopt the term 'postmodern' to describe his theory. Fashion thus provides an important constituent of the process of modernity which will lead to postmodernity. Fashion for Baudrillard simulates *l'actualité*, the new, the latest, the most up-to-date, as it recycles past forms and models. Consequently, 'fashion is paradoxically the out-of-date, the non-contemporary (*l'inactuel*)' (*ES*, p. 132). Simulating 'joy in appearances' and 'the innocence of becoming,' fashion represents the triumph of the artificial and of models, 'the seizure of the living by the dead' (*ES*, p. 133). Fashion is thus 'the frivolity of the *déjà-vu*' in its incessant replacement of one series of (recycled) forms by another. This constant turnover and replacement is also 'linked to the spectacle of an incessant abolition of forms,' so that one could say that 'the desire for death is recycled in fashion' (*ES*, p. 133). (In the next section we will see how death haunts all of life in the postmodern carnival.)

Fashion is inextricably linked to the social, but to a 'theatrical sociality' which is subversive in totalitarian or puritanical societies, yet controlled by the machinations of the fashion industry: 'Even if fashion is enchanting, it remains the enchantment of merchandise and – still further – enchantment of simulation, of the code and the law' (*ES*, p. 144). Indeed, fashion comes to colonize even sexuality, to code and modify sexuality, transforming it from a mode of bodily pleasure into a sign scene, a mode of looking. 'Fashion is certainly that which neutralizes sexuality most efficaciously (a made-up woman is one whom one does not touch) . . . precisely because fashion is a passion, not an accomplice to but a competitor to sexuality over which it is triumphant' (*ES*, pp. 145–6).

Baudrillard argues that within the system of fashion no subversion, no emancipatory gestures, are possible; for fashion is able to recuperate everything (blue jeans are his example):

> Fashion also does not leave room for revolution except to return to the genesis of the sign which constitutes it. And the alternative to fashion is not in a 'freedom' [from fashion] or a transcendence of some sort toward a truth of the world and referentials. It is rather a deconstruction of the form of the sign of fashion and of the very principle of signification – as the alternative to political economy can only be in the deconstruction of the commodity form and of the very principle of production. (*ES*, p. 151)

Rejecting moralistic condemnation of fashion, Baudrillard claims that the dialectics of fashion can be reversed only through deconstruction of its system – which apparently requires replacing it with a system of symbolic exchange which valorizes spectacle, festival and waste for their own sake, rather than for the sake of being fashionable, of submitting to the dictates of fashion for the end of prestige, social approval or recognition. Once again Baudrillard fails to specify a position from which he could criticize the system of fashion and replace it with another mode of appearance, though there are hints throughout *L'échange symbolique* of a critical perspective toward the system of fashion and valorizations of its deconstruction and replacement by symbolic exchange.

The fashion scene points once again to the growing independence and importance of the sign in contemporary life. Fashion produces, regulates and organizes signs into a 'fairy world' that is both enchanting and vertiginous, for the signs of fashion are free-floating and not grounded in any referential. Thus they invade ever new areas of experience, just as the models of entertainment, high fashion and advertising enter the domains of politics, economics and culture. Fashion signs are free to commutate and permutate in this world without limits, thus representing another colonization of social life by the code; for ultimately fashion mobilizes desire into socially defined and organized models of dress, appearance, behavior and so on. These are then organized into a fashion system, a life-style or mode of life.

Baudrillard's most important point concerns the spiraling expansion of fashion and its penetration into ever more domains of experience, a process which he describes as 'the inexorable investment of all domains by the code' (*ES*, p. 131). As social life is increasingly penetrated by simulation, it is 'haunted by fashion,' as models come to determine fashion not only in the sphere of 'light' signs – that is, clothing, the body, objects – but also in the domain of 'heavy' signs – politics, morals, economics, science, culture and sexuality. Presumably Baudrillard is describing a condition whereby fashion is totalized through every region of society, as politics, behavior, entertainment and art, theories and ideas, all go through cycles of popularity, in which one exemplar and model follows another. Fashion itself thus becomes a sign of the postmodern, interpreted as a scene of inexorable change in which signs enter cycles of transmutation and combination with other signs.

Likewise, in one of his studies of simulations later in the decade, 'Publicité absolue, publicité zéro,' Baudrillard describes the totalizing of advertising (*publicité*).[7] He begins by claiming that one of the fundamental processes of the contemporary age involves the absorption of all modes of expression by that of advertising, 'because it is without depth, instantaneous and instantly forgotten. [Advertising is] the triumph of superficial form, the smallest common denominator of all significations, the zero degree of meaning, the triumph of entropy over all possible tropes' (*S & S*, p. 133). Consistent with his media theory in which 'the medium is the message' (3.1), it is the form of advertising, its ubiquity, its saturation and neutralization of all possible meanings which is significant for Baudrillard.

Baudrillard sees a convergence since the late 1920s of propaganda and advertising; thus advertising today tends to be propaganda for itself and for whatever product, politician, idea or life-style it is trying to sell. 'This convergence defines our society where there is no longer any difference between the economy and politics because the same language reigns there from one end to another, in a society therefore where political economy, speaking literally, is finally fully realized' (ibid.). The ubiquity of advertising is part of the end of the social, the political, of meaning and so on, which advertising desperately tries to revive, but, through its destruction of stabilities and its neutralizing and banalizing effects, only helps to destroy (*S & S*, pp. 140ff.).

It appears that Baudrillard is developing critical perspectives vis-à-vis fashion and advertising. Yet, in *De la séduction*, fashion and cosmetics become part of 'that radical metaphysics of appearance' which is part of the game of seduction (*SED*, pp. 126ff.). In these writings, Baudrillard valorizes appearances per se against depth models, and presents positively Baudelaire's celebration of fashion and make-up (see the discussion in 5.3). In this context, fashion becomes part of a celebration of artifice, appearance and sign games, and is thus positively valorized as part and parcel of Baudrillard's ideal of seduction. Likewise, although Baudrillard himself does not develop these perspectives, one might interpret fashion as an expression of modernity, as a total system governed by rules of style, color and product coordination, systems of makeup, jewelry and so on, where all parts of the fashion system are rigorously governed by rules and codes. Postmodern fashion, by contrast, is ruled more by artifice for the sake of artifice, fashion for the sake of fashion; it thus allows for more disordered and nonsystematic combinations which mix clothes, styles, looks and the rest from various periods, subcultures, classes and so forth into the form of fashion pastiche, eclecticism, populism and so on.

Sexuality also mutates in the transformation from modernity to post-modernity, and in the next section we shall examine Baudrillard's analysis of its vicissitudes.

The Sexual Carnival

In a study of 'The Body or the Carnality of Signs,' Baudrillard takes us on some excursions into the sexual carnival. The modern body is a *marked* body, a body marked by the signs of fashion and sexuality (*ES*, pp. 155ff.). Just as primitive tribes decorated their bodies with the signs of their cultural codes, so, too, modern bodies apply makeup, cosmetic aids, jewelry, rings, ties, gloves and other pieces of clothing and accoutrements which mark the body as belonging to a system of signification, as fitting into a place in the differential code. In particular, the body is organized into a system of sexual exchange value 'organized entirely around the fetishization of the phallus as the general equivalent' (*ES*, p. 155).

Although *L'échange symbolique* contains many polemics against Freud, Baudrillard privileges Freud's theory of castration and the phallus in describing the phenomena of the sexual carnival: 'Fashion, publicity, nude-look, nude theater, strip-tease: everywhere, it's the scenodrama of erection and castration' (*ES*, p. 155). Baudrillard proceeds to engage in a detailed discussion of fashion and sexuality from the standpoint of the phallus and castration, interpreting a variety of phenomena – including makeup, gloves, ties, stockings, striptease, nudity – as fetishistic displays of the phallus to alleviate castration anxiety. In the entire system of fashion and sexuality, 'castration is *signified* . . . and thus misrecognized' (*ES*, p. 156).

In particular, Baudrillard rejects models which describe fashion, or even sexual activity, as expressive or emblematic of desire. Rather than seeing the profusion of sexual signs in contemporary society as an expression of libido, of sexual desire, Baudrillard interprets sexuality as a sign game in which castration plays the key role.

> The line of the stocking across the thigh: the erotic power of this image does not come from its proximity to real sex and its *positive* promise . . ., but from an apprehension of sex (the panicked recognition of castration) which is *arrested upon the mise en scène of castration* – this inoffensive mark of the line of the stocking . . . and the naked thigh and metonymically the entire body, becomes through this caesura a *phallic effigy*, a fetish object of contemplation and of manipulation stripped of all menace. (*ES*, p. 156)

Baudrillard's analyses are so extremely reductive and so excessively Freudian that his readings can be interpreted as a reductio ad absurdum of the Freudian theory of sexuality, as taking the categories of the phallus and castration to and beyond their limits, using them as the master code to interpret *all* manifestations of sexuality – although he presents his readings straightforwardly as revealing the truth about sex.[8] These studies thus go as far as is possible in interpreting sexuality as sign play, as a reflection of castration anxiety and as phallic display. Desiring to divest the theory of sexuality from Freudian and other theories of desire which would make primordial sexual desire, or a libidinal economy, the truth of sex and the telos of liberation, Baudrillard takes his interpretations in the opposite direction, and views sexuality as a play of signs governed by a logic of lack and anxiety. This obsession with signs and reduction of political economy, sexuality and eventually all social and material reality to sign play leads me to describe Baudrillard's theory as a *sign fetishism* which henceforth will mark the secret origins of his thought games – a theme to which I shall recurrently return.

Perhaps the most interesting analysis of sexuality in *L'échange symbolique* deals with what Baudrillard calls 'managed narcissism' (*ES*, pp. 171ff.), which relates to pleasure in the marked body, the body as a display of the signs of fashion and sexuality. 'This *neo-narcissism* attaches itself to the *manipulation* of the body as value. It's a managed economy of the body, founded upon a scheme of libidinal and symbolic destructuration, of dismantlement and of managed restructuration of libidinal investments, of "reappropriation" of the body according to directive models and thus under the control of meaning, of transference of the wish-fullfilment of desire upon the code' (*ES*, p. 172). This managed narcissism 'rewrites' the body as 'a "personalized" Eros, that is to say, an Eros indexed upon functional collective models. It is a body homogenized as the place of industrial production of signs and differences, mobilized under the sign of programmatic seduction. It is an interception of the ambivalence of the body in the profit of a total positivization as a scheme of seduction, of satisfaction and of prestige. The body as the *summation* of partial objects of which the subject is the you of *consumption*' (*ES*, p. 173).

We encounter here one of Baudrillard's last references to social control by means of a system of consumption in which the body is interpreted in terms of the 'total system of signs ordered by models, under the general equivalent of the phallic cult, as capital becomes the total system of exchange value under the general equivalent of money' (*ES*, p. 173). *L'échange symbolique* is thus one of Baudrillard's last texts to use the categories of political economy. Henceforth, it will be simulation models – and not the mode, or code, of production or consumption – that will be the demiurges of postmodernity, independent of political economy.

In *De la séduction*, for example, it is *cloning* on which Baudrillard's analysis of the body fixates, and he delineates what he sees as transformations of the body and sexuality in postmodern society.[9] Cloning, Baudrillard suggests, makes possible an extension and multiplication of the body, which transforms the very nature of the body, sexuality and human being itself. Highly impressed by stories of a 'clone boy' reproduced from a gene in the United States, Baudrillard sees this as a future model of reproduction which eliminates the need for sexuality as a mode of reproduction and will make possible a new kind of narcissism, new bodies and new personalities.

In Baudrillard's (science fiction) vision, the genetic information contained in an individual's genes can be used to clone exact replications of him or herself. No longer caught up in the oedipal drama of the family triangle (or circle), the clone child in effect engenders itself, rather than being a product of 'the duel' between the genetic information of the sperm and that of the egg and between the mother's and father's personal influence (*SED*, pp. 229ff.). The end of Oedipus, the end of psychoanalysis. 'Father and Mother have disappeared to the profit of *a matrix called a code*. No more mother: a matrice' (*SED*, p. 230).

Cloning will also put to an end to the body as we have so far known and suffered it. Henceforth the body will not be the unique singularity generated from an aleatory conjuncture of one's parents' genetic traits and one's personal and environmental experiences, but will be an extension of cloned cells. Sexuality will thus become unnecessary, and death too loses its sting when one can clone oneself indefinitely in a series of extensions of one's favorite cell. One's entire body will be an extension of one's genes, and will thus be artificially produced and reproduced: 'The prostheses of the industrial age are still external, *exotechniques* – those which we recognize [in cloning] are ramified and interiorized: *esotechniques*' (*SED*, p. 233).

Baudrillard concludes thus:

We are now in the age of soft technologies, of genetic and mental software. The prostheses of the industrial age, the machines, could still impact on the body in order to modify its image – they themselves being metabolized in the imaginary, in which this metabolism constituted part of the image of the body [that is, as a machine or whatever]. But when one attains a point of non-return in simulation, when prostheses infiltrate the anonymous and micro-molecular heart of the body, when they are imposed on the body as its very matrix, burning all ulterior symbolic circuits, every possible body being only its immutable repetition – this is the end of the body and of its history: the individual is henceforth only *a cancerous metastasis of its basic formula*. (*SED*, p. 233)

'Cancerous metastasis' is henceforth Baudrillard's key metaphor for the very processes of the postmodern body. 'Cancer is indeed the illness which commands all contemporary pathology because it is *the very form of the virulence of the code*: an exacerbated redundance of the same signals, an exacerbated redundance of the same cells' (*SED*, p. 234). We see here how this theory of the postmodern body instantiates Baudrillard's focus on models of simulation in genetics, miniaturization and modulation through the code. This analysis is paradigmatic of a postmodern theory of a fundamental rupture, which brings an end to previous problematics of the body, sexuality, reproduction and so forth. The end of psychology and psychoanalysis:

> The digital Narcissus replaces the triangular Oedipus. The hypostasis of an artificial double, the clone will henceforth be your guardian angel, the visible form of your unconscious and flesh of your flesh, *literally and without metaphor.* Your 'neighbor' will henceforth be this clone of an hallucinatory resemblance, consequently you will never be alone again and no longer have a secret. 'Love your neighbor as yourself': this old problem of Christianity is resolved – your neighbor, *it's yourself.* Thus love is total. And so is self-seduction. (*SED*, p. 235)

Such cloned narcissism will produce a total mutation in society and history, Baudrillard suggests. 'The masses are themselves a product of cloning which functions from the same to the same without passing through the other. They are only at bottom the sum of the terminals of all systems – a flowing network of digital impulses: it is that which makes them mass. Insensitive to external injunctions, they constitute themselves in integrated circuits given up to manipulation (self-manipulation) and to "seduction" (self-seduction)' (ibid.).

The postmodern body is thus immersed in a network of self-seduction and cool fascination and seduction by the objects, novelties and events which solicit it to join in and 'network' with media, computers, information systems and so on. Consequently the body itself (and its neighbor the subject – see 6.1 below) are undergoing fundamental mutations. Yet the body – so far at least – must still undergo death and come to terms with its finitude. Indeed, Baudrillard will claim that contemporary culture can itself be characterized as a death culture, a culture in which repression, projection and externalization of death become a fundamental organizing principle.

4.2 LIFE, DEATH AND SIGN FETISHISM

Some of Baudrillard's most provocative ideas in *L'échange symbolique* concern his analyses of death, his critiques of Freud's theory of the death instinct, and what he sees as the repression of death in Western thought since the sixteenth century. In these analyses he combines some insightful, often brilliant, Foucaultian genealogies of death as a social construct in different historical epochs with a Derridean deconstruction of the antinomy of life and death in Western thought. Baudrillard claims that this opposition is the basic binary structural principle upon which Western metaphysics, Freudian psychoanalysis and much modern misery is based. Against the repression of death in Western society, Baudrillard offers as a model the incorporation of death into life and symbolic exchange between life and death in various primitive societies which serve as examples of a mode of life which escapes fundamental binary structures, division and repression.

Baudrillard begins by pointing to the extradition of the dead in Western societies and the sharp distinction between life and death, the living and the dead. The 'human,' he suggests, was always defined by what it excluded – nature, animals, minerals, the nonliving – or women, other races, the insane and so on (*ES*, pp. 193ff.). Consciously building on Foucault's genealogies,[10] Baudrillard points out that 'racism' against the dead is 'modern,' and can be contrasted to quite different attitudes toward death and modes of relating to the dead in different societies and epochs. He claims that 'From savage societies to modern societies, the evolution is irreversible: little by little *the dead cease to exist*. They are thrown outside of the symbolic circulation of the group' (*ES*, p. 195). They are placed in cemeteries – which are moved further and further away from the center of town – and which Baudrillard sees as the first ghettoes: centers of exclusion for the undesirable.

Psychologically too our modern societies want to repress death, to not think or talk about it. All value is placed on life and on the living and thus '*it is not normal to be dead*' (*ES*, p. 196). Yet this exclusion of death from 'normality' means that it haunts us all the more powerfully, it also covers over the fact that our culture is a death culture, that 'our modern cities are dead cities and cities of death' (ibid.). The fundamentality of the very distinction between life and death means that our society is heavily invested in separating the two, and thus in repressing death, which ensures that our lives will be haunted by a fear of death and obsessed with a desire for immortality.

Things were quite different, Baudrillard claims, in other societies. In so-called primitive societies there was no real division between life and death. One lived with the dead – their spirits, memories, achievements – and was early on initiated into the realm of the dead oneself, dying a symbolic death and being reborn into a symbolic world in which there was no difference between life and death. In these societies, symbolic exchange between life and death continuously took place, with gifts and ceremonies honoring the dead and favors or hostilities being visited on the living by the dead. In such societies, there need be no fear of death or obsession with death, for it is an integral part of everyday life.

This was also true of the West at one time. The Middle Ages had its Dance of Death, its elaborate homages to the dead and its expectations of the Kingdom of Heaven, the Last Judgment, which would bring Paradise Now. In addition, death was integrated into life and was an integral part of collective social activity. It is only during modern times, beginning in the sixteenth century, that death becomes individualized, repressed and excluded from social life. This segregation of death from life aids, first, the guardians of the afterlife in the Church, and then the protectors of life in the here and now, the State. Following Max Weber's analysis of *The Protestant Ethic and the Spirit of Capitalism*, Baudrillard suggests that fear of death and desire to prove one's immortality, one's divine election, fueled the era of production and accumulation in industrial capitalism.

Further, Baudrillard suggests that repression of death is the fundamental mechanism which produces an unconscious rooted not in sexual guilt or inhibition but in a socially mandated fear of death. This, in turn, gives rise to an autonomous psychic sphere marked by desires 'TO KILL, TO POSSESS, TO DEVOUR – our entire individual unconscious is organized around these terms and around the phantasms which encircle them under the sign of repression' (*ES*, p. 214). In primitive societies, by contrast, a different social organization and different values are operative: 'TO GIVE, TO RENDER, TO EXCHANGE – everything is played in primitive societies within the collective exchange manifested around these three terms, in the rituals and myths which support them' (ibid.). Consequently, from a psychological point of view – and, as we shall soon see, from a sociological point of view as well – our society is a death culture, while societies organized around symbolic exchange are beyond binary oppositions between life and death.

What I have called Baudrillard's 'primitive communism' (see 2.2) is especially evident in these studies of cycles of symbolic exchange of life and death in primitive societies. Both industrial capitalist and contemporary Communist socities, by contrast, exclude death from life and are haunted by death in subjectivist and individualist modes. In a penetrating analysis, Baudrillard discusses how interiorization of the fear of death helps to produce a modern individualist subjectivity in which death is the repressed double (of the subject, of life) that haunts the body and nourishes further doubling of the subject in the soul (which yearns for immortality) and conscience (which disciplines the subject so that he or she can obtain this divine eternity and salvation). Deprived of the intimate relation with death of a primitive society, the modern individual lives haunted by the fear of death, and readily submits to social authorities (the Church, the State) which promise immortality or protection from death.

One of Baudrillard's most provocative claims concerns the argument that the division between life and death serves as foundation for social exclusion. On this argument, the dead are the paradigm of social exclusion and discrimination. Historically, inequality before death served as a paradigm of inequality in societies such as that of Egypt, in which only the kings and nobility were accorded honors of immortality. Metaphysically, Baudrillard claims, the separation of life and death is the fundamental distinction and social division, serving as an archetype of separation between humans and nature, men and women, and individuals and their own death. Social power over death also provides an archetype of the power of society over the individual: 'All forms of power will always have something of this odor around them, because it is in the manipulation, in the administration of death that power is founded in the last instance' (*ES*, p. 201). The abstraction of one's death from one's life, he suggests, as a final end somewhere in the distant future, provides the foundation for all other abstractions and alienations.

What Baudrillard calls 'the symbolic,' by contrast, puts an end to all disjunctions between life and death, soul and body, humans and nature, the real and the nonreal (*ES*, pp. 205ff.). 'The symbolic' refers to a mode of thought beyond the binary oppositions of the terms of Western metaphysics and rationality, and in symbolic operations these terms lose their distinctiveness and penetrate each other. Baudrillard's discussion contains a highly deconstructive argument against the absolutizing of distinctions between life and death in contemporary society and against binary oppositions in general. He claims that all such metaphysical divisions contain the projection of an imaginary of its opposite by the privileged term. Thus, 'In the partition human/nature, nature (objective, material) is only the imaginary of the human thus conceptualized. In the sexual partition between masculine/feminine, a structural and arbitary distinction which grounds the principle of sexual "reality" (and sexual repression), woman as thus always defined is never more than the imaginary of man. Each term of the disjunction excludes the other which becomes its imaginary' (*ES*, p. 205).

Thus, in our distinction between life and death, our conception of death is only a fantasy, an imaginary, of the living – but one that haunts us continually. Indeed, Baudrillard claims that 'all of the disjunctions which found the different structures of the real . . . have their archetype in the fundamental disjunction of life and death. That is why, in whatever field of "reality," each separated term, for which the other is its imaginary, is haunted by the other one as *by one's own death*' (*ES*, p. 206). This mode of binary thinking also structures our political thought: 'Thus the peoples of the Third World (Arabs, Blacks, Indians) serve as the imaginary of Western culture (just as much as an object/support of racism as the support of revolutionary hope). Inversely, we – the technological and industrial West – are their imaginary, what they dream of in their separation. This founds the *reality* of world domination' (ibid.).

It is thus the symbolic which would bring to an end the structure of metaphysical binary oppositions which constitutes our modern thought; and such deconstruction should begin, according to Baudrillard, by taking apart the opposition between life and death. Out modern societies go further than past eras in disassociating life and death and in attempting to abolish and repress death. 'To abolish death, this is our fantasy which is ramified in all directions: that of survival and eternity for religion, that of truth

for science, that of productivity and accumulation for the economy'
(*ES*, p. 225). All these valorizations serve to positivize and absolutize life, to
make it the ground of value. Modern thought strengthens this tendency.
Baudrillard claims that Christianity, Marxism and existentialism are united
in seeking a triumph over death – Christianity with its promise of eternal
life, Marxism with its promise of control of productive forces and nature to
maximize the preservation of life, and existentialism with its promise that
only an individual who recognizes his or her finitude can lead an authentic
life (*ES*, p. 228).

According to Baudrillard, only Freud and more marginal thinkers like
Bataille recognize the radicality of death, its otherness. Yet Freud's theory of
the death instinct founders on its ambivalence as to whether the instinct is
biological or psychological, somatic or psychic, and whether it or the so-
called life instinct, eros, is primary (*ES*, pp. 232–5). There is also confusion
in Freudian theory, Baudrillard claims, concerning whether the concept is to
be taken as a scientific theory or a myth. Bataille goes much further,
Baudrillard believes, both in recognizing the primacy and fundamentality of
death and in overcoming the metaphysical distinction between life and
death.[11] For Bataille there is no difference between death and sexuality, life
and death: both provide a 'paroxysm of exchanges,' both have the sense of
expenditure, waste and a festival in which nature celebrates its excess. Both
are seen as part of a cycle of symbolic exchange, and oppose the rationality,
utility and linearity of the system of economy.

Consistent with his political (metaphysical) vision of the time, Baudrillard
thus celebrates symbolic exchange over control by the code of political
economy. In the remaining studies of the political economy of death, he
describes various ways in which society's control of death extends social
control over the individual (*ES*, pp. 242–82). The form of his argument is
deconstructive: society is interpreted as a death culture, and its means of
processing and even preventing death are interpreted as means of controlling
life and extending the reign of a dead society over living individuals.
Meanwhile, death is interpreted as an event whose repression in this life
renders the individual subject to control by social powers.

Modernity itself is thus characterized in part by the repression of death
and the production of an individual subject who, haunted by the thought of
his or her own death, takes refuge in the Church, the State, the accumulation
of goods and wealth, or his or her own anxious inner life as fundamental
protector and guarantor of survival. Such refuge weakens social life, subjects
the individual to control by external powers, and unleashes untold amounts
of repressed aggression and death in social life. In postmodernity, one might
argue, signs of death proliferate and play an even more intense role in the
social imaginary, nurturing terrorism and fears and fantasies of mass death,
as well as nihilism. Note that I said that *signs* of death proliferate, not
numbers of deaths. In view of the great numbers of violent deaths in World

War I, under fascism and Stalinism, and in imperialist wars and pogroms, one can not really claim that there is a social acceleration of death in contemporary societies; but one might perhaps argue that there are more signs of social death and of violent death than ever before in a media-saturated society which thrives on spectacle and violent mass images.[12]

Postmodern culture is thus a culture in which free-floating signs come to constitute a new world of experience. Baudrillard's analyses of the body, sexuality, death and terrorism point to the fundamental role which he ascribes to *signs* in contemporary society. Furthermore, his rather macabre celebration in *L'échange symbolique* of sacrificial death and his dream of death as a symbolic exchange between life and death point once again to his *sign fetishism*, his fascination with the play and exchange of signs. At bottom, he translates a biological necessity and finality (death) into part of a sign game, and interprets contemporary modes of representing death (such as automobile accidents,, natural catastrophes, murder, suicide) as means of transfiguring a natural event into a sign spectacle. Yet he valorizes symbolic exchange of life and death in primitive society, in which there is allegedly no radical separation between life and death, thus pointing again to his fascination with the primitive as a sign culture, as a society in which culture and the play of signs took precedence over the economy and material necessity.[13]

Yet does the sort of symbolic exchange which Baudrillard advocates really provide a solution to the question of death? Baudrillard's notion of symbolic exchange between life and death and his ultimate embrace of nihilism (see 4.4) is probably his most un-Nietzschean moment, the instant in which his thought radically devalues life and focuses with a fascinated gaze on that which is most terrible – death. In a popular French reading of Nietzsche, his 'transvaluation of values' demanded negation of all repressive and life-negating values in favor of affirmation of life, joy and happiness. This 'philosophy of value' valorized life over death and derived its values from phenomena which enhanced, refined and nurtured human life.[14] In Baudrillard, by contrast, life does not exist as an autonomous source of value, and the body exists only as 'the carnality of signs,' as a mode of display of signification. His sign fetishism erases all materiality from the body and social life, and makes possible a fascinated, aestheticized fetishism of signs as the primary ontological reality. This way of seeing erases suffering, disease, pain and the horror of death from the body and social life, and replaces it with the play of signs – Baudrillard's alternative. Politics too is reduced to a play of signs, and the ways in which different politics alleviate or intensify human suffering disappears from the Baudrillardian universe.

Consequently Baudrillard's theory spirals into a fascination with signs which leads him to embrace certain privileged forms of sign culture and to reject others (that is, the theoretical signs of modernity such as meaning, truth, the social, power and so on) and to pay less and less attention to materiality (that is, to needs, desire, suffering and so on), a trajectory that will ultimately lead him to embrace nihilism (see 4.4). Thus Baudrillard's interpretation of the body, his refusal of theories of sexuality which link it with desire and pleasure, and his valorization of death as a mode of symbolic exchange – which valorizes sacrifice, suicide and other symbolic modes of death – are all part and parcel of a fetishizing of signs, of a valorization of sign culture over all other modes of social life. Such fetishizing of sign culture finds its natural (and more harmless) home in the fascination with the realm of sign culture which we call art. I shall argue that Baudrillard's trajectory exhibits an ever more intense aestheticizing of social theory and philosophy, in which the values of the representation of social reality, political struggle and change and so on are displaced in favor of a (typically French) sign fetishism. On this view, Baudrillard's trajectory is best interpreted as an increasingly aggressive and extreme fetishizing of signs, which began in his early works in the late 1960s and which he was only gradually to exhibit in its full and perverse splendor as aristocratic aestheticism from the mid-1970s to the present. Let us now trace the evolution of his fascination with art, a form of sign culture which Baudrillard increasingly privileges and one which provides an important feature attraction of the postmodern carnival.

4.3   POSTMODERN ART, ARCHITECTURE AND SIGN CULTURE

Baudrillard began his analysis of art with a discussion of pop art in *La société de consommation* in terms of the dramatic transformations of art objects in the early twentieth century.[15] Whereas previously, art was invested with psychological and moral values which endowed its artifacts with a spiritualistic-anthropomorphic aura, by the twentieth century art objects 'no longer live by proxy in the shadow of man and begin to assume extraordinary importance as independent elements in an analysis of space (cubism, etc.)' (p. 33). Soon – and Baudrillard likes to move quickly through the terrain of modern art – art objects exploded to the point of abstraction, were ironically resurrected in Dada and surrealism, then destructured and volatilized by subsequent movements toward abstract art. Yet today 'they are apparently reconciled with their image in New Figuration and Pop Art' (ibid.).

Baudrillard then raises the question of whether pop art is an authentic art form of the society of signs and consumption or simply an effect of fashion and thus a pure object of consumption itself. He indicates that the question cannot be answered unambiguously, for pop art, like advertising, fashion and so on is apparently both. In interpreting pop art, he argues that it follows the logic of consumption in eliminating representation as a privileged vehicle of meaning (through sign value and exchange value) and, like commodification, reduces the artwork to the mere status of a sign:

> Whereas all art up to Pop was based on a vision of the world 'in depth', Pop on the contrary claims to be homogeneous with their industrial and serial production and so with the artificial, fabricated character of the whole environment, homogeneous with this *immanent order of signs*: homogeneous with the allover saturation and at the same time with the culturalised abstraction of this new order of things. (Ibid.)

Baudrillard raises the question of whether pop art should be interpreted as a resacralization of things through the aesthetic investment of art or a banalizing of art, a reducing it to a commodity object, to a reproduction of the signs of the commodity world:

> Some will say (and Pop artists themselves) that things are really more simple: they say this because they are taken with them; after all, they are having a good time, they look around and paint what they see, it's spontaneous realism, etc. This is wrong: Pop signifies the end of perspective and the end of evocation, the end of testimony, the end of the active creator and by no means least of all, the end of subverting the world and of iconoclastic art. Not only does it aim for immanence of the 'civilised' world, but for its total integration in this world. There is a crazy ambition here: to abolish the rituals (and foundations) of a whole culture, that of transcendence – perhaps also quite simply an ideology. (p. 34)

Pop art thus constitutes a turning point in the history of art in Baudrillard's view, the point at which art becomes quite simply the reproduction of signs of the world, and in particular the signs of the consumer society which itself is primarily a system of signs. Triumph of the sign over its referent, the end of representational art, the beginning of a new form of art which he will privilege with his term 'simulation': art as the simulation of models. Baudrillard insists that it is wrong to criticize pop art for its naive Americanism, its crass commercialism, its flatness and banality, for precisely thereby it reproduces the very logic of contemporary culture, 'and Pop artists could not be reproached for making it evident. . . . The worst thing that could happen would be for them to be condemned and so re-invested, with a sacred function. It is logical for an art which does not oppose the world of objects, but explores its system, to enter into the system itself. . . . Throughout its predilection for objects, throughout its commercial success, Pop is the first to explore its own status as an art object which is "signed" and "consumed" ' (ibid.).

Yet Baudrillard sees some dangers lurking in a too enthusiastic embrace of pop art. For pop is close to a naive celebration of pure authenticity, bourgeois spontaneity, the authentic artist as the one who most accurately reproduces the world around him or her. Connected with this danger is the 'dangerous aspect of *initiation*' associated with the belief proclaimed by some pop artists that their art is accompanied by discovery of a whole new world, the world of consumption, full of fascinating new objects and commodities, which serve as inspiration for a new reconciliation with the existing universe. Finally, there is a danger that pop artists may fall prey to, and thus disseminate: a new essentialism, a new belief that art can grasp and reproduce the essence of things, rather than just reproduce signs. It seems, then, that for Baudrillard, pop art is valuable mainly as a sign of the logic of consumer society, as a replication of the processes of signification (sign value, abstraction, repetition and so forth) which he was at that time describing on a theoretical level. A similar interest in using art to exhibit his own theoretical positions is evident in the two essays on art in *For a Critique of the Political Economy of the Sign*. The study 'Gesture and Signature: Semiurgy in Contemporary Art' illustrates his theory of how the system of objects (and needs) in consumer society is organized into a system of signs. Baudrillard's example is the painting as a signed object (signature) and a gestural object, the product of artistic gestures or practices.

He begins by making the point that in today's art world the painting only becomes an art object with the signature of the painter, with the sign of its origin, which situates it as a '*differential* value' within the system of signs, the series of works, which is that of the oeuvre of the painter (*CPES*, p. 102). Baudrillard points out that copies, or even forgeries, were previously not denigrated the way they are in the contemporary world, in part because art was more the collective product of artist's studios, and because today art is supposed to be the 'authentic' product of an individual creator as part of his or her oeuvre. 'Modernity' in painting begins when the work of art is not seen as a mosaic of fragments of a general tableau of the universe, but as a succession of moments in the painter's career, as part of a series of his or her works: 'We are no longer in space but in time, in the realm of difference and no longer of resemblance, in the series and no longer in the order [that is, of things]' (*CPES*, p. 104). It is the act of painting, the collection of the painter's gestures in the individuality of the oeuvre, that is established with the painter's signature which constitutes the sign value of the work as a differential item in the series whereby the work is inserted into the system of art and receives its place (and value).

Painters like Rauschenberg and Warhol who produce almost identical series of works present 'something like a truth of modern art: it is no longer the literality of the world, but the literality of the gestural elaboration of creation – spots, lines, dribbles. At the same time, that which was representation – redoubling the world in space – becomes repetition – an indefinable redoubling of the act in time' (*CPES*, p. 106). In other words, precisely the seemingly peculiar gestures of pop artists repeating almost identical works in series points to the very nature of modern art, which establishes itself not as a representation of the world, but as a series of gestures, the production of signs in the series of an oeuvre. This practice also points out the naiveté, Baudrillard maintains, of believing that the function of art is to (re)grasp the world, to refresh ways of seeing, to provide access to the real; for such art, all art, is merely a set of signs, the product of 'the subject in its self-indexing' within a series (*CPES*, p. 107). Thus, rather than art being interpreted as the product of a sovereign subject who, in the gesture of creation, provides critical commentary on the real or subjective expression, the 'subjectivity in action' in painting points only to the way in which all gestures in the contemporary world are assigned their meaning as gestures within coded series, as part of a homogeneous system of signs, as emblems of everydayness itself, which like the painting, is 'difference in repetition' (*CPES*, pp. 108–9).

Thus Baudrillard interprets painting as emblematic of sign culture, of the reduction of culture to a system of signs within which 'art' often plays a privileged role. Art is thus subject to the same rules and system of signification as other commodities, and follows as well the codes of fashion, determination of value by the market and thus commodification. Baudrillard concludes his exercise with a polemic against the very notion of critical or contestatory art:

> Only recognition of this structural homology between a systematized world and art that is itself serial in its most profound exercise permits one to grasp this contradiction of modern art – which is deplored everywhere, even by artists themselves as a fatality. Modern art wishes to be negative, critical, innovative and a perpetual surpassing, as well as immediately (or almost) assimilated, accepted, integrated, consumed. One must surrender to the evidence: art no longer contests anything, if it ever did. Revolt is isolated, the malediction 'consumed.' All the more reason there would seem to be, then, to abandon all nostalgia, resign negativity and admit finally that it is in the very movement of its authenticity, in systematizing itself according to a formal constraint, in constituting itself according to a play of successive differences, that the work of art offers itself of its own initiative as immediately integrable in a global system that conjugates it like any other object or group of objects. (*CPES*, p. 110)

Modern art, *all* modern art, is thus for Baudrillard an '*art of collusion vis-à-vis* the contemporary world. It plays with it and is included in the game. It can parody this world, illustrate it, simulate it, alter it; it never disturbs the order, which is also its own' (ibid.). This passage is extremely interesting because it points to a continuity in Baudrillard's work underlying the discontinuities that I have been stressing, in that, up to the present, he has consistently denied the critical and negative function of art and has seen its surrender to and collusion with the existing society as a fatality, a necessity of the current situation. Just how fatal this necessity is we shall see in chapter 6, but here, in a relatively early work, we find a preview of Baudrillard's later surrender to the world of things.

It is also noteworthy how Baudrillard consistently uses his studies of art to illustrate his theses concerning developments in contemporary society (see, for example, *CPES*, chapters 4 and 5), and throughout the 1970s, he continued to use analysis of art to illustrate his theoretical positions. He frequently referred to baroque art as a sign of the process of signification transcending representation and as beginning a move toward a self-sufficient series of signs; on the other hand, his frequent references to ultra-realist *trompe l'oeil* paintings were used to illustrate the ways in which simulacra came to replicate reality and the process whereby it became increasingly difficult to tell the difference between simulacra and reality and whereby hyperreal models came to dominate and determine art and social life. He also began writing introductions to art exhibition catalogues and monographs for various museum installations.[16]

His theories of simulation and hyperreality even came to influence new movements in the art world, especially in the 1980s. Indeed, Baudrillard became a major theoretical guru in the world of modern art, a theoretical icon increasingly referred to and cited in discussions of the contemporary art scene. In particular, a trend of simulation art attempted to embody his theory of simulations, while hyperrealist art movements illustrated his theory of hyperreality. A statement by one of Baudrillard's followers, Peter Halley, illustrates his influence:

One can refer to it as either postmodernism or as neo-modernism, but what is characteristic of this order is that the elements of modernism are hyper-realized. They are reduced to their pure formal state and are denuded of any last vestiges of life or meaning. They are re-deployed in a system of self-referentiality which is itself a hyper-realization of modernist self-referentiality – though it is now detached from the modernist dream of revolutionary renewal. In post – or neo-modernism – the syntactical elements do not change. The vocabulary of modernism is retained, but its elements, already made abstract, are finally and completely severed from any reference to any real.[17]

The new hyperrealist, simulationist, or neo-geo, artists do not attempt to represent any objects or social reality, but simply reproduce hyperreal models or simulations through abstract representations of signs that simulate or pastiche former paintings, abstract and representational, attempt to represent scientific paradigms or models or those of cybernetic languages, or simulate commodity and image production.[18] In the words of art critic Hal Foster:

> Halley assumes a drastic Baudrillardian perspective, according to which our new dynamic of electronic information and mass media has made of social space a total system of cybernetic networks, at all levels of which is repeated one model: 'cells' connected by 'conduits' (thus, according to Halley, the cell-and-conduit system of the computer, of the office with its electronic lines, of the city with its transportation network, etc). It is this abstract field, this putative 'formalism of the cell and the conduit,' that Halley depicts with color-coded rectangles and 'Cartesian' lines, painted iconically on partially stuccoed grounds.[19]

These movements were deflated, but not yet volatilized, by Baudrillard's distancing himself from them during a lecture at Columbia University in the spring of 1987. According to one report, Baudrillard

> sent shock waves through the New York art world when he publicly refused to associate himself with the work of artists such as Peter Halley, Ross Bleckner, Jeff Koons, Haim Steinbach and Philip Taaffe. These artists are identified with so-called 'Simulationist' or 'Neo-Geo' art, one of the hottest new trends to come out of New York in several years. This work has received a great deal of critical attention, at least in part because it is allegedly based on Baudrillard's controversial analysis of postmodern culture. Halley actually claims to provide visual equivalents for Baudrillard's theory.[20]

Evidently, Baudrillard did not like the work with which his theory was being associated, was reluctant to promote any artistic movement, or believed in a separation of theory and art.

In the 1970s Baudrillard began to refer more frequently to architecture. As a result, his works started being discussed in architectural circles as well. His discussions of architecture, like those of art, were usually to illustrate his social theory, as in the case of his discussion of the twin towers of New York World Trade Center, which was used to illustrate his theory of the new system of deterrence through binary regulation (while the old New York skyscrapers pointed to an earlier world of competitive capitalism with each building – read: individual, corporation, nation-state – aggressively trying to outdo the other (see 3.3). His most detailed analysis of architecture is found in his study 'The Beaubourg-Effect: Implosion and Deterrence.'[21] Here, Baudrillard carries out a detailed analysis of the new Parisian Beaubourg culture center, an ultramodern multistoried structure housing art exhibits, films, video rooms, libraries, offices and a lecture hall designed to exhibit all forms of contemporary culture. Baudrillard was both fascinated and appalled by the center, which he took as an illustration of his main theses concerning contemporary society and culture:

> Beaubourg-Effect . . . Beaubourg-Machine . . . Beaubourg-*Thing* – how can we name it? The puzzle of this carcass of signs and flux, of networks and circuits . . . the ultimate gesture toward translation of an unnamable structure: that of social relations consigned to a system of surface ventilation (animation, self-regulation, information, media) and an in-depth, irreversible implosion. A monument to mass simulation effects, the Centre functions like an incinerator, absorbing and devouring all cultural energy, rather like the black monolith of *2001* – a mad convection current for the materialization, absorption, and destruction of all the contents within it. (p. 3)

Baudrillard uses his analysis of Beaubourg to illustrate in particular his theories of implosion and deterrence. Beaubourg allegedly absorbs and neutralizes all cultural energies which implode in a deterrence system that mirrors the political and social systems; thus it illustrates in a microcosm the fundamental processes at work in the larger society. 'Beaubourg is nothing but a huge mutational operation at work on this spendid traditional culture of meaning, transmuting it into a random order of signs and of simulacra that are now (on this third level) completely homogeneous with the flux and tubing of the facade. And it is really to prepare the masses for this new semiurgic system that they are summoned – under the pretext of indoctrination into meaning and depth' (p. 6). Beaubourg thus really contributes to the death of meaning, to the demise of high culture, and can therefore be seen as 'a *monument of cultural deterrence.*'

Baudrillard thus sees Beaubourg as 'a brilliant monument of modernity . . . the most exact reflection possible of the present state of affairs' (p. 4). Curiously, Baudrillard is using this piece of architecture as some cultural theorists used art – and Baudrillard, McLuhan and Kroker are three contemporary examples – to reveal the real, to illuminate contemporary conditions, to serve as a privileged vehicle of insight and understanding. In particular, Beaubourg represents for Baudrillard the implosion of culture into the masses and their initiation into a new era of disconnected flow, recycling and massification. Yet while Baudrillard finds Beaubourg highly instructive, he also finds it appalling, for its populist display of culture for the masses 'is, in any case, antithetical to culture, just as visibility and multipurpose spaces are; for culture is a precinct of secrecy, seduction, initiation and symbolic exchange, highly ritualized and restrained. It can't be helped. Too bad for populism. Tough on Beaubourg' (p. 5).

Once again, Baudrillard affirms his aristocratic values and fetishes of seduction and symbolic exchange against the cultural populism of Beaubourg.

He takes particular delight in reflecting on the phenomenon of the masses of the 'silent majorities' pouring into this cultural center, filling it up to the point that the very structure of the tubular building was buckling and threatening to collapse. Not surprisingly, Baudrillard finds the whole spectacle exemplary of the implosion of the social and the cultural into the masses, as illustrating his position that the masses were absorbing and neutralizing all contents of culture, information, meaning and so forth, just as Beaubourg-Thing was supposedly neutralizing cultural energies. Indeed, in his most amusing thesis, Baudrillard claims that rather than seeing Beaubourg as a work of cultural mystification of the masses, 'the masses fall on Beaubourg to enjoy this execution, this dismembering, this operational prostitution of a culture that is at last truly liquidated, including all counterculture, which is nothing but its apotheosis. . . . *the masses themselves will finish off mass culture*' (p. 7).

Indeed, Baudrillard claims that the real content of Beaubourg consists of the masses themselves, whose programmed flow through the museum replicates the flow of energy, information and goods through networks of social life. Indeed, the models of culture in Beaubourg point to the ways in which social (simulation) models produce the very massification of the masses:

> Everywhere in the 'civilized' world the buildup of stockpiles of objects entails the complementary process of human stockpiling: lines, waiting, bottlenecks, concentrations, camps. That's what 'mass pro-duction' is – not massive production or a utilization of the masses for production, but rather a production *of the mass(es)*. The mass(es) is now a final product of all societal relations, delivering the final blow to those relations, because this crowd that they want us to believe *is* the social fabric, is instead only the place of social implosion. *The mass(es) is that space of ever greater density into which everything societal is imploded and ground up in an uninterrupted process of simulation.* (pp. 8–9)

The masses go to Beaubourg to see a painting, a film (or other people – who cares?). Baudrillard goes to see the masses. The masses see objects and people. Baudrillard sees implosion, deterrence and simulation. This ability to see one's categories instantiated in various domains of social life is both the talent of the theoretician and a mark of sign fetishism, of seeing signs – of one's theory or whatever – where other people see things, events, humans and so on. It is also remarkable how Baudrillard is able to identify with these masses – who are 'ourselves (there is no longer any difference)' (p. 6) – and to read their secret designs and thoughts. 'The people want to accept everything, swipe everything, eat everything, touch everything. Looking, deciphering, studying doesn't move them' (p. 10). Henceforth Baudrillard will be the mouthpiece of the masses, giving voice to the silent majorities and to the things themselves, enlightening us as to what is really going on, speaking for the abused yet seductive object world. The social theorist of the society of signs and simulations will soon become the metaphysician of the new world into which we are entering (see chapters 6 and 7).

As he turned to metaphysics, Baudrillard soured a bit on art, believing that it had exhausted itself and might not have much to offer (which did not keep the art world from enthusiastically pursuing him as a prophet and privileged mouthpiece). In the interview 'Game with Vestiges' Baudrillard claims that in the sphere of art every possible artistic form and every possible function of art has been exhausted. Furthermore, against Benjamin, Adorno and other cultural revolutionaries, Baudrillard again claims that art has lost its critical, negative function:

> Truly, art can no longer operate as radical critique or destructive metaphor. So art at the moment is adrift in a kind of weightlessness. It has brought about a sphere where all forms can co-exist. One can play in all possible ways, but no longer against anyone. There is no longer an enemy, no longer any system. . . . Of course, there is still one, but it no longer has the specific power of, for example, capital or the political in their hey-day. Accordingly there is a disappearance of the horizon of a political order, a cultural order. It amounts to this: art is losing its specificity. It is brought back to itself again in a kind of self-reference and it continues to operate in all its tableaux. That is to say, it is becoming 'mosaic' as McLuhan put it. It cannot do anything more than operate out of a combinatory mode.[22]

Baudrillard then describes the postmodern as

> the characteristic of a universe where there are no more definitions possible. It is a game of definitions which matters. It is also the possibility of resuscitating images at the second level, ironically of course. It all revolves around an impossible definition. One is no longer in a history of art or a history of forms. They have been deconstructed, destroyed. In reality, there is no more reference to forms. It has all been done. The extreme limit of these possibilities has been reached. It has destroyed itself. It has deconstructed its entire universe. So all that are left are pieces. All that remains to be done is to play with the pieces. Playing with the pieces – that is postmodern. (p. 24)

Baudrillard thus argues, rather contentiously, that all possible art forms have been produced, as well as attacked, revived, deconstructed and put back together in combination with other forms. All the targets of oppositional art, he claims, once again highly dubiously, have been destroyed so that art has lost its power of negativity – of negating what exists – and of effectivity. All art – and presumably theory, politics and individuals – can do is to recombine and play with the forms already produced. As he put it at the end of the interview:

> Postmodernity is neither optimistic nor pessimistic. It is a game with the vestiges of what has been destroyed. This is why we are 'post' – history has stopped, one is in a kind of post-history which is without meaning. One would not be able to find any meaning in it. So, we must move in it, as though it were a kind of circular gravity. We can no longer be said to progress. So it is a 'moving' situation. But it is not at all unfortunate. I have the impression with postmodernism that there is an attempt to rediscover a certain pleasure in the irony of things, in the game of things. Right now one can tumble into total hopelessness – all the definitions, everything, it's all been done. What can one do? What can one become? And postmodernity is the attempt – perhaps it's desperate, I don't know – to reach a point where one can live with what is left. It is more a survival among the remnants than anything else. [Laughter!] (p. 25)

4.4　NIHILISM AND POSTMODERNITY

Baudrillard's narrative concerns the end of the era of modernity dominated by production and industrial capitalism and the advent of a new postmodern era constituted by 'simulations' and new forms of technology, culture, society and experience. Whereas modernity was distinguished by expansion, differentiation, energy and movement, as well as by theoretical and artistic projects which sought to represent and interpret the real, postmodernity is distinguished by implosion, de-differentiation, reproduction of models of the hyperreal and inertia. This new social order is distinguished by the disappearance of all the big signs of modernity – production, meaning, reality, power, the social and so forth – and the appearance of a new type of social order and modes of experience.

Indeed, in Baudrillard's post-1976 writings, it appears that political economy, the media and cybernetics coalesce to produce a new social order beyond the stage of capitalism described by Marxism, which could be interpreted as an altogether new type of postmodern society. Yet until 1980 – and to some extent thereafter as well – Baudrillard persisted in describing the contemporary social scene as 'our modern society,' 'modern times' and 'our modernity.'[23] Indeed, it is not until the postmodern craze of the 1980s that Baudrillard explicitly takes up the term in relation to his own work. In *L'échange symbolique* he generally referred to the focus of his analysis as

modernity, or our 'modern society' (*SE*, pp. 7ff., *passim*), and in later 1970s
texts he also referred to 'our modern society' and 'our modernity' (see *SSM*,
pp. 2, 101), a tendency which he continued into the 1980s (see 6.4). In an
article 'On Nihilism,' first delivered as a lecture in 1980 and then published
in 1981, however, he describes for the first time his theory as an analysis of
'postmodernity.'[24] In this essay Baudrillard describes 'modernity' as 'the
radical destruction of appearances, the disenchantment of the world and its
abandonment to the violence of interpretation and history' (p. 38).
Modernity was the era of Marx and Freud, the era in which politics, culture
and social life were interpreted as epiphenomena of the economy, or
everything was interpreted in terms of desire or the unconscious. These
'hermeneutics of suspicion' employed depth models to demystify reality and
show the underlying realities behind appearances, the factors that constituted
the facts.

The 'revolution' of modernity was thus a revolution of meaning grounded
in the secure moorings of the dialectics of history, the economy or desire.
Baudrillard scorns this universe and claims to be part of a 'second
revolution, that of the 20th century, of postmodernity, which is the immense
process of the destruction of meaning, equal to the earlier destruction of
appearances. Whoever lives by meaning dies by meaning' (pp. 38–9). The
postmodern world is devoid of meaning; it is a universe of nihilism in which
theories float in a void, unanchored in any secure harbor by any secure
moorings. Meaning requires depth, a hidden dimension, an unseen yet stable
and fixed substratum or foundation; in postmodern society, however,
everything is visible, explicit, transparent, ob-scene and unstable. The
postmodern scene exhibits signs of dead meaning and frozen forms mutating
into new combinations and permutations of the same.[25] In this accelerating
proliferation of signs and forms, there is an ever accelerating implosion and
inertia, characterized by growth beyond limits, turning in on itself. The
secret of cancer (and AIDS?): 'Revenge of excrescence on growth, revenge of
speed in inertia' (p. 39).

Acceleration of inertia, the implosion of meaning in the media, the
implosion of the social in the mass, the implosion of the mass in a dark hole
of nihilism and meaninglessness: such is the Baudrillardian postmodern
vision. Fascinated by this void and inertia, Baudrillard privileges the scene of
nihilism over the phantasy of meaning, arguing that – and this is as good an
expression of his postmodern position as any – 'If being nihilist is to
privilege this point of inertia and the analysis of this irreversibility of
systems to the point of no return, then I am a nihilist. If being nihilist is to be
obsessed with the mode of disappearance, and no longer with the mode of
production, then I am a nihilist. Disappearance, aphanisis, implosion, Fury
of the *Verschwindens*' (p. 39).

Baudrillard's nihilism is without joy, without energy and without hope
for a better future. 'No, melancholy is the fundamental tonality of functional

systems, of the present systems of simulation, programming and information. Melancholy is the quality inherent in the mode of disappearance of meaning, in the mode of volatilisation of meaning in operational systems' (*ibid.*). In fact, Baudrillard's postmodern mind-set exhibits a contradictory amalgam of emotions and responses, ranging from despair and melancholy to vertigo and giddiness to nostalgia and laughter. Analysis of the 'mode of disappearance' constitutes a rather original contribution to contemporary social theory; and indeed, he has been true to this impulse to describe without illusions or regret what is disappearing in our society and culture. Indeed, Baudrillard concludes 'On Nihilism' by linking his theory with 'intellectual terrorism':

> If being nihilist is to take, to the unendurable limit of the hegemonic systems, this radical act of derision and violence, this challenge which the system is summoned to respond to by its own death, then I am a terrorist and a nihilist in theory as others are through arms. Theoretical violence, not truth, is the sole expedient remaining to us.'
>
> But this is a utopia. For it would be admirable to be a nihilist, if radicality still existed – as it would be admirable to be a terrorist if death, including that of the terrorist, still had meaning.
>
> But this is where things become insoluble. For opposed to this nihilism of radicality is the system's own, the nihilism of neutralisation. The system itself is also nihilist, in the sense that it has the power to reverse everything in indifferentiation, including that which denies it. (p. 39)

This passage points to the cul-de-sac into which Baudrillard had theorized himself. While previous radical theory had valorized negation, Baudrillard claims that it is the system itself which is truly negating previous values and is therefore truly nihilistic, so that radical negation simply mimics the system's own processes and contributes to destruction of meaning. Indeed, he claims that the production of meaning itself contributes to an oversaturation and neutralization of meaning, thus robbing radical social theory of another oppositional strategy. From his perspective, postmodernity represents a new stage of nihilism, a new situation in which the highest values are exhausted, comparable to, yet different from, the nihilism diagnosed by Nietzsche during an era in which Christian and supernatural metaphysical values had supposedly collapsed:

> Nihilism no longer has the dark, Wagnerian, Spenglerian, sooty complexion of the end of the century. It no longer arises from a Weltanschauung of decadence or from a metaphysical radicality born of the Death of God and of all the consequences that can be derived from this. Nihilism today is the nihilism of transparency and in a way

it is more radical, more crucial than in its earlier historical forms, for this transparency, this floating is irresolvably a floating of the system and of all theory that still claims to analyse it. When God is dead, Nietzsche was still there to say it – that great nihilist before the Eternal and the cadaver of the Eternal. But before the simulated transparency of everything, before the simulacrum of the materialist or idealist fulfilment of the world in hyperreality (God is not dead, he has become hyperreal), there is no longer any theoretical and critical God to recognise his own. (p. 38)

Just as Nietzsche proclaimed the death of all previous (transcendent) values, so too Baudrillard proclaims the death of all the values of modernity – production, revolution, the social, meaning and the rest. Like Nietzsche, he wants to derive value from the order of appearances without appeal to a supernatural world, a *hinterwelt* or a deep reality. Like Nietzsche, he appeals to aristocratic values by privileging such activities as expenditure, the duel, seduction, ritual and so on. Yet significant differences from Nietzsche now also emerge. Baudrillard completely divests himself of any Nietzschean vitalism or celebration of life and the body. Nietzsche's 'gay science' and moods of joy also dissipate in the Baudrillardian atmosphere of melancholy. Further, whereas Nietzsche celebrated the sovereignty of the superior individual as the mode of transition to a higher stage of being, Baudrillard comes to attack the subject itself and to advocate quite different theoretical perspectives (see chapter 6).

Yet at the same time Baudrillard is moving into the ever more pronounced aristocratic aesthetic and metaphysical tradition associated with Nietzsche and French Nietzscheans like Bataille, Klossowski, Blanchot and others. A new relation to the past and to an aestheticized historicism also emerges. In the interview 'Game with Vestiges,' Baudrillard again characterizes his thought in terms of 'postmodernity,' describing it as a response to emptiness and anguish which is oriented toward 'the restoration of a past culture' that tries 'to bring back all past cultures, to bring back everything that one has destroyed, all that one has destroyed in joy and which one is reconstructing in sadness in order to try to live, to survive. Really, that is the tendency. But I hope it won't finish there. I hope there is a solution that is more original than that. For the moment one really doesn't see it [Laughter].'[26]

Baudrillard may laugh during this interview, but Nietzsche's cheerful laughter is not his dominant mood; and for the most part throughout the 1980s, Baudrillard does not offer an explicit theory of postmodernity beyond the few comments which I have cited, mostly from interviews during the 1980s in which he was pressed on the issue of postmodernity or in which he broached the issue himself. (To date the essay 'On Nihilism' is the only one of his major texts in which he actually presents his own theory as delineating a new postmodernity.) Thus in his 1970s texts in which he explicitly referred to new social conditions, to dramatic changes taking place, Baudrillard described them as taking place within modernity, and hesitated to name the new. Further, in his 1980s texts which we will examine in the last two chapters, Baudrillard continues to use the term 'modernity' as the global framework of his analysis, and the few times that he mentions a 'postmodern' phenomenon, he tends to be a bit churlish and critical, and so far has resisted spelling out a theory of postmodernity (though one could – as I have tended to do in the last two chapters – find something of a proto-postmodernist theory operative in Baudrillard).

As Baudrillard developed his theory of the new stage of society and the break with the previous social order, his polemical position toward other contemporary theories of the present age intensified, and it is to an examination of these polemics that we shall turn in the next chapter.

5

Provocations

From the early 1970s to the present, Baudrillard has been aggressively criticizing and eventually dismissing the positions of, first, the master thinkers of his generation Marx and Freud, and second, his competitors on the French scene, such as Foucault, the Freudo-Marxists and the French feminists.[1] These polemics emerge from a matrix of factors closely connected with the shifting position of the intellectual in French society in a rapidly mutating political and cultural environment. Simply put, from the late 1960s to the early 1970s it was chic to be associated with Marx and Freud, and most of the dominant intellectuals positioned themselves positively with regard to these masters of modern thought, either absorbing Marxian and Freudian ideas into their own work or positively citing or referring to them. Both Marxism and psychoanalysis were 'in,' and most of the more visible French writers of the era, including Baudrillard, took up positions accordingly.

Inevitable reaction against a too uncritical appropriation of the master thinkers set in by the early 1970s, and many critiques emerged of both orthodox Marxism and Freudianism and the attempts to synthesize them into Freudo-Marxism which blended calls for political revolution with calls for sexual revolution. The reaction against Marx and Freud and the attempt to merge them in theories of 'libidinal revolution' and 'the micropolitics of desire' was also conditioned by the failure of the May 1968 revolts to produce more dramatic and lasting changes. Disillusionment and 'left melancholy' set in, and thinkers like Baudrillard began to abandon their revolutionary hopes and pretensions. Baudrillard himself began directing his critical energies toward new targets, including some of the icons and sacred cows of the previous era of 'revolutionary' aspirations.

Polemics against Marx by former radicals, including Baudrillard, began appearing in the early 1970s, and culminated in the relentlessly anti-Marxian polemics of the 'new philosophers.' Fewer anti-Freudian polemics circulated, but some reactions against the hyper-Freudianism of the French intellectual milieu began to appear, such as Deleuze and Guatarri's *Anti-Oedipus* (1972), and a critic like Baudrillard could attract attention in this milieu by attacking the father of psychoanalysis and the modern discourse of sex.[2] Likewise he sensed the growing importance and influence of Foucault and Freudo-Marxism, and in 1977 published a broadside attack *Forget Foucault* against his chief competitors on the French cultural scene. And when feminism became increasingly influential, Baudrillard turned to the highly provocative practice of attacking and ridiculing feminism, as well as male theorists like Deleuze and Guattari and Lyotard, in *De la séduction* (1979). Thus Baudrillard, in line with his attacks on the current radical discourses, was one of the few males to polemicize against French feminism.

Consequently, Baudrillard eventually emerged as one of the major figures in the move against Marx and Freud and the attempts to combine them into a Freudo-Marxism. His polemics were among the sharpest and the most aggressive; he thus positioned himself as one of the chief critics of the master thinkers, taking extreme positions in the battles against Marx and Freud and his polemics against all his contemporaries and competitors in the struggle for cultural capital positioned him as a major provocateur in the contemporary French intellectual scene.

During this period, not only were there major, dramatic theoretical shifts within the French intelligentsia, but the very social role and function of the intellectual began to shift in French society.[3] Sartre and others had called for a new sort of political intellectual in the aftermath of the May 1968 upheavals, and the most advanced theorists of the time, including Baudrillard, saw themselves as 'revolutionary' theorists engaged in producing 'revolutionary theory.' Eventually, however, there was a reaction against the politics of the 1960s, and thinkers like Baudrillard began to revert to (modernist/avant-garde) models of intellectuals as critical thinkers, as specialists in the art of negation whose destiny was to negate *all* positive doctrines, politics and so on. At the same time, however, intellectuals were tempted by media power, and many French intellectuals saw themselves elevated to celebrity status: the critic as star, the theorist as media or cultural hero – a temptation that Baudrillard at first resisted strenuously, then succumbed to with the celebratory media reception of his diaries and aphorisms *Cool Memories* in 1987 (see 7.2).

If Baudrillard played revolutionary theorist through his first five books, culminating in *L'échange symbolique et la mort* (1976), in the works succeeding these, he played the games of hypercritic, iconoclastic destroyer of received wisdom, avant-garde avatar of the new, and visionary prophet of postmodernity. In this chapter I will discuss some of Baudrillard's most striking provocations as hypercritic, while explicating and attempting to appraise the worth of his polemics. I will guide my inquiry by the following questions: Are Baudrillard's polemics fair and accurate? Does he offer illuminating insights into deficiencies and limitations of the targets of his provocations? Is his own position any more convincing or useful than those he rejects?

Baudrillard, of course, would disdain any judgment of his work according to criteria of accuracy, fairness or use value, categories which he would assign to the illusions of the past. But using such categories and modes of thought against his own positions may be precisely what will help us to both make sense of Baudrillard's enterprise and discern its contributions and limitations.

Before beginning, however, I might note that, as far as I know, Baudrillard has never really engaged in any polemics with another of his chief competitors, Jacques Derrida. As I have suggested, Baudrillard appropriates and reconstructs in his own way some of Derrida's terminology, theses and deconstructive method. Nevertheless, in his published works, Baudrillard has not explicitly engaged in polemics with Derrida. Moreover, while he generally uses the term 'deconstruction' as a positive element in his method, it is not clear to what extent his method is similar to or different from Derrida's deconstruction. For while there are significant deconstructive moments and arguments in *L'échange symbolique*,[4] he never discusses Derrida's work in any detail. Later, I will suggest that Baudrillard is not sufficiently deconstructive himself, and that his own thought requires deconstruction (6.4).

5.1   BEYOND FREUD AND THE MIRROR OF DESIRE

Having smashed the 'mirror of production' and declared the end of political economy, Baudrillard next attacks the phantasm of the unconscious and the phantasmagoria of psychoanalysis. In *L'échange symbolique*, he describes Freudian theory as the 'mirror of desire,' and the unconscious as 'our modern myth,' with psychoanalysis as 'its prophet, the liberation of the unconscious (the revolution of desire) is its millenarian heresy' (*ES*, p. 220). On an Freudian reading, one might see the ferocity of Baudrillard's attacks on Marx and Freud in terms of an oedipal revolt against the father and an attempt to assert his own independence. There does seem to be an exaggerated need on Baudrillard's part to separate himself from his theoretical mentors and strike out on his own. Part of Baudrillard's 'anxiety of influences' might be market-determined: for to sell and position himself in the cultural market requires differentiation from his forerunners and competitors. Yet there also seems to be a rather pronounced desire to free himself from previous influences, to attack sharply his former mentors and establish his own distinctive theoretical positions.

Baudrillard's polemic against Freud is somewhat surprising, for much of his early writing traversed the field of Freudo-Marxism. As he confessed in 'The Ecstasy of Communication,' his early work confronted two logics: the logic of objects (heavily influenced by Marx) and 'a phantasmatic logic that referred principally to psychoanalysis – its identifications, projections and the entire imaginary realm of transcendence, power and sexuality operating at the level of objects and the environment'.[5] In this sense Baudrillard was engaging in a psychoanalysis of objects, showing how people invested and projected value, desire and so on into objects like cars, houses or furniture. This Freudo-Marxist exploration of the commodity world thus combined a reconstructed version of the Marxian logic of commodity production with the Freudian logic of symbolic projection.

Baudrillard's project in *L'échange symbolique* is to counterpose a concept of symbolic exchange to Marxian and Freudian notions of economic and libidinal exchange, and to valorize the realm of the symbolic against political economy and libidinal economy (a term used by Freudo-Marxists to refer to the political economy of desire and the instincts, e.g. investment, circulatory, expenditure, etc.).[6] In addition, there was another reason, why Baudrillard felt impelled to polemicize against Freud in this book and his subsequent writings. It has to do with the prestige in France at the time of Jacques Lacan and his Freudian theory of language and the unconscious.[7]

In Lacan's writings, linguistic categories like the symbolic, the imaginary and the subject were merged with Freudian concepts in an impressive and influential synthesis of linguistics and psychoanalysis. The Lacanian reading of Freud was taken up in turn by linguists, literary and cultural critics, and social theorists. In the light of the growing influence of Lacan's theory, Baudrillard criticized not only attempts to synthesize Marx and Freud, but also those syntheses of Freud, linguistics and semiology associated with Lacan, Barthes and the *Tel Quel* group. Thus Baudrillard attacked Freudo-linguistic theory (though there is no sustained polemic against Lacan), and attempted to develop his own theory of language and the symbolic against those who would make Freudian theory central to their work.

The general project of *L'échange symbolique* is to valorize a theory of symbolic exchange against orthodoxy within Marxism, linguistics, psycho-analysis and anthropology, all of which Baudrillard felt underplayed its revolutionary importance (see 2.2). This involved valorization of Saussure's anagrams (word games) against structural linguistics, Mauss's theory of gift giving against anthropological and Marxian theories of exchange, and a reading of Freud's theory of the death instinct against conventional Freudian psychoanalysis. This project required turning

Mauss against Mauss, Saussure against Saussure, Freud against Freud. We must line up the principle of reversion (the countergift) against all the economistic, psychological, or structuralist interpretations to which Mauss's work has led. We must oppose the Saussure of the *Anagrams* against that of the linguistics and even against his own restrictive hypothesis about the anagrams. The Freud of the death instinct must be played off against the whole previous edifice of psychoanalysis, and even against Freud's own version of the death instinct. (*ES*, p. 8).

In all these cases Baudrillard wants to show that theories of symbolic exchange offer more revolutionary perspectives on language, social relations and life than the orthodoxy contained within linguistics, psychoanalysis and anthropology. He is thus still operating within a framework of the politics of critique and revolution, believing that he has discovered three phenomena – Mauss's concept of the gift, Freud's death wish deconstructed and reinterpreted, and Saussure's anagrams – whose revolutionary potentials have hitherto been overlooked.

The strategy of Baudrillard's critique of Freud and psychoanalysis is to attack the universalizing pretensions of Freudian theory and undermine its claims of universal truth and validity. In a discussion of 'The exchange of death in the primitive order,' Baudrillard criticizes the universalizing claims of the Freudian unconscious and oedipal complex (*ES*, pp. 202ff.). His strategy is parallel here to his critique in *The Mirror of Production* of Marxian anthropologists who attempt to impose Marxian explanatory schemes on primitive societies by using notions of the primacy of the mode of production to interpret social life in its entirety, thereby frequently distorting cultural and social practices in societies organized around symbolic exchange, rituals and the like, and not production (see 2.2).

Baudrillard is also concerned to raise some general questions concerning the validity of Freudian (and Lacanian) concepts. He begins by interrogating the Lacanian scheme of the symbolic/real/imaginary. While 'the symbolic' for Lacan referred to the structures of language and discourse, as when a child begins interpreting his or her experience in terms of the categories and schemata appropriated during language acquisition and thereby constructs stable identities, for Baudrillard, 'The symbolic is neither a concept, an instance nor a category, nor is it a "structure," but is an act of exchange and *a social relation which puts an end to the real*, which resolves (*résout*) the real and at the same time the opposition between the real and the imaginary' (*ES*, p. 204).

Playing with the Lacanian concept of the imaginary, Baudrillard claims that the very Freudian notion of a reality principle, or the Lacanian concept of 'the real,' is itself only 'the imaginary of another term' (the pleasure principle, the psychic, the symbolic and so on). For symbolic exchange, by contrast, there is no longer any distinction between real and unreal, ideal and material, the visible and the invisible. Baudrillard illustrates this point by analyzing some of the ways in which primitive tribes process death, as by enacting a ritualistic death, thereby relativizing the distinction between life and death, so that, in effect, they have already died, are already dead, and thus henceforth live their death during their daily lives. In this ritualistic experience, the (imagined, ritualized) death is no more imaginary or unreal than fornication or excretion. Moreover, it has the benefit of allowing so-called primitives to incorporate death into their lives so that, presumably they are not haunted by continual fear of death (*ES*, pp. 205–6). (Similarly, the 'real' event of death is then 'imaginary,' or rather, beyond the distinction of real and imaginary).

Baudrillard claims that 'This reciprocity of life and death, in so far as they are exchanged in a social *cycle* rather than being ordered according to a *linear* biology and the *repetition* of a phantasm . . . all of this puts in question the very hypothesis of an unconscious' (*ES*, p. 208). He suggests that it is the very repression of the fear of death, of nonbeing, which produces the structure of the unconscious, so that if this fear were to disappear – or were never to exist – so too would repression and the unconscious (see 4.2). Baudrillard then builds on some anthropological studies which suggest that neither the oedipal complex nor the unconscious can be postulated as existing in primitive societies. He concludes by drawing a parallel between reductionistic schemes in Marxism and psychoanalysis (*ES*, p. 215).

Baudrillard claims that in both there is 'the same misrecognition (*méconnaissance*)' which fails to see that if the economic is hidden and latent, then it is not determinant or primary; while if the unconscious becomes manifest, it is no longer 'unconscious.' In relation to Freudian psycho-analysis, Baudrillard attacks 'the double' of the unconscious and 'the doubling' game of psychoanalysis. He claims that our culture is haunted by this absent double of the unconscious or desire which is parallel to a primitive animism or mana which exerts its mysterious force on our entire life. From this perspective, he mocks psychoanalysis as, echoing Nietzsche, 'our profound depth, a supernatural world (*Hinterwelt*)' which exhibits 'the omnipotence of thoughts, a magic narcissism, a fear of death, a primitive animism or psychicism which we gently fold back upon savages in order to recuperate them in our world as "archaic sediments"' (*ES*, p. 219). Psychoanalysis thus exhibits a 'reductive operation' which provides an inadequate model for interpreting societies other than our own and which cannot understand and thus represses symbolic exchange (*ES*, pp. 219–20).

Similar arguments are regularly made by anthropologists who would deny the universalist pretensions of Freudian theory. Indeed, they were widely disseminated in France in Deleuze and Guattari's *Anti-Oedipus*, which was the publishing sensation of its era.[8] More original is Baudrillard's general claim that psychoanalysis is a simulation machine, and that all its concepts are the imaginary of desire, projections which in effect create the unconscious and its effects. For without Freudian theory and its widespread dissemination, we would probably not even speak of an unconscious, an oedipal complex, castration anxiety and the like.

The most surprising and unusual aspect of Baudrillard's polemic against Freud, however, is his interpretation and reconstruction of Freud's theory of the death instinct, which he then turns against orthodox psychoanalysis. For

Baudrillard, the death instinct is a rationalization of a destructive, violent society whose destructiveness is in a sense naturalized by Freud's instinct theory. In Baudrillard's reading, Freud posits death as a metaphysical finality opposed to life, and thus operates with a dualistic theory which Baudrillard believes needs to be deconstructed (see 4.2).

Baudrillard's critique of the Freudian theory of the unconscious is another important aspect of his polemic against Freud. In an essay translated as 'Beyond the Unconscious: The Symbolic,' originally published in *L'échange symbolique*, Baudrillard presents his own concept of the symbolic, and polemicizes against the Freudian concept of the unconscious by arguing that the concept of the symbolic is more useful in explaining such things as jokes, poetic language and so on than Freud's concept of the unconscious.[9] The critique is elaborated by posing the question of whether there is a special affinity between poetic and psychoanalytic discourse. The strategy is to show how Freud's theories of the joke and poetic language – which utilize the notion of the unconscious – fail to properly elucidate these phenomena. Baudrillard criticizes, first, the psychoanalytic theory of humor and then what he takes to be the conflation of poetic and psychoanalytic discourse in certain contemporary French linguistic/poetic theories. He argues instead for their difference, claiming that poetic discourse follows a different logic from psychoanalytic discourse, in that it is not simply a circuitous expression of repressed desire, but another kind of autonomous linguistic creation altogether.

Baudrillard interprets jokes and the poetic as a pure expenditure, a pure waste (of desire, language, activity and the like), in which pleasure is gained purely from the expenditure, the waste and the play for pure activity. Note how Baudrillard is once again building on Bataille's anthropology (see 2.2) and how he opposes subversion of meaning to meaning, non-sense to sense. Psychoanalytic theory, by contrast, discovers meaning behind every joke, slip of the tongue, dream, textual production and so on, and thus operates within an economy of meaning, within the confines of a code. Baudrillard sees psychoanalytic theory as operating within a rigorous binary code of conscious/unconscious, primary/secondary process, pleasure principle/ reality principle, Eros/Thanatos and so forth, which imposes a code of interpretation, a theoretical grid, upon the entirety of experience which is processed, interpreted and explained in terms of its concepts. The symbolic for Baudrillard – like deconstruction, to which the concept is related – unties all these binary oppositions, and operates in a (more primordial? more free? more emancipatory?) realm beyond these distinctions. Baudrillard thus sees Freudian theory as a rationalistic and reductive code, as a simulation model, as the mirror of desire which – like Marxism – imposes its code on experience in an imperialistic and terroristic manner (that is, to the extent that it privileges its discourse and/or rejects other discourses or imposes its categories on primitive societies which are organized fundamentally differently from ours).

The autonomy of poetic discourse is explained in a similar fashion, Baudrillard claims. Rather than seeing the poem as an expression of the poet's unconscious which gains its effects through resonance with the unconscious of the reader, Baudrillard sees it as an autonomous discourse which works on language, which gains its effects through its explosion of unities and its polyvalencies of meaning, and which undermines reference and denotation through its use of the symbolic. Baudrillard seems to posit an inherently emancipatory dimension to the symbolic per se, connecting his concept of the symbolic with Bataille's notion of expenditure, Derrida's notion of dissemination and Saussure's anagrams, all of which celebrate a radical proliferation and dispensing of meaning – which for Baudrillard, at least, is a dissemination without surplus, remainder or utility.[10]

For Baudrillard 'the symbolic' thus stands for the *extermination* of the sign, the destruction of meaning, escape from all determination and all codes, 'thereby opening upon all possible meanings' (p. 68). In a concluding section entitled 'Beyond the Unconscious,' Baudrillard claims that the concept of the symbolic explodes all binary oppositions; for 'the symbolic is already that realm beyond the unconscious and psychoanalysis, that realm beyond the libidinal economy, as it is beyond the realm of value and political economy' (p. 82). Baudrillard concludes:

> The difference between the symbolic and the libidinal unconscious is at present greatly obscured by the privilege of psychoanalysis, but it must be reinstated – psychoanalysis must be prohibited from making incursions into realms where it has nothing to say. Concerning poetry (the work of art), the symbolic, (primitive) anthropology, neither Freud nor Marx were able to say anything that was not reductive, either to the Mirror of Production or to repression and castration. In those areas where psychoanalysis and Marxism break down, we must not be tempted to cast them aside as either angels or beasts; rather they must be analyzed relentlessly in terms of what escapes them. The limitations of each are at this time the strategic points of any revolutionary analysis. (p. 83)[11]

At the time of publication of *L'échange symbolique* Baudrillard was still searching for a revolutionary theory. Neither Marx nor Freud were sufficiently radical, because their attempts to produce a political economy and a libidinal economy respectively merely mirrored the systems already established. Both were interpreted as simulation machines, as mirrors of production and desire respectively, which did not break radically enough with the established society and its values of utility, investment, production and gratification and their alleged repression of death, waste and everything nonassimilable to the code of production and utility. Symbolic exchange, by contrast, is 'perhaps more radical in the long run than those [conceptions] of Freud or Marx' because it reveals 'here and now, a realm beyond value, a realm beyond law, beyond repression, beyond the unconscious. These things happen' (p. 83).

Baudrillard wants to go beyond libidinal economy, as he wants to transcend political economy. He seeks his alternative to the discourses and practices of the productivist society in a new sphere of the symbolic. It is not clear if this involves regression behind the reality already constructed, to a more 'primordial' and 'authentic' state, or to a new mode of being that is not really specifiable or ascertainable. Neither Marx nor Freud, in his view, escaped the limitations of the social reality and the reality principle which they were putting in question. According to Baudrillard, both abstracted from the symbolic, from a more multidimensional reality, and 'neither of them takes a critical attitude concerning the respective separation of their fields. They are not conscious of the rupture (*coupure*) that founds them. They are critical symptomatologies which subtly turn their respective symptomatic fields into the determining field. Primary processes, mode of production, "radical" terms, irreducible schemes of determination – those are the grounds on which they export their concepts and practice imperialism' (p. 84).

The structure of Baudrillard's polemics against Marx and Freud at this point are similar. Both are reductionistic; both would reduce cultural expression, to the logic of production or a libidinal economy respectively; neither can sufficiently explain certain cultural phenomena which follow a different logic; both use representational modes of thought which suppress more radical views of language and symbolic exchange; and neither offers adequate alternative perspectives to the existing order of production and exchange. Moreover, current attempts to mix Marxism and psychoanalysis are likewise doomed to failure, because both are 'coherent only within their partial circumscriptions, and are therefore not generalizable schemes of analysis' (p. 84). Baudrillard thus concludes: 'Neither their "synthesis" nor their contamination – only their respective extermination – can provide a foundation for radical theory. Marxism and psychoanalysis are going through a crisis. We must telescope and precipitate their respective crises rather than using one to support the other. They can still do each other a great deal of harm. We must not deprive ourselves of this spectacle. They are only critical fields' (p. 84).

Yet it is not clear that Baudrillard's replacement theories (here the symbolic) are any more useful in explaining the phenomena analyzed by Freud, just as it was not clear that Baudrillard offered a useful replacement to Marxian political economy in his theory of simulations. Nonetheless, Baudrillard's provocations here are useful to the extent that they provoke further thought about the limitations and contributions of Marx and Freud, and offer perspectives that enable one to rethink and develop better theories of the topics under investigation. Just as I argued earlier that reconstructed Marxian theories continue to be of use, I would also argue that Freud's perspectives on the unconscious, repression, sexuality and behavior continue to be of use. Concerning Freudian interpretations of jokes and poetry which Baudrillard takes as the target of his polemical critiques, I would argue that a reductive use of the Freudian model as the sole means of interpretation clearly limits our comprehension of these phenomena, but that Freudian perspectives also provide useful insights into them, insights evident in the vast and rich body of critical Freudian interpretation.

Likewise, I would argue that Freud continues to provide useful perspectives for critical social theory and cultural critique. While one should certainly avoid sole use of any one perspective (including Baudrillard's!) on complex social and cultural phenomena, a variety of critical perspectives, by contrast, enriches one's critical arsenal. Consequently I would argue that Baudrillard's attacks on Marx and Freud are too undialectical and denunciatory, and that they often fail to extract or properly valorize what might still be valuable. Against Baudrillard, I would argue that Marx's and Freud's theories, whatever their problems and limitations, continue to provide useful contributions to the study of social and psychological phenomena. Although Baudrillard's polemics against Freud are not anything like as denunciatory and dismissive as his polemic against Marx, he tends nonetheless, in his succeeding writings to imply that Freud's thought is generally an obstacle to properly explaining and understanding psychological and social phenomena today (though when it comes to analyzing sexuality, I note that Baudrillard still makes significant use of Freudian theories – see 4.1). In addition, he constantly implies that psychoanalysis is itself of dubious value, both as a theory and as a therapy, and he frequently claims that fascination with psychoanalysis is over.[12]

Yet we shall see that in his later writings, Baudrillard tends to drop the concept of the symbolic and replace it with 'seduction' (see 5.2 and 5.3), which becomes his preferred alternative to the hated code of production and utility. Further he began to move away from the rhetoric of revolution and to radically question *all* revolutionary theory, and the very concept of revolution itself, a critique that begins with his confrontation with Michel Foucault.

5.2 *FORGET FOUCAULT*

In his early works, Baudrillard generally cited Foucault positively, and often borrowed terminology, examples and strategies from him. As already noted, Baudrillard's genealogy of the order of simulacra followed the model of Foucault's *epistèmes*, or structures of knowledge; in addition, in other mid-

1970s texts, Baudrillard frequently cited Foucault's work.[13] In 1977, however, he launched a broadside attack, *Forget Foucault*, at the time when Foucault was becoming a major figure in the pantheon of French theory.

In many ways *Forget Foucault* marks a turning point and point of no return in Baudrillard's theoretical trajectory. In this text he turned away from his previous apotheosis of a politics of the symbolic, and moved into a more nihilistic, cynical and apolitical theoretical field. He also began to question more aggressively some of the basic concepts of radical social theory – power, desire, revolution and the social itself – and distanced himself from the other major theorists of the French scene, directing intense, uncompromising polemics against them, while crafting an increasingly hermetic theory of his own, which inhibited dialogue with his contemporaries, who henceforth were condemned for inhabiting an obsolete theoretical and political universe.

On one account, the occasion of the polemic against Foucault was the proposed formation of a study group consisting of Baudrillard, Foucault, Lyotard, Deleuze, Guattari and others, for which Baudrillard presented a position paper.[14] Baudrillard's polemic was so aggressive and his critique of his French contemporaries so extreme that after heated debate the group disbanded. The principle of *difference*, which had become a rallying cry and a battering ram for New French Theory, had evidently proliferated to such a degree that civil discussion and debate were impossible. The 'end of the social' that Baudrillard was to announce in his next work, *In the Shadow of the Silent Majorities* (see 3.4), was anticipated in the uncivil and asocial polemics against his fellow theorists.

Forget Foucault is therefore an important document within Baudrillard's trajectory, because it clearly delineates his differences from some of the other New French Theories produced in the 1970s, and provides formulations of the positions that would define his thought and writing for at least the next decade. He opens his provocation with some critical remarks on Foucault's theory of power and sexuality, but then quickly turns to polemicize against the Freudo-Marxian theories of desire which were so popular at the time, especially those of Deleuze and Guattari and Lyotard. In this way, he continues his polemics against Marx and Freud, and provides alternative perspectives on power, production and desire to Foucault and to Freudo-Marxian theories. In the last section of his study, Baudrillard contrasts these positions with his own theories of seduction, simulations and the hyperreal.

Baudrillard begins by describing Foucault's style and how his writing reproduces the very ways in which he conceptualizes the trajectory of power in contemporary societies (*FF*, pp. 10–11). Yet he immediately claims that Foucault's analysis of power, however elegant, is now obsolete in a new social era: 'What if Foucault spoke so well to us concerning power . . . only because power is dead? Not merely impossible to locate because of dissemination, but dissolved purely and simply in a manner that still escapes us, dissolved by reversal, cancellation, or made hyperreal through simulations (who knows?)' (*FF*, pp. 11–12). In short, Baudrillard is proposing that we 'forget Foucault,' because his theory is obsolete in the new postmodern society of simulations and determination by models, codes, information, media and so on. Previous discourses on power and sexuality, like Foucault's, Baudrillard suggests, are obsolete precisely because the phenomena which they describe (and helped constitute) have radically changed. Power no longer resides securely anchored in spheres like the economy or in institutions like the state, prisons and so on, but is radically dispersed throughout society in an era in which postmodern semiurgy proliferates signs of power, and power comes to reside in codes, simulations, media and the like, rather than in actual institutional forces and relations.

While Foucault also dispersed power through a multiplicity of sites, discourses, practices and strategies, he failed to analyze *simulations* of power, the ways in which power is feigned, masqueraded and simulated, and the ways in which signs of power often displace and replace actual relations of force and discipline. For Baudrillard, therefore, power in the society of simulations becomes increasingly abstract, since it is grounded in simulations rather than in actual social relations and forces. Further, it is volatilized into signs of *dead* power, which proliferate and fascinate in their very unreality and hyperreal dissemination: 'The universal fascination with power in its exercise and its theory is so intense because it is a fascination with a *dead* power characterized by a simultaneous "resurrection effect," in an obscene and parodic mode, of all the forms of power already seen – exactly like sex in pornography' (*FF*, p. 61).

As pornography replaces real sex with obscene (that is, totally explicit and hyperreal) signs of sex, so too in a media society signs of power, power simulations, replace the real exercise of power, as when Ronald Reagan governed by simulations, by exhibiting signs of power, rather than, say, by political insight, expertise and action. Although Baudrillard does not make this point himself, it is striking that Foucault never analyzes the role of communications media in transmitting discourses and relations of power, and thus neglects completely the whole issue of media power and simulations which Baudrillard himself inhabits. Consequently, while it is not clear that we can safely 'forget Foucault,' there is an important dimension missing (the media, communications, information, simulations) in Foucault's account of power, which Baudrillard supplements.

Baudrillard thus argues in effect that Foucault's theory of power conceptualizes an earlier stage of social structure in which power took discernible forms and was actively visible, and suggests that this stage of history is over. Foucault saw power not as something to be described in terms of abilities and forces of prohibition, coercion and domination, but rather in relational structures in which discourses, institutions, norms and practices induced individuals to produce, conform and act in certain ways.[15] In other words, power was to be conceptualized as a positive, productive and generative force, and not as a solely repressive, negative and prohibitive force. Furthermore, there was no essence or basic structure of power but ' "it is the name that one attributes to a complex strategical situation in a particular society" (Foucault, *The History of Sexuality*, p. 93)' (*FF*, p. 101). In Foucault's view power operates in a variety of complex micrological ways in different societies at different times, and theories of power should try to discern and describe all these. It is therefore ironic that Baudrillard takes Foucault to task for ascribing a discernible, describable structure to power, since he had polemicized against the reductive theories of power of previous thinkers on the grounds that they centralized power in privileged sources and institutions – that is, the economy, the state, patriarchy and so on – and usually ascribed to it an unchangeable essence or nature. Instead, Foucault argued, power is more diffuse, decentralized, disseminatory and complex.

Still, Baudrillard believes that in contemporary postmodern society the proliferation of signs of power and simulation models have so radically decentered power that it has now mutated into signs of dead power which float through the postmodern scene. In this context, power is so dispersed, pulverized, and dematerialized that it is seemingly impossible to chart its trajectories, structures, relations and effects. Moreover, Baudrillard claims that power was never as structured and ordered as classical theories affirmed; nor was it something that could be accumulated indefinitely: 'Something in us disaccumulates unto death, undoes, destroys, liquidates and disconnects so that we can resist the pressure of the real and live. Something at the bottom of the whole system of production *resists the infinite expansion of production* – otherwise, we would all be already buried. There is something in power that resists as well as we see no difference here between those who enforce it and those who submit to it' (*FF*, pp. 41–2).

We see in this passage how Baudrillard grounds his theory of (simulated) power in certain metaphysical assumptions and sociological claims. Following Bataille's anthropology, Baudrillard claims that there is a propensity to disaccumulate, waste and expend that resists imperatives to accumulate and preserve (wealth, power and so on) (see 2.2). Further, he claims that power by its nature is reversible, that the dominated can always become the ones who dominate, that the terms of power are always subject to radical reversal, and that power relations are thus always becoming undone, reversing and redefining themselves. And this, Baudrillard claims, is intrinsic to the very nature of power (note the metaphysical turn in Baudrillard's thought, which will become increasingly pronounced).

Consequently Baudrillard claims that today dominant relations of power have supposedly come undone in a semiological situation in which models of power generate dead signs of simulated power, which spiral and disseminate in contradictory ways throughout society. A similar process is occurring, he claims, with sexuality, and understanding these mutations will put in question dominant Freudo-Marxist theories of sexuality and the micro-politics of desire.

Sexuality and the Micropolitics of Desire

In *Forget Foucault* Baudrillard also argues that sexuality no longer exists in the forms described by Foucault and classical discourses on sexuality (that is, psychoanalysis). During the bourgeois era, according to Baudrillard, sexuality referred to a localized domain of erotic practices, surrounded by well-defined, well-known prohibitions, and discourses on sexuality referred to these practices (either inhibiting or encouraging them), while marking 'abnormalities' and 'perversions.' Today, however, sexuality has presumably proliferated to such a degree in cultural semiurgy that it permeates society and, according to Baudrillard, refers to something different from the sexuality of the previous era. That is, in a society in which sexuality speaks in advertising, fashion, the media and other popular discourses, it is manifest and open throughout social life. With sexuality no longer private and hidden or repressed, its discourses presumably take on new meanings and have different effects, tending to encourage sexual behavior, all forms of sexual practice, rather than limiting or prohibiting sexual activity.

The argument seems to be that with sexuality completely out in the open and encouraged from every official site (with pornography merely the most explicit public display of a completely explicit sexuality), it loses its mystery, as an alluring special and private activity, or as a zone of the forbidden and the taboo. Thus sexuality is no longer a private, individualized, personal affair, but is socially mandated, defined, normalized and proliferated. In this situation, sexuality is reduced to an imperative to have sex, to release sexual tensions, to deploy sexual pleasure according to social models and codes, and such activity supposedly divests sexuality of its seductive charms and its allure as a forbidden fruit. Sexuality is henceforth something that is encouraged, organized and colonized by social discourses, rather than something that could at least be a rebellion against social codes and prescriptions.

Furthermore, *'everything is sexuality'* now, so it no longer has its more localized significance (*FF*, p. 14). And if everything is sexuality, then nothing is really sexuality any more. In an argument parallel to his claim that Foucault is able to describe power so well simply because it no longer exists, Baudrillard then asks:

And what if Foucault spoke to us so well of sexuality (at last an *analytical* discourse on sex) . . . only because its form, this great *power* (that too) of our culture, was like that of power, in the process of disappearing. Sex, like man, or like the category of the social, may only last for a while. And what if sex's reality effects, which is at the horizon of the discourse on sexuality, also started to fade away radically, giving way to other simulacra and dragging down with it the great referents of desire, the body, and the unconscious – that whole recitative which is so powerful today? (*FF*, pp. 88–9)

Since sexuality, like power and everything else, has fallen prey to the logic of simulations, new analyses are needed in an era of simulations, and since Foucault presumably does not analyze sexual simulacra, his theory is now obsolete and cannot adequately conceptualize new postmodern sexuality. On this view, which is congruent with the guiding positions of New French Theory, sexuality, power and all other social phenomena are social constructs, the products and effects of dominant discourses. Thus Baudrillard can refer to Freudian psychoanalysis as a 'simulation machine' which constructs the unconscious and proliferates this discourse and model throughout society (*FF*, pp. 30–1), and can claim that this simulation machine is obsolete because the theory does not take account of the manifold ways in which new discourses on sexuality are simulated and proliferated. Yet Baudrillard does not really discuss in any detail the postmodern, or new, sexuality that supposedly replaces the previous form of sexuality described by Foucault; thus one might be skeptical concerning the disappearance of sex in the postmodern scene.[16]

It should now be clear that Baudrillard's fundamental project in the 1970s was to put in question the major concepts that Marxists, Freudians, the various adherents of Freudo-Marxism and others were using to radicalize contemporary thought and politics. The underlying argument was that contemporary social conditions had changed to such an extent that the categories used to describe previous social formations were no longer relevant or valid. At stake is whether Baudrillard is right in saying that we have *already* entered a new era of history in which power, discipline, sexuality and so on are *completely different* from what they were in the previous era, so that previous forms of power, sex and so on are 'dead' and the theories describing them are 'obsolete,' or whether instead, as I shall argue, we are in a transition period, when we need new syntheses of theories like these of Foucault and Baudrillard to make sense out of what is going on.

It soon becomes clear that the central targets of *Forget Foucault* are the Freudo-Marxian theories of repression and liberation which Baudrillard believes combine problematic discourses of power and sexuality. Baudrillard claims that Lyotard and Deleuze and Guattari use the same model of desire that Foucault uses of sex and power: a disseminatory production machine in which desire flows through intensities and trajectories where it attempts to break through repression and interdiction, thereby providing a foundation for resistance and revolution (*FF*, pp. 17ff). Indeed, by the mid-1970s these

Freudo-Marxian theories of liberation and a micropolitics of desire were becoming increasingly influential. Such theories called for a micropolitics of everyday life in which subversive desire could be turned against repressive institutions to begin a transformation of everyday life that would be part of a process of total revolution.[17]

By the time of *Forget Foucault*, however, Baudrillard had turned against the politics of desire completely, concluding: 'When power blends into desire and desire blends into power, let's forget them both' (*FF*, p. 19). He argues that the problematics of both desire and power follow the dynamics of a production model, shifting from 'a violent and archaic model of socialization (work) to a more subtle and fluid model which is at once more "psychic" and more in touch with the body (the sexuality and the libidinal)' (*FF*, p. 20). That is, whereas previously socialization was harsh and involved the imposition of labor and discipline in the work place as the primary mode of social organization, in neo-capitalist societies, it was claimed, socialization took place through the channeling of desire, through managed gratification. Unleashing desire against its socially hegemonic forms, advocates of libidinal revolution were claiming, would produce a revolution of desire which would be the motor of a process of social revolution and restructuring.

Against this 'micro-politics of desire,' Baudrillard is arguing that both the older Marxist and the newer Freudo-Marxian models operate under the binary logic of production and repression versus liberation. In all cases, production becomes the dominant goal, for liberated labor as for desire. In the classical Marxian project the goal is to produce more use values, goods, democracy, satisfaction and so on, whereas in the Freudo-Marxian model, the goal is to produce more pleasure, release, gratification and so on. Yet this emphasis on the liberation of the unconscious, desire, sexuality or the body reproduces, according to Baudrillard, precisely the imperatives of capital for maximal production and circulation:

> The compulsion toward liquidity, flow and an accelerated circulation of what is psychic, sexual, or pertaining to the body is the exact replica of the force which rules market value: capital must circulate; gravity and any fixed point must disappear; the chain of investments and reinvestments must never stop; value must radiate endlessly and in every direction. This is the form itself which the current realization of value takes. It is the form of capital and sexuality as a catchword and a *model* is the way it appears at the level of bodies. (*FF*, p. 24)

Baudrillard thus suggests that the discourse of liberation – be it the liberation of labor or sexual liberation – is reproducing *capitalist* rationalist and rationalizing discourses of production. By contrast, he advocates discourses and practices that break more radically with capitalist logic and discourses. The radical alternative to productivist sexuality is, he argues,

seduction, which, we shall see, he defines in idiosyncratic ways (see 5.3).
Against the injunctions toward the liberation of desire, Baudrillard contrasts

> cultures which maintain long processes of seduction and sensuousness
> in which sexuality is one service among others, a long procedure of
> gifts and countergifts; love-making is only the eventual outcome of
> this reciprocity measured to the rhythm of an ineluctable ritual. For us,
> this no longer has any meaning: for us, *the sexual has become strictly
> the actualization of a desire in a moment of pleasure* – all the rest is
> 'literature.' What an extraordinary crystallization of the orgiastic
> function, which is itself the materialization of an energetic substance.
> (*FF*, pp. 23–4)

Our society, by contrast, he claims,

> is a culture of premature ejaculation. More and more, all seduction, all
> manner of seduction (which is itself a highly *ritualized* process),
> disappears behind the *naturalized* sexuality imperative calling for the
> immediate realization of a desire. Our center of gravity has in fact
> shifted toward an unconscious and libidinal economy which only
> leaves room for the total naturalization of a desire bound either to
> fateful drives or to pure and simple mechanical operation, but above all
> to the imaginary order of revolution and liberation. (*FF*, p. 23)

Baudrillard thus contrasts the logic of production which governs Freudo-
Marxian theories of sexual liberation with his own theory of seduction
which will soon be the central positive category of his project: '*Seduction* is
that which is everywhere and always opposed to *production*; seduction
withdraws something from the visible order and so runs counter to
production, whose project is to set everything up in clear view, whether it be
an object, a number, or a concept' (*FF*, pp. 21–2).

Baudrillard's analysis of the similarities between Foucault's discourses on
power and sex and Freudo-Marxian theories of libidinal economy and the
theories of revolution and liberation shared by both is provocative, as is his
claim that these discourses are linked with the logic and values of capitalism.
This latter argument is especially clever and perhaps troubling for his French
compatriots who were competing to see who was both the most radical
and most anti-capitalist revolutionary. Against those who, like Foucault,
Lyotard and Deleuze and Guattari, celebrate a molecular politics of desire,
defined as a micropolitics of everyday life, Baudrillard utilizes Jacques
Monod's theory of DNA and the genetic code to put in question the
celebration of the molecular in these theories. For Baudrillard suggests that
precisely on the most microscopic level of the molecular, the DNA code
dominates and controls flows and intensities of behavior, and that therefore

to fetishize a molecular politics or a micropolitics of desire might be to advocate a politics of liberation in a sphere which itself may be controlled by coercive, and in some cases unknown, powers. Thus, Baudrillard warns, 'Beware of the molecular!' (*FF*, p. 36).

After concluding his critique of Freudo-Marxism and Foucault's theory of power, Baudrillard's polemic in *Forget Foucault* loses steam, ending with a series of cryptic aphorisms which are supposed to illuminate his position, but which probably shed more darkness and confusion than light, and which might be read as symptoms of the increasing incoherence and hermeticism of his own position (*FF*, pp. 49ff.). Yet his polemic raises the question as to whether we should forget Foucault and previous theories of society and power as outmoded dinosaurs which have little to offer to contemporary theory and politics. Is this the case? Or should we forget Baudrillard?

For Baudrillard and Foucault: Toward Multiperspectival Social Theories

Once again, while Baudrillard's critiques of Foucault and other New French Theorists are often provocative, he fails to articulate convincingly a coherent and attractive counterposition. As in the case of Marx and Freud, he finds little worth preserving in Foucault or Freudo-Marxism, and rather ungenerously dismisses them wholesale, without attempting to salvage what is valuable in their work. Yet, despite Baudrillard's telling criticisms, should we conclude that Foucault's attempts to chart the trajectories of power in contemporary society through studies of hospitals, mental institutions, prisons and other disciplinary institutions are completely obsolete? Are Foucault's studies of the discourses which legitimated and were part of these institutions and the conjunctures of power and knowledge in these discourses and practices irrelevant in the allegedly completely new postmodern society?

Baudrillard suggests that both Foucault's and previous theories of power assumed that there was something behind power, secret sources and modes of power, and that the task of radical critique was thus to lay bare how power functions in modern society, how sometimes hidden forces wield power for their own ends. The analysis also presupposes that power is used for specific individual ends against other individuals, and intrinsically serves the ends of domination and control. For Baudrillard, on the contrary, these uses of power are only simulacra of power. Real power, if it ever existed, is dead, and all that remains is the illusion of power, the mirage of power, the signs of power behind which exist only other signs, or, strictly speaking, nothing. Baudrillard's agnosticism concerning the reality of power in contemporary society is thus consistent with his skepticism concerning the real, the social, the political, the signified, desire and all causal modes of thought which attempt to detect causes behind effects, structures behind appearances. This is not possible, Baudrillard believes, in a simulation-saturated society in which the interplay of codes and simulacra replaces relations of power and domination. Rather, 'power' (under erasure) is at once everywhere, in every code and simulation, and nowhere, in no particular centralized locus.

Foucault is therefore dismissed, because he believes that he can provide an analysis of the complex ways in which power functions in the modern world. Baudrillard urges us to forget these illusions and move on to other problematics. But can we so easily escape the imperatives and urgencies of desire, power and resistance? Have power and oppression ceased to play an important role in our lives and societies? Or is it simply that it has become more difficult to grasp and conceptualize the ways in which power functions? If so, is the proper approach to abandon inquiry into these topics, as Baudrillard proposes, or to undertake new ways of studying sexuality and power, as Foucault does? Or – better – to attempt to combine Baudrillardian and Foucaultian perspectives on power?

In fact, can we have a radical politics without theories of desire and power? Traditional political theories focus on who has power and how they get it and use it, and perhaps on who they use it against, as well as how the powerless adapt to or struggle against their situation. The goal of critical political theories, from liberalism to Marxism, is to see how power can be more equably distributed or how the have-nots can get more power to use against the haves. Radical social theory, whether it thematizes this or not, is concerned with human suffering and with removing the causes of suffering; for power is what enables its possessors to inflict pain and suffering on the dispossessed, and the winning of power becomes part of the goal in the struggle against human suffering and oppression. The problematic of revolution or radical social change therefore turns to some extent on reversing and undoing current power relationships and producing new ones. Thus the concept of power has been central to a variety of traditional and contemporary political theories, and continues to be part of political discourse today.

The crux of Baudrillard's case against Foucault is that the latter seems to be too much of a structuralist and not enough of a poststructuralist. That is, Baudrillard seems to be faulting Foucault for believing that there are determinate structures, relations and practices of power, whereas in Baudrillard's poststructuralist universe there is only the play of simulations, without any anchoring in the real. Foucault, on the other hand, attempts to delineate the ways in which power informs discourses, institutions and social practices, all of which Baudrillard sees as being dissolved in the hyperrealism of simulations.

At this point, it is hard to keep from losing patience with Baudrillard, given that we live in a world in which unequal power relations and repression produce massive suffering, incarceration, torture, murder and the slow death of lifeless life on a massive scale. A comparison of Foucault's theories with those of Baudrillard would allow us to show what is wrong with Baudrillard's ways of seeing and theoretical perspectives. On Baudrillard's account, such things as human suffering and institutions that produce suffering, like prisons, mental institutions, sexual repression and practices, and the work place have no real significance; they are simply simulations without real power, efficacy or importance for the critical critic. But while these phenomena may not be real for the postmodern theorist sitting in his Paris apartment, puffing on his Gaulois or Cuban cigar with defiant pen in hand, for those condemned to work for a living or condemned to live in prisons, hospitals and mental institutions, they are all too real.

Furthermore, power functions in a multitude of ways in everyday life that should not be ignored. Dominant forms of power often focus on and attempt to shape and channel desire in such a way that desire and power become interrelated, especially in the consumer society and in the mass politics of the twentieth century. Fascism managed to channel desire into symbols, politics and figures which the fascists presented, and Reich, Bloch and others claimed that the Left had to engage in similar attractive and desirable political practices if they were to succeed. In our capitalist democracies, political advertising and politically managed media politics attempt to manipulate desire and fear into channels sympathetic to various power elites and their values and institutions. Here a combination of Foucaultian and Baudrillardian analysis might help us to examine current forms of desire and power. Whereas Foucault analyzes discourses, practices and institutions which exercise power and knowledge, Baudrillard analyzes how media, information technologies and simulations function to transform contemporary society and everyday life.

Foucault's merit in comparison with Baudrillard is the care with which he studies the institutions, discourses, archives, practices and so on which illuminate the workings of power and oppression. Yet Foucault, as noted, bypasses the media, simulations and semiurgy. Hence Baudrillard's focus on these phenomena does add an important dimension to discourse about power and knowledge, thereby forcing us to engage in more multi-dimensional analysis and critique. Let us make use of both Foucault and Baudrillard, then, forgetting neither as we forge our own theories of contemporary society. Thus I would argue for social theories that make use of a multiplicity of perspectives to analyze the phenomena and dynamics in our current social situation. Baudrillard, by contrast, believes that the rupture in history is so significant and the novelty of the new social conditions so extreme that only radically new theories can account for the new social conditions. Against this position, I would propose adopting Ernst Bloch's notion of nonsynchronicity, and would argue that we are currently in a transitional nonsynchronic social situation in which we live in many worlds at once, and thus need a multiplicity of viewpoints to make sense out of various domains of our social experience.[18] That is, at times we still find ourselves victims of oppressive bureaucracies such that Weber's 'iron age' and Kafka's novels provide illuminating perspectives; at other times we are confronted with the more subtle forms of disciplinary or normalizing power or the panoptic powers of surveillance which Foucault describes so well; and sometimes we find ourselves in the new situations which Baudrillard evokes, as when we are confronted with political or religious simulacra or with media signs which attempt to seduce us into purchases, normalized behavior, voting or whatever. Furthermore, sometimes we need to mobilize classical strategies of political struggle to fight against certain kinds of classical political power, as in struggles against imperialist foreign policies or repressive legislation; at other times, however, more Foucaultian strategies of resistance may be in order, as when we refuse or seek to undermine certain policies in the various departments of our universities; and in other circumstances a Baudrillardian reversal of power relationships may be possible through 'seduction' or what he later calls 'fatal strategies' (more on these in 5.3 and chapter 6).

The point is that we frequently need a variety of theoretical and political theories and strategies to deal with situations in which we find ourselves. No one theoretical perspective will always be illuminating, and no one political strategy can always work to solve the problems we face (one could make a similar argument for the need for a variety of critical strategies in the theory and practice of interpretation). Consequently, it seems a mistake to adopt a Baudrillardian position of theoretical purity or to assume the absolute validity and superiority of any one social theory or political strategy over others.

In fact, there are similar limitations in both Foucault's and Baudrillard's theories of power and society. Power is too decentered in *both* theories, to an extent that one loses sight of institutional loci of power like corporate capital or patriarchy, to which Marxists or feminists call attention. Further, both theorists undertheorize the dimension of resistance, via a primary focus on power and domination (although Baudrillard's is far more aleatory and simulational than Foucault's). Both in fact – as Habermas has suggested of Foucault[19] – have a primarily negative view of the social, and cannot set forth a point of view from which to justify critique, resistance and struggle. Thus both fail to theorize an adequate normative basis from which to criticize and attack power. Thus there are limitations in both perspectives that require us to turn to other positions to provide more adequate theories of power in contemporary society.

As we shall see, Baudrillard's polemics against his contemporaries and his rejection of their theories and concepts is part of an attempt to create his own language and theories, and to 'liberate' himself from the illusions of the tradition and his contemporaries. Yet is Baudrillard himself the victim of the liberationist ideologies which he criticizes in *Forget Foucault*? Or is his attempt to concoct his own discourse and theory independent of his contemporaries itself an effect of a consumer society which imposes imperatives of product differentiation and individualization as a counter-tendency to massification and homogenization? *De toute façon*, after *Forget Foucault*, Baudrillard rarely uses his contemporaries' terminology, theories and positions, and resolutely sets out to create his own little thought world, his own theoretical kingdom. *Forget Foucault* thus marks something of a rupture in his theoretical production, even though it is part of a series of polemics that continues through the 1970s and to some extent into the 1980s. From now on Baudrillard is completely Baudrillardian, so to say, as he produces increasingly iconoclastic simulacra of theoretical texts.

5.3 BAUDRILLARD'S AFFRONT TO FEMINISM: *DE LA SÉDUCTION*

In 1979 Baudrillard published a highly provocative little book entitled *De la séduction* (republished in 1981), which can be read, among other ways, as an attack on feminism. To continue my analysis of Baudrillard's provocations I shall read it in this way here, even though I use this text in other discussions, and thus propose other possible readings and uses of the book as well.

De la séduction is an important text, which marks Baudrillard's move to his current theoretical matrix. Henceforth *seduction* will replace symbolic exchange as the privileged oppositional term to the world of production and utility which Baudrillard continues to combat. He begins with a discussion of how, for religion, seduction was a strategy of the devil, the sorceress of love (*SED*, pp. 9ff.). On this view, seduction is always evil and worldly. It is 'the world's *artifice*.' Seduction is also a polemical target of the philosophers, who, since Plato, have worried about misguided souls being seduced by appearances and missing out on the reality behind the seductive veil of perceptual illusion. Thus, in the philosophical tradition, seduction is traditionally taken as the realm of artifice and appearance, versus that of nature and reality.

The bourgeois revolutions, according to Baudrillard, unleashed an era dedicated to production and to the domination of nature. This was the heroic era of industrial capitalism, of the unleashing of productive forces, in which seduction had to take a back seat to both production and industry. For Baudrillard, it is the aristocratic order of seduction, 'which is the order of sign and ritual,' that is opposed to the holy order of production. Thus, while the bourgeoisie were forced into the order of production and procreation, a presumably 'emancipated' neo-aristocracy, which Baudrillard dreams about and desires to prefigure, would be freed from the divine orders of production and procreation, and would be able to engage in the ruses and artifices of seduction.

The crux of Baudrillard's argument concerns the alleged opposition of seduction and production which I cited in the discussion of *Forget Foucault*, and which he repeats verbatim in *De la séduction*. Baudrillard interprets seduction not primarily in the sense of enticing someone to have sexual intercourse, but as a ritual, a game, with its own rules, charms, snares and lures. It takes place on the level of appearance, surface and signs, and is thus fundamentally artificial, unlike the 'natural' pursuit of sexual pleasure. Baudrillard associates seduction with the 'feminine,' arguing that the 'feminine' is precisely that principle of reversibility, nondifferentiation and indifference which characterizes artifice, whereas 'the masculine' is precisely that which is ineluctably marked, defined and differentiated (*SED*, pp. 10, 17ff.).

It is important to see that Baudrillard is distinguishing between sexuality and seduction. While nothing seems more confused and indeterminate than sexuality today, Baudrillard claims that sexuality itself *is* (as Freud assured us) *masculine*: 'Freud is right: there is only one single sexuality, one single libido – masculine. Sexuality is this distinct structure which is discriminating, centered on the phallus, castration, the name of the father, repression. There isn't any other. It serves no purpose to dream of some non-phallic sexuality, that is neither barred nor marked' (*SED*, p. 16).

Seduction, by contrast, is 'feminine,' and Baudrillard slyly insinuates that those French feminists (like Derrida or Luce Irigaray) who want to redefine sexuality in 'feminine' terms are in fact operating with a masculine 'productivist' model of sexuality. Irigaray, for example, takes feminine sexual pleasure and orgasms as the model of sexuality, arguing that a 'feminine,' nonphallocentric model of sexuality would be polymorphic, disseminatory, plural and multiple, rather than linear, phallic and ejaculatory. It would be most visibly instantiated in the female sexual pleasures that Irigaray celebrates in a passage cited by Baudrillard which describes the specific female sexual *jouissance* derived from women's anatomy (*SED*, p. 20).

But the joy of polymorphic sexual pleasure is not the 'femine' for Baudrillard: 'The feminine, however, is elsewhere, it is always somewhere else: this is the secret of its power' (*SED*, p. 17). Baudrillard claims that feminists who speak of women's specific sexual pleasures, writing and discourse naturalize the 'feminine,' and present it as the voice of the body, the voice of nature, as if language or writing could be a natural expression of pre-existing biology (*SED*, p. 20–1). Baudrillard brings the same complaint against sexual liberationists and those who, like Deleuze, champion the freeing of (natural) desire from its social constraints. Both are caught up, Baudrillard suggests, in metaphysical essentialism and the discourse of nature and truth, in which the (feminine or desiring) body and unconscious speak the truth of nature, and express the primordial reality of human being.

Baudrillard claims that the nature and power of women does not lie in their biology, but rather that the 'power of the feminine is that of seduction' (*SED*, p. 18). In addition,

> The decline of psychoanalysis and of sexuality as strong structures, their retraction into a psychological and molecular universe (which is nothing other than that of their definitive liberation) allows us to envisage another universe . . . which is no longer interpreted in terms of psychic or psychological relations, nor in terms of repression or of the unconscious but in terms of play, of challenge and defiance, of duelling relations and the strategy of appearances: that is, in terms of seduction. No longer at all in terms of structure and of distinctive oppositions, but of seductive reversibility – a universe where the feminine is not that which opposes itself to the masculine, but which *seduces* the masculine (*SED*, p. 18).

In other words, seduction is precisely that which subverts fixed dualities between masculine and feminine and eludes definition and differentiation. Thus the 'feminine' for Baudrillard is not to be interpreted as a mark of nature or of culture, 'but as a *trans-sexuality of seduction* which all organizations of sexuality tend to put down' (*SED*, p. 19). Seduction in turn '*represents the mastery of the symbolic universe, while power only represents the mastery of the real universe*'; seduction is '*the strategy of appearances*' which opposes, is other than, relations of power. Baudrillard claims that feminists who reject seduction as a form of male domination and exploitation fail to see that this is precisely to surrender women's mastery of the symbolic and their sole viable alternative to, and means of undermining, male power.

Continuing his provocations against French feminism, Baudrillard next attempts to provide an answer to Freud's claim that 'anatomy is destiny.' He argues that feminists who claim the superiority of women's anatomy or biology or psychology or writing over those of men are merely reproducing Freud's position on another level (*SED*, pp. 19–22). Against this position, Baudrillard repeatedly insists that seduction alone can be radically opposed to 'anatomy as destiny,' and only that seduction can provide a genuine reversal of the (male/productivist) social order. He continues his play of reversals, ironies and provocations throughout the book. Although he scores points off feminists like Irigaray who attack sexist views of women and then celebrate 'feminine' biological nature as superior to masculine (as if biology *was* destiny), one can easily turn poststructuralist and more advanced feminist arguments against Baudrillard's own positions, and insist that 'masculine' and 'feminine' are social constructs, as is sexual behavior in its dominant forms and practices. If this is the case, as it arguably is, it is perverse to equate the 'masculine' or the 'feminine' with specific sexual traits or behaviors such as production (which for Baudrillard is the realm of the 'masculine') and seduction (which is the realm of the 'feminine'). (I put these terms in quotes because, contra Baudrillard, they designate social constructs rather than ontological realities.)

Indeed, Baudrillard utilizes an essentialist discourse of a 'feminine nature' when, for instance, he discusses characterizations of 'the feminine' as depth or as surface and concludes that the authentically 'feminine' is 'indistinction between surface and depth' or 'indifference between the authentic and the artificial' (*SED*, pp. 22–3). To be sure, Baudrillard is positively valorizing 'appearance,' and thus 'the feminine,' over depth, but it is not clear what is to be gained by essentializing differences between the 'masculine' and 'the feminine' in any manner, since these oppositions are social constructs and the loci of oppression which progressive individuals should work to dissolve and overcome.

Continuing his essentializing discourse, Baudrillard raises the question of whether there are properly 'masculine' and 'feminine' figures of seduction, or whether there is but one ungendered form (*SED*, pp. 121–2). He claims that seduction 'oscillates between two poles – that of strategy and that of animality' (*SED*, p. 122). Not surprisingly he equates animality with the female seductress and strategy with the male seducer. Female seduction involves animal charm, makeup and artifice, while male seduction involves a conscious strategy – though Baudrillard claims that the seducer is himself generally the one seduced. Explicitly provoking feminist orthodoxy of the day, Baudrillard defends 'artificial' over 'natural' beauty, claiming that it is artifice which is truly seductive (*SED*, p. 125). He offers a 'praise of the sexual object' (*SED*, pp. 127ff.), utilizing Baudelaire's reflections on women's use of makeup as evidence of the mastery of the symbolic universe and the manipulation of seductive appearance. This praise of Baudelaire was presumably designed to provoke feminists who were attacking makeup and fashion and calling for more 'natural' looks and behavior, in contrast to a sign fetishist like Baudrillard who was naturally going to prefer artifice.[20] Indeed, for Baudrillard, seduction resides solely in the realm of artifice, appearance and game, and thus on the level of signs and objectification. Throughout his later work, one notes a fetishism of signs which become for him the most highly charged 'reality' and the locus of value. (Despite frequent attacks on the concepts of reality and value, Baudrillard has his own valuations and obsessions, which he invests with at least the effect of value and reality.)

As mentioned, while Baudrillard attributes an animal charm and ruse to female seductiveness, he attributes strategy to the male seducer. Here Baudrillard utilizes Søren Kierkegaard's highly masculist and misogynist text 'The Diary of the Seducer' as the basis for his model of seduction. He takes Kierkegaard's aesthete (a barely disguised alter ego) who devises incredibly complicated strategies and ruses to fascinate an 'innocent' young virgin in a long series of preludes to the eventual sexual conquest as the model for the highly ritualistic game that he is valorizing as the alternative to the order of production.[21] In this way Baudrillard interprets seduction as an elaborate ritual or game which breaks with the logic of both production and desire, and which pursues its own aesthetic play on the levels of appearance, signs and fascination.

While feminists would probably find this peculiar theory of seduction highly distasteful, there have been few feminist polemics against Baudrillard,[22] with the exception of Jane Gallop, who cites some of the logical inconsistencies in Baudrillard's theory, and then criticizes his prescriptions for 'the proper course for women. "Now [Baudrillard writes], woman is only appearance. And it's the feminine as appearance that defeats the profundity of the masculine. Women instead of rising up against his 'insulting' formula would do well to let themselves be seduced by this truth, because here is the secret of their power which they are in the process of losing by setting up the profundity of the feminine against that of the masculine" (p. 22.)'[23] Gallop finds Baudrillard's presumption in prescribing 'the proper course for women' itself insulting, and attacks his assumption of a 'position of superiority, of speaking the truth' for women.

Pursuing a critique of Baudrillard's position, one might argue that seduction might more plausibly be seen as a form of aggressive masculist behavior *and* as a form of behavior forced on women, as well as part of mating rituals or as something forced on women by economic necessity. On this reading, seduction is thus a form of socially constructed game playing, which would be opposed in the name of more reciprocal, egalitarian sexual relations, without pursuer and pursued, seducers and seducees, subjects and objects of seduction.[24] Yet Baudrillard goes even further in his provocations to feminism. Consistent with his critique of Foucault's theory of power, he insists that feminist theories of patriarchy, of male power over women, are a mirage, *'un gigantesque contre-sens'* (*SED*, p. 29). For Baudrillard, the counter-hypothesis is 'perfectly plausible' and 'more interesting': 'women were never dominated; they were always dominant' (*SED*, p. 29). By this, Baudrillard does not mean 'the feminine precisely as sex, but as a transversal form of all sexuality, of all power, as the secret and virulent form of insexuality (*l'insexualité*)' (*SED*, p. 29).

In other words, Baudrillard claims that women are dominant because the 'feminine' supposedly incarnates a principle of reversibility, of transexuality, of undecidable transition from 'masculine' to 'feminine,' from dominant to dominated, which perpetually troubles the allegedly fixed male order of sexuality. (Recall that earlier Baudrillard had argued that the very principle of sexuality was male and fixed, whereas 'the feminine' was a principle of reversibility and de-differentiation.) In view of the history of the oppression of women, such sophistry might be regarded as highly offensive; but Baudrillard would find objection to it to be 'an expression of sexism and racism itself: commiseration' (*SED*, p. 34). The proper response to male power, in Baudrillard's view, is not to challenge it or to try to transform sexual relations or practices, but to more effectively carry out the age-old strategy of seduction, whereby women use their charms, wiles and mastery of the symbolic and ritualistic to advance their aims.

Baudrillard's most interesting analyses in *De la séduction* concern what he calls 'cold seduction' in the society of media, simulations and information (see 3.1). Collapsing McLuhan's distinction between hot and cool media, all media become cool for Baudrillard, seductive instruments of fascination. Seduced by cinema and the cult of film stars (*SED*, pp. 130ff.), 'our modern idols exert a *cool* seduction, being at the intersection of a cool medium of the masses and the cool medium of image' (*SED*, p. 132).[25] He claims that the society of simulation exerts a ludic and cool seduction (*SED*, pp. 213ff.) throughout all domains of social experience. Imbricated within a network of communication terminals, 'each of us is offered a light, psychedelic vertigo of multiple or successive branching of connections and disconnections. Each of us is invited to become a miniaturized "system of games," a micro-system capable of play. . . . Seduction/simulacra: communication like the social functions in a closed circuit, redoubling by signs an undiscoverable reality. And the social contract has become a pact of simulation, sealed by the media and information' (*SED*, pp. 221–2).

Repeating his analysis of the end of the social (see 3.4), Baudrillard suggests that in response to media simulation, the masses respond with a simulation of meaning and response: 'To this deterrence, they respond with disaffection, to this lure they respond with an enigmatic belief' (*SED*, p. 222). What is crucial, however, is not that individuals believe in specific messages from the media, but that they plug into various communications systems and participate in television, radio, telephone, computer and other communications and information networks. In this way individuals become terminals in communication matrices, and are "seduced" into participation through their pleasures and play within these networks. Baudrillard claims that this gives rise to a new sort of self-seduction, or cool narcissism:

> The group connected to the video is also only its own terminal. It records itself, self-regulates itself and self-manages itself electronically. Self-ignition, self-seduction. The group is eroticized and seduced through the immediate command that it receives from itself, self-management will thus soon be the universal work of each one, of each group, of each terminal. Self-seduction will become the norm of every electrified particle in networks or systems. (*SED*, p. 225)

Ultimately, seduction becomes a metaphysics for Baudrillard, and the term becomes one of his basic categories to describe both contemporary society and a form of alternative, aristocratic behavior which escapes the logic of social determination. A contradiction emerges at this point in

Baudrillard's work. On the one hand, seduction describes how society works: it is our destiny and the way of the (postmodern) world (*SED*, pp. 238ff.). On the other, it is Baudrillard's ideal, his alternative to production, which replaces symbolic exchange as his privileged form of behavior. From this perspective, seduction is the negation of the seriousness of reality, the exigencies of production, meaning and truth; it involves the charms of pure and mere games, superficial rituals. It is that which profoundly undermines demands for production, meaning and morality (*SED*, pp. 115ff.). Yet Baudrillard's theoretical-political project becomes ensnared in its own ruses; for he cannot really delineate an alternative sense of seduction against the cool seduction which characterizes postmodern society. He wants to valorize seduction as an alternative to production and so on, but more and more he suspects that cool seduction by postmodern society is our destiny. In any case, as we shall see, Baudrillard is himself thoroughly seduced eventually by the objects of his analysis, and gives up the very principle of sovereignty and subjectivity. (See 6.1 for the surprising turn in Baudrillard's quixotic battle against the destiny of the system of objects whose trajectories he has been charting.)

In sum, *De la séduction* appears to be more of a provocation to feminists than a serious study of contemporary sexuality or seduction in their manifold forms. Yet the book is also a desperate attempt to stake out a radical alternative to the mode of production and to delineate a sphere of practice which would undermine and reverse the dominant logic and reality principle (Marcuse undertook a similar attempt in *Eros and Civilization* in his valorization of eros and play).[26] As noted, Baudrillard replaces symbolic exchange by seduction as his preferred alternative, possibly because symbolic exchange has overtones of pre-capitalist 'primitivism' which would expose Baudrillard to charges of nostalgia for bygone eras, retrogression to idealization of earlier forms of society. Seduction thus surpasses a pre-modern primitivist ideal with a postmodern neo-aristocratic ideal which preserves the emphasis in symbolic exchange on reversibility, play and exchange on the level of the symbolic, expenditure and waste, excess and aesthetic display (better postmodern than pre-modern). Henceforth Baudrillard's aristocratic aestheticism will valorize seduction as a preferred form of symbolic behavior.

While Baudrillard is frequently playful, ironic and teasing in the book, *De la séduction* also occasionally takes on a weighty, lugubrious tone, as if Baudrillard were mourning the end of desire and sexuality (one of his postmodern themes). Indeed, sometimes it is ponderous and didactic, as if Baudrillard were still trapped in the prison-house of academic discourse, too tired to fight his way out. At other times it is metaphysical and prophetic, as if Baudrillard had found a new philosopher's stone from which to gain insight, one which he could use to seduce his readers. After *De la séduction*, in fact, the polemical élan evaporates somewhat, giving way to a metaphysical world-weariness and a grim fascination with the decline of Western civilization which characterize most of Baudrillard's work of the 1980s, which we will take up in the final two chapters.

5.4　BAUDRILLARDIAN POLEMICS AND THE FRENCH CULTURAL SCENE

Baudrillard's polemics and provocations are among the most distinctive features of his thought during the 1970s. Yet why, one might ask, did Baudrillard engage in such aggressive polemics against his contemporaries and against the most distinguished thinkers of his time? In a curious way, Baudrillard can be read as a product of the very sociocultural situation that he constantly denounces. In reading Baudrillard, one sometimes gets the impression that his writing increasingly becomes a simulation of criticism – that is, it becomes hypercriticism, a desperate attempt to imitate and surpass critical models which, like the hyperreality he attacks, becomes more critical than critical with every outing, so that eventually it becomes a caricature of itself and degenerates into mere hype.

Indeed, there is a sense in which his social critique and theoretical polemics become more and more similar to advertising sloganeering, in which 'messages' are compressed into slogans which are endlessly repeated and recycled, much like advertising campaigns which build on previous images and slogans which are recycled for the current intervention into commodity struggle. Baudrillard's texts could be profitably studied from this vantage point, as a series of campaigns in the French cultural market which attempt to sell his product and to position it as a model superior to those of his competitors. In this way, one could read his language and images as hyperreal simulations which must compete with media communication and the texts, lectures, media appearances and cultural presences of his competitors, and that must therefore defeat and destroy his competitors, rather than mediating other positions with his own theory.

Indeed, I think that Baudrillard's trajectory can be read in terms of his interventions within the French cultural milieu of the last two decades, and some of his more puzzling simulations can be interpreted and understood within this context. During the 1970s, French intellectuals gained increased access to the mass media – radio, television and newspapers – and gained new opportunities for prestige, power and profit from magazines, journals and the publishing industry.[27] Meanwhile, the French university scene continued to offer its most successful practitioners traditional rewards and prestige, as well as a field in which to perpetrate seduction of various sorts. In terms of Debray's framework, it seems that Baudrillard wanted at once to be writer, teacher and celebrity, and to excel in all these roles.

In such a competitive intellectual milieu, it was necessary both to play to existing trends and to distinguish oneself from the competition in order to get ahead. This required gaining access to the sources of cultural capital, and effectively manipulating publishing, mass communications and academic media. The system also rewarded those who were able to generate controversy and to differentiate themselves from the competition that way. In this regard, at least, Baudrillard has been a relatively successful player in the game of intellectual competition for the past decade or so; he has had a profusion of books published by important presses, and has had articles and cultural commentary accepted by prestigous journals and even by newspapers. He has successfully differentiated himself from the competition, yet has played successfully to dominant cultural trends. Although there has been little response to his polemics in France, he has managed to circulate his texts, especially in English-, Italian- and Spanish-speaking countries, and has been particularly successful in linking his thought with the poststructuralist, post-Marxist and postmodernist currents sweeping through the world in the 1970s and 1980s. Moreover, although he resisted mass media appearances for many years, when the media turned to him to celebrate his simulated confessions/notebooks, *Cool Memories*, he took to the broadcast waves for his fifteen minutes of media celebrity.

Yet the most curious effect of his polemics has been their neglect and lack of effects. Indeed, hardly anyone has taken up Baudrillard's multifarious theoretical challenges since the beginnings of his polemics against Marxism in the 1970s. I have found few attempts to respond to Baudrillard's critique of Marxism in *For a Critique of the Political Economy of the Sign* and *The Mirror of Production*.[28] I have found no attempts to respond to his polemics against Marxist anthropology or his similar critiques of the Freudian theory. Likewise, as far as I can discern, no Foucaultian has attempted to answer his critiques of Foucault; nor have Deleuze, Guattari, Lyotard or their contemporaries attempted to respond in writing to his critiques of their positions. And, despite the highly charged polemical atmosphere concerning French feminism and French Leftist politics, I have found few polemics against his critiques of feminism or the French Left parties.

There is a certain pathos in the failure of Baudrillard's French contemporaries to take up his theoretical challenges to their positions, since for Baudrillard the very concept of 'the challenge' (*le défi*) has a certain metaphysical and political resonance. In *De la séduction* he claims that the challenge is

> bewitching, like a meaningless discourse, to which, *for this absurd reason*, we cannot help but respond. Why do we answer a challenge? This is the same mysterious question as: what is it that seduces?
>
> What could be more seductive than a challenge? To challenge or seduce is always to drive the other mad, but in a mutual vertigo, madness from the vertiginous absence that unites them and from their

mutual involvement. Such is the inevitability of the challenge and consequently the reason why we cannot help but respond to it: for it inaugurates a mind of mad relations, quite different from communication and exchange . . . [the challenge contains] an unremitting obligation to respond and to outdo, governed by a fundamental rule of the game and proceeding according to its own rhythm. (*SED*, pp. 113–14; *SW* 161)

Baudrillard was obviously seduced by many of his contemporaries' theoretical positions and by the radical politics of the day. Accepting their challenge, he launched his own, hoping thereby to seduce his interlocutors into a counter-challenge. Eschewing the desire for consensus favored by Habermas and others, Baudrillard wished to establish dueling relations with his theoretical antipodes and competitors. But it seems that in France, at least, Baudrillard has been ignored by his opponents, who on the whole have chosen not to respond to his provocations. Baudrillard's most receptive audience seems instead to be in the English-speaking world, where his positions have been positively received, and he has been able to exert a seductive force and challenge some of us to respond. Yet, despite neglect by his competitors, Baudrillard has continued to be one of the most prolific and provocative writers of his generation. Thus he has ultimately triumphed in the realms of sign value and exchange value, even if it is not yet clear what use value his theories ultimately possess.

6

The Metaphysical Imaginary

During the excursions into the postmodern carnival, and perhaps tired of polemicizing against his contemporaries, Baudrillard began to construct a metaphysical imaginary. Forsaking the political imaginary and the imaginary of social theory and critique, his thought in the 1980s gravitated toward metaphysics. This turn is not especially surprising, since metaphysics provides a transcendental refuge for those who are dissatisfied with reality as it is and impatient with designs for social transformation. Traditionally the metaphysical imaginary inscribed the contours and basic features of a higher reality, which was established in categories which purport to conceptualize the features of the really real, the universal and essential features of an ultimate reality, beyond the facticity of the empirical and the banality of everyday life. Yet, after the poststructuralist critique of metaphysics and of the very concept of 'the real' – a critique in which Baudrillard participated – the return to metaphysics is highly ironic. Indeed, Baudrillard offers one of the most ironic metaphysics in the history of philosophy.[1]

Despite his earlier critique of metaphysics, Baudrillard's thought was always metaphysical in some ways. His early writings were informed by the Marxian and Freudian imaginaries, but were always complemented by alternative theoretical perspectives, ranging from his concept of symbolic exchange to his theory of simulations. Then, having smashed the mirrors of production and desire, and having rejected the conceptual universe of Foucault and the other luminaries of New French Theory, Baudrillard undertook to produce a novel metaphysics as social theory or – why not? – social theory as metaphysics. For in a sense, Baudrillard's metaphysics derives from his social analysis and notion of the end of modernity, the disappearance of the social, the political, meaning, reality and so forth, in our new and original social situation. Baudrillard's postmodernism thus provided the impetus and ground for a new metaphysics. Hence, strictly speaking, Baudrillard does not in the final analysis provide a *social theory of postmodernity* – that is to say, an adequate account of historical stages or ruptures in history and society in the transition from modernity to postmodernity, accompanied by a systematic analysis of the contemporary era.[2] Rather, his work terminates in a postmodern metaphysics which ignores the critique of metaphysics carried out earlier by Derrida and other poststructuralists.

Baudrillard himself points to his metaphysical turn in an interview entitled 'Forget Baudrillard': 'Well, let's be frank here. If I ever dabbled in anything in my theoretical infancy, it was philosophy more than sociology. I don't think at all in those terms. My point of view is completely metaphysical. If anything, I'm a metaphysician, perhaps a moralist, but certainly not a sociologist. The only "sociological" work I can claim is my effort to put an end to the social, to the concept of the social.'[3] Yet, as noted, the metaphysics emerges from certain social experiences. As he put it in the interview 'Le cristal se venge', 'The problem is a little like knowing if this thing that interests me is a detour or a modern movement (*peripetie moderne*), or if it is a question at bottom of a metaphysics. I believe that it is both. For me, there is a dimension more and more metaphysical, or anti-metaphysical, but which reappears just the same and nevertheless it is the contemporary modern conjuncture which interests me.'[4] Following this perspective, I will suggest below that Baudrillard's flights into the metaphysical imaginary were motivated both by what he saw as certain social developments (connected with what we are calling 'postmodernity' for want of a better word) and by a certain political impasse upon which we will focus in the concluding chapter.

Baudrillard's movement toward the metaphysical imaginary is apparent in *L'échange symbolique et la mort* and even more so in *De la séduction*, while his exercises in social theory published in *Simulacres et Simulation* also reveal a metaphysical trend in his thought. But his full-blown metaphysical imaginary is first made manifest in *Les stratégies fatales* (6.1), and is elaborated in *America* (6.2), *Forget Baudrillard*, *L'autre par lui-même* (translated as *The Ecstasy of Communications*), *Cool Memories* and his other 1980s texts (6.3). In this chapter, I shall accordingly focus on Baudrillard's metaphysics, and will conclude with some critical reflections on his specific brand of metaphysics and on metaphysics as a particular mode of thought and discourse (6.4).

6.1 FATAL STRATEGIES AND THE SUPREMACY OF THE OBJECT

For centuries, metaphysics has provided many delights and compensatory pleasures. Unable to change the world through politics or social action, the metaphysician can create his or her own conceptual reality. Metaphysics thus provides the narcissistic gratification of enjoying the creation and observation of one's own world. The metaphysician is a god (often a quite minor one) who dares to produce his or her own conceptual universe. Part of the metaphysical lust is a drive to produce a better world, or at least a conceptual universe in which one feels more at home and comfortable. Often frustrations in one's personal life or one's sociopolitical conjuncture drive one to leave the more modest realm of social theory and research for the loftier realm of metaphysics. The metaphysical imaginary thus provides a useful vehicle for sublimation, frustration and projection. Thus, if the impasse of the Left in France and elsewhere – or some personal blockage – sapped his one-time revolutionary political thought of its energy and telos, Baudrillard could at least channel his energies into a new sort of metaphysics born out of his experiences in the postmodern carnival.

Baudrillard first elaborates his new metaphysics in some detail in his 1983 text *Les stratégies fatales*. This book contains a strange, fatalistic view of the world, and manifests a somewhat new tone, style and eccentricity by comparison with his previous works.[5] While Baudrillard repeats many earlier positions, and utilizes many of his old categories – seduction, the obscene, terrorism, hyperreality, the media and so on – he finds new illustrations and instantiations of them, and adds some new concepts and positions. He also employs a more anecdotal method, filling his treatise with short stories and parables which illustrate his theoretical positions and concepts. The book also exhibits the strong influence of Nietzsche and the French Nietzschean cynical-nihilist tradition (Nietzsche as mediated by Sade in the works of Bataille, Blanchot, Klossowski and the like, lightened by the pataphysics of Alfred Jarry discussed later in this section).

The book opens on a prophetic note: 'Things have found a way to elude the dialectic of meaning which bored them: it is to proliferate to infinity, to fully realize their potentialities (*de se potentialiser*), to surpass their essence in going to extremes, in an obscenity which henceforth takes the place for them of an immanent finality and of an insane rationality' (*SF*, p. 9). This passage highlights the focus and thesis of the book. Consistent with his earlier work, Baudrillard is analyzing the trajectory of objects and what he sees as metaphysical developments in the object world whereby objects surpass all assigned boundaries and limits to act in ways which subvert all previous metaphysics and theories.

Baudrillard's theme in *Les stratégies fatales* is the triumph of objects over subjects within the obscene proliferation of an object world so completely out of control that it surpasses all attempts to understand, conceptualize and control it. His 'system' of concepts is relentlessly dualistic and nondialectical. Categorical oppositions (like subject and object, masculine and feminine, seduction and production and so on) parade one after another, without mediation, although his categories often incarnate themselves in social processes and phenomena. He claims: 'The universe is not dialectical, it moves toward extremes and not towards equilibrium. It is devoted to radical antagonism and neither to reconciliation nor to synthesis. Such is also the principle of evil and it expresses itself in the evil genius of the object, it expresses itself in the ecstatic form of the pure object, in its victorious strategy over that of the subject' (*SF*, p. 9).

One might note the oracular, metaphysical tone of Baudrillard's new discourse, and might conclude that in his celebration of extremes and his rejection of dialectics and synthesis he is conflating the universe with his own mode of thought. His scenario has to do with the proliferation and growing supremacy of objects over subjects and the eventual triumph of the object. In a discussion of 'Ecstasy and Inertia,' Baudrillard discusses how objects and events in contemporary society are continually surpassing themselves, growing and expanding in power. The 'ecstasy' of objects is their proliferation and expansion to the nth degree, to the superlative; ecstasy as going outside of or beyond oneself: the beautiful as more beautiful than beautiful in fashion, the real more real than the real in television, sex more sexual than sexuality in pornography. Ecstasy is thus the form of obscenity (fully explicit, nothing hidden) and of the hyperreality described by Baudrillard earlier, now taken to a higher level, redoubled and intensified. His vision of contemporary society exhibits a careening growth and excrescence (both *croissance* and *excroissance*), expanding and excreting ever more goods, services, information, messages and demands, surpassing all rational ends and boundaries in a spiral of uncontrolled growth and replication. Yet, as the society is saturated to the limit, it implodes and winds down into inertia and entropy. This process, as we will see, leads to catastrophe for the subject, for not only do the acceleration and proliferation of the object world add an aleatory dimension of chance and nondeterminacy, but the objects themselves take over, in a 'cool' catastrophe for the exhausted subject, whose fascination with the play of objects turns into apathy, stupification and an entropic inertia.

More than he did before, Baudrillard takes a broad philosophical view of ultimate reality (which has disappeared to the masses lost in simulations, but reappears to Baudrillard sitting high above the silent majorities on his philosopher's throne), and pontificates as if he were the scribe of Hegel's Absolute or the Voice of the Order of Things. Key sections of *Les stratégies fatales* describe 'the evil genius of the object,' 'the supremacy of the object' and the revenge of the object, culminating in the stunning disclosure that *'le cristal se venge'* – the object strikes back. This ominous phrase is hidden among some letters on the cover of the book, and will come to signify the triumph and revenge of the object and object world over the subject who for centuries had tried to control and dominate them.

Baudrillard proclaims the 'supremacy of the object,' and claims that in the past, philosophers and others have always experienced and celebrated the splendor of the subject and the misery of the object. It was the subject who made history, who dominated nature, and who was the foundation and guarantor of knowledge. One might add that this was particularly true of the philosophy of subjectivity from Descartes to phenomenology and Sartre, where this philosophy of subjectivity endowed the subject with all the splendid features of freedom, creativity, imagination, certitude, objectivity and knowledge, while the poor object was conceptualized as an inert thing in a causal order, part of a quantitative nexus whose being was defined by number or dead matter, though some more generous souls allowed the object quality and even an *élan vital* (Bergson).

The subject thus provided the foundation for knowledge in rationalist metaphysics, and the object was merely the prey and booty of the knowing subject. Even worse, as Baudrillard points out, the object was often declared to be unintelligible or even 'contemptible, obscene, passive, prostituted and the incarnation of evil, of pure alienation' (*SF*, p. 163). For an idealist or subjectivist metaphysics, the object was a being-in-itself lacking the being-for-itself of consciousness (Hegel and Sartre). The object was also a slave in the dialectic of master and slave, in which the subject attempted to dominate nature and to bend and control the object for its own purposes (we've already heard part of this story from the Frankfurt School).

Against this metaphysics of the subject, Baudrillard claims that he will be the first to intuit and conceptualize the 'sovereign power of the object,' and to pay the object its metaphysical due (*SF*, p. 164). Indeed, for years he has been observing the power of objects to overpower and seduce human beings: commodities, capital, fashion, the sexual object, media, politics, information, codes and models. All Baudrillard's dominant themes instantiated the growing supremacy of the object over the subject, and his writings described its growing fascination, seductiveness and ultimate supremacy.

Baudrillard thinks that if we understand seduction properly, then we can grasp the ubiquity and supremacy of objects in our lives. For he believes that it is an illusion to think that the subject is the aggressor in the game of seduction: rather, the object is the matrix of fascination and the subject falls prey to its charms and traps (see *SF*, p. 174). In fact, he suggests that the subject has been seduced by objects all along, and was deluded if it thought that it was in control. Baudrillard thus recommends that we abandon a privileged position for the subject, with its fiction of a will, a conscience or an unconscious (*SF*, p. 164). But it is not clear how far he wants to go with this idea. Clearly he wants us to abandon illusions about the supremacy and pre-eminence of the subject, and wants us to take objects more seriously, to perceive their powers and qualities and learn to live with and get along with them. But he also seems to be darkly implying that it may be too late to enter some 'gentleman's agreement' with objects and harmonize our relations with them because we have tried to master and manipulate them for our own purposes for far too long, and now the objects are rebelling and taking revenge (*SF*, p. 165).

Indeed, the pride, hubris, inexhaustible will to power, transcendence, narcissism and dramaturgy of the subject appear so extreme to Baudrillard that the subject may not even be capable of reform and learning how to get along with objects. Thus, while one could read Marcuse as recommending a new way of living with and using objects, Baudrillard seems to doubt whether this is any longer possible. For Baudrillard announces in italics that *'the position of the subject has become simply untenable'* (SF, pp. 165–6). Consequently he recommends that one move on and take up the position of the object, learning its ruses, strategies and modes of seduction.

This is precisely what Baudrillard is up to in *Les stratégies fatales*, which describes the 'fatal strategies' whereby objects come to fascinate, challenge, seduce and ultimately overpower the subject. The triumph of the object is connected with the end of the political and the emergence of *'figures du transpolitique'* (SF, pp. 37ff.). The 'transpolitical' 'is the transparency and obscenity of all structures in a destructured universe, of change in a dehistoricized universe, of information in a universe devoid of events,' yet saturated with media, information networks and messages. Transparency, ecstasy and obscenity characterize the mode of being of things and objects in a society in which everything is exhibited, marked, numbered and tracked, including the social in a mass society, the political in the age of terrorism, and the body in hygenics and genetic cloning (ibid.). These examples, as well as the many others that he explores, all point to the subject's decline, diminution and possible disappearance in the new postmodern universe. The process seems to be what one might call the 'hyperization of the object' in Baudrillard's theory. For the object takes on ever more overwhelming, extreme and seductive powers.

The transpolitical is also a mode of *disappearance* of history, politics, sexuality, subjectivity and so on. It is henceforth the mode of disappearance, Baudrillard believes, and not the mode of production which should be of interest for social theory (SF, p. 37). In effect, he continues here his inquiries into what might be called a postmodern society that is completely transforming all modes of life and thus requires new categories and modes of thought. Baudrillard's method is to appeal to a 'redoubling,' or extension, of quantity, size, speed and so on that will produce qualitative change: the development of objects and phenomena beyond the previous boundaries and ends which serve only to bring to a halt the previous state of history and being, thereby opening the door to a new stage. As before, he claims that the 'hyperreality of simulations' in the media are more real than real, and come to produce and define a new reality. The hypercorporeality of the body in obesity and the hyperobscenity of sexuality in pornography are more corporeal than the corporeal and more obscene than the obscene, and point to mutations of the body, sexuality and society in the postmodern world.

Thus in his discussion of obesity – using as examples, what he sees, rather unkindly, as a typical proliferation of bodies out of control in the United States – Baudrillard claims that this excrescence of the body beyond all previous boundaries is related to cancer, and that both are symptomatic of social processes which exhibit a similar obesity. Both the body and society, as we have previously known and defined them, disappear in this process of proliferating growth and metastasis (*SF*, pp. 41ff.). He also describes such exponential growth as a 'genetic' revolt, and as a revolt of objects against their intended and supposed purposes and limits. Likewise, the transpolitical drama of terrorism is more real (in our media world) than the politics of the assembly, and is symptomatic of a political world that is out of control and has surpassed its previous boundaries and rules.

In retrospect, the growing power of the world of objects over the subject has been Baudrillard's theme from the beginning, thus pointing to an underlying continuity in his project. In his early writings he explored the ways in which commodities fascinated individuals in the consumer society, as well as ways in which the world of goods was assuming new and greater value through the agency of sign value and the code – themselves part of the world of things, the system of objects (see chapter 1). His polemics against Marxism were fueled by the belief that commodities, fetishism, and ideology were more pervasive than even Marx imagined in constituting contemporary society (see chapter 2). At that time, reflections on the media came to the forefront of his thought: the television object was at the center of the home in Baudrillard's earlier thinking, and the media, simulations, hyperreality and implosion eventually came to obliterate distinctions between private and public, inside and outside, media and reality (see chapter 3). Henceforth everything was public, transparent, ecstatic and hyperreal in the object world which was gaining in fascination and seductiveness as the years went by.

In this scenario, fascination with the object was accelerating rapidly, and the subject found him or herself more and more immersed, plugged in, networked and seduced by the world of things, which henceforth became the master, while the once mighty subject found itself overpowered by this new object world. Moreover, it appears that Baudrillard believes that there is now not much that the subject can do to regain his or her diminished sovereignty (if, indeed, he or she ever reigned supreme). Yet he seems to believe that we – that is, subjects – can learn something from the 'fatal strategies' of objects. In a new emphasis on 'strategic discourse,' Baudrillard distinguishes between banal, ironic and fatal strategies. Ironic strategies are grounded in a belief in the omnipotence of thought and the 'fundamental irreality of the world. . . . All existing mythologies, all new-born religions, have experienced a violent denegation of the real, a violent challenge to existence' (*SF*, p. 114). To some extent, Baudrillard has himself gone over to the side of (metaphysical) irony of this sort, by valorizing appearance, artifice, signs, seduction and other 'unreal' phenomena over 'reality,' nature, production and so on.

Yet *fatal* strategies are of more interest to him than ironic strategies. Fatal strategies are those of 'the evil genius of the object,' and they are distinguished from banal strategies, which involve efforts of the subject to master and control the object. Banal strategies involve belief in referents such as the subject, power, revolution, the real, desire and so on, which Baudrillard believes have disappeared (*SF*, p. 80). The chief difference between banal and fatal strategies or theories is that 'in one the subject believes itself to always be more clever than the object, whereas in the other the object is always supposed to be more shrewd, more cynical, more brilliant than the subject' (*SF*, pp. 259–60). Whereas in banal strategies, the subject believed itself to be more masterful and sovereign than the object, in fatal strategies, the subject recognizes the supremacy of the object, and therefore takes the side of the object and attempts to reproduce its strategies, ruses and rules.

In particular, such 'fatal strategies' require taking a thought or course of action to its furthest extremities, pursuing something to the nth degree, attempting to surpass previous boundaries and thus enter a new conceptual field. Baudrillard claims it is precisely these fatal strategies that objects – media, information, masses and so on – have pursued, and that in so doing, they have defeated the subject. The 'evil genius of the object,' Baudrillard claims, is to elude scientific and cognitive understanding and control. Although previously objects submitted to conceptual schemes and laws devised by science, they are also capable (he fantasizes?) of resisting control and revolting against the models made to capture their movements (*SF*, pp. 115ff.). Matter, or objects, are thus not to be characterized as dead stuff, he warns, but as genial and rebellious active agents, like the protons which escape comprehension and control (*SF*, pp. 117ff.) (or perhaps the AIDS virus?). Likewise, within the human sciences, one cannot be certain that the objects of investigation, the masses, are actually revealing their true nature or submitting to the conceptual schemes which social scientists impose on their behavior. In both cases, Baudrillard suggests, the objects of investigation may resist observation and interrogation, and may respond by disappearing, refusing to be questioned, rebelling or other ruses. Moreover, not only can objects fool or escape control by subjects, they can also come to seduce the subject, thereby reversing relationships of power and sovereignty. Baudrillard concludes that a projective vision of such an unknowable, powerful and uncontrollable object world is a consequence of modern physics (that is, of indeterminacy, uncertainty, relativity and the like), and lies in waiting for us at 'the unavoidable extremities of all physics' (*SF*, p. 120).

What is most audacious in Baudrillard's metaphysical scenario is his claim that the objects of *both* the natural and the physical sciences resist control by the subject (and thereby impede knowledge of them). Baudrillard also argues for a version of 'predestination' in which human life is controlled by powerful forces beyond its control.[6] He is thus affirming the supremacy of objects over subjects, and is telling us to reverse our previous subjectivist evaluations and commitments to the subject. In his attempt to reverse the positions of subject and object, good and evil, Baudrillard argues that 'it's not evil that is interesting, it's the spiral of the worst (*la spirale du pire*)' (*SF*, p. 261). The 'spiral of the worst' signifies the triumph of the object over the subject, and thus the triumph of evil (defined tautologically as the triumph of the object over the subject). Indeed, the object becomes more malignant and threatening as the story goes on, for there are no beautiful sunsets or blue orchids in Baudrillard's object world. 'The object desires to be worst and demands what is worst. It bears witness to a negativity more radical,' which ultimately disobeys completely the laws and order of the subject and returns to its origin, whereby the ruses of the object control the universe and the subject is not part of the action (*SF*, pp. 261–2).

This position emerges in Baudrillard's 'theory' of catastrophes, which appear as often in his writings as disasters in contemporary societies thereby infusing his writings with a strong reality effect. Catastrophes seem to represent for Baudrillard the rebellion of the object world against the laws, expectations and desires of the subject, as well as the tendencies of objects – and nature – to exceed themselves, to spontaneously produce spectacle, to careen toward catastrophe. This also signifies the end of the problematic of liberation, because the defeat of the subject by the object renders dreams of liberation a mirage and illusion. Catastrophes confirm the power of the object over the subject, and delight people in their spectacular excess, just as humor which subverts the order of language produces pleasure. Following this line of thought a bit, as objects gain in supremacy, we should probably expect more catastrophes, and indeed, Baudrillard implies that this will be our destiny.

He thus concludes that we should submit to the supremacy of the object and go with the flow into the spiral of the worst. For those of us still attached to the subject, there is 'one and only one fatal strategy: theory' (*SF*, p. 259). Presumably if we understand what is going on through better theories – namely, Baudrillard's – we won't be undone by the worsening spiral of catastrophes which the objects are inflecting upon us and using to avenge themselves. Yet a 'fatal theory' must renounce subject positions and the projection of subjective passions, preferences and fantasies onto objects. Instead, it must take the position of the object, and conceptualize the 'ceremony of the world' from this point of view. In the concluding pages of *Les stratégies fatales*, Baudrillard asks what we can do in the face of the triumph of the object (*SF*, p. 268), and, admitting that his proposal is an enigma, concludes:

It's true that this is an obscure and difficult option: to pass to the side of the object, to take sides with the object. To search for another set of rules, another axiomatic system: there's nothing mystical in this, there's no otherworldly delirium of a subjectivity entrapped and fleeing forward in a paroxysmal (*paroxystique*) description. But simply to outline this other logic, to unfold these other strategies, to leave the field open for objective irony is also a challenge, possibly absurd, which runs the risk of that which it describes – but the risk is to be taken: the hypothesis of a fatal strategy can only be fatal itself. (*SF*, p. 271)

Baudrillard concludes his book with an outline of a mysterious, enigmatic metaphysics of appearance, disappearance and metamorphosis. His metaphysics of 'reversible imminence' projects a cyclical view of the world which breaks with linear temporality and posits a cycle of appearance and disappearance that valorizes metamorphosis. It is difficult to understand what Baudrillard is proposing here, but his references to fatality in terms of a 'second birth, the true one,' predestination and a 'necessary return' of events seem to imply a modified version of Nietzsche's eternal return, in which one inevitably returns to an earlier situation, receives a second chance and reverses a temporal development. Metamorphosis is the privileged figure for this process, in which one transforms oneself into an opposite (subject into object? male into female? human into nonhuman?). This doctrine is neither illustrated nor elucidated in *Les stratégies fatales*, although it seems to point to a mystical and esoteric turn in Baudrillard's thought which has been rendering it increasingly hermetic and inaccessible.

Baudrillard as Pataphysician

In *Les stratégies fatales* and his other recent writings, Baudrillard seems to be taking social theory into the realm of metaphysics; but it is a specific type of metaphysics, deeply inspired by the pataphysics developed by Alfred Jarry. For Jarry,

> pataphysics is the science of the realm beyond metaphysics. . . . It will study the laws which govern exceptions and will explain the universe supplementary to this one; or, less ambitiously, it will describe a universe which one can see – must see perhaps – instead of the traditional one. . . .
>
> Definition: pataphysics is the science of imaginary solutions, which symbolically attributes the properties of objects, described by their virtuality, to their lineaments.[7]

Like the universe in Jarry's *Ubu Roi, The Gestures and Opinions of Doctor Faustroll* and other literary texts, as well as in his more theoretical explications of pataphysics, Baudrillard's universe is a totally absurd place in which objects rule in mysterious ways, and people and events are governed by absurd and ultimately unknowable interconnections and by predestination (the French playwright Eugene Ionesco is another good source of entry into this universe). Baudrillard follows Jarry in inventing a universe in line with the fantasies, hallucinations and projections of its creator. Like Jarry's, Baudrillard's universe is ruled by surprise, reversal, hallucination, blasphemy, obscenity and a desire to shock and outrage.

We thus see how Baudrillard's sign fetishism has driven him to produce a world of his own signs. Like Jarry after the death of God in the earlier stage of nihilism, the pataphysician Baudrillard aspires to the status of a god, and desires to usurp God's power of creation and judgment. Like Jarry, Baudrillard projects a malefic vision of a universe ruled by baser instincts and objects in which 'good' and subjective designs are foiled and come to naught. Yet there is a fundamental, substantive difference between Jarry's and Baudrillard's pataphysics. Jarry's subjects – Ubu Roi, Faustroll and the rest – heroically, albeit foolishly, try to master the universe and remake reality according to their imaginary designs, ambitions and desires. But for Baudrillard, this game is over: the subject has been defeated, the reign of objects has commenced, and we had better recognize the new rules of the game and make the necessary adjustment.

Pataphysics aside, it seems that Baudrillard is trying to end the philosophy of subjectivity which has controlled French thought since Descartes by going over completely to the other side. Descartes' *malin genie*, his evil genius, was a ruse of the subject which tried to seduce him into accepting what was not clear and distinct. But Descartes was able to master his subjectivity and ultimately to prevail. By contrast, Baudrillard's evil genius is the object itself, which is much more malign than the merely epistemological deceptions of the subject faced by Descartes, for it constitutes a fatal destiny that demands the end of the philosophy of subjectivity. Yet, by renouncing subjectivity and the possibility of changing, transforming and restructuring objects and situations, one is affirming a hyperconformity that will allow objects to follow their own laws and impulses, and sweep the subjects blindly along. Such a renunciation is equivalent to renouncing all possibility of effective intervention in the world. Indeed, Baudrillard affirms a rather bizarre form of predestination which rules out in advance any possibility of subjective intervention by denying human agency and even indeterminacy. For a good deconstructionist, this opposition would be undecidable, since it is impossible to gain the information which would allow one to decide whether certain events are determined, and since arguments for both positions tend to break down. Such deconstruction would give us the license to move on and perhaps read a good book or fight against the reactionary powers which achieved dominance in most quarters in the 1980s when Baudrillard was dispensing his new metaphysical wisdom.

But no, Baudrillard is not just going to deconstruct the chance-determinism dichotomy by showing all the problems involved in believing in either chance and necessity or free will and determinism, thereby dismantling metaphysical positions on both sides. Yet he ends by affirming a rather strange notion of predestination. We might note that the subtitle of the English translation of the section of *Les stratégies fatales* in which he argues for his version of fatalism is 'Beyond the Uncertainty Principle.' Baudrillard has become certain that everything is interconnected, that chance does not exist, that destiny and predestination are the human fate. 'What one must never doubt is that destiny, not chance, is the "natural" course of things. . . . Contrary to all our virtuous morality, things may have a predestined interconnection. Instead of unfolding according to a genesis and an evolution, they are inscribed in advance in their disappearance. Prophecy, then, distinguishes them, not prediction.'[8]

Baudrillard does not tell us precisely how he knows this; nor does he give the usual type of philosophical arguments, preferring bald assertion and prophecy to argumentation. Instead, he tells a story to illustrate a predestined interconnection and hidden order between the only two people of whom he has dreamed for years, one of whom he abandoned and the other who abandoned him; they were connected by having the same first name. Now it cannot be decided from this illustration whether we are to infer that he has taken leave of his television and seduction, and has through some means gained insight into the secret relations of the subject and the object and between the interconnections and mysteries of the object world; or whether our pataphysician is just playing and putting us on, or telling us a story that charms and amuses him.[9]

In fact, one of his 'arguments' for his theory of predestination is that we *prefer* belief in chance over causal necessity, but do not like the sense that there is no order and determinacy in the world; hence we *prefer most of all* to think that there is 'fatal interconnection' and predestination in the world, or at least that certain sequences of our experience are fatally interconnected and predestined.[10] This metaphysics seems to have a deep affinity with a cynical Stoicism which submits to the dictates of a sovereign fate and rejects as illusory any possibility of changing the world (see 6.3 for documentation of Baudrillard's adherence to this position in his recent writings). Further, Baudrillard's stoical (or opportunistic) capitulation to the object world is linked with a contempt for what is human, accompanied by an admiration for what is inhuman.[11] From the beginning, Baudrillard subscribed to what might be called a 'theoretical anti-humanism' which privileged objects, commodities, signs, codes, models and simulations over individuals or people en masse. In his earlier writings, 'meaning' was a function of differential relations between signs or objects, not the product of human creativity or the interaction among people or between people and objects. In his 1980s texts, which proclaim the triumph of the object, Baudrillard seems to affirm the superiority of the nonhuman over the human. Evidence of this superiority is found, Baudrillard suggests, conveniently forgetting Greek and Christian religions, in religions in which the gods take nonhuman form

(*SF*, p. 262). Thus, 'one must be respectful of the inhuman,' as in fatalistic societies 'which found their commandments on the side of the inhuman, on the side of stars or animal gods, in constellations or in a divinity without image' (*SF*, p. 262). But should not one be equally respectful of the human? – or is it hopelessly corrupted and defeated? Marx's favorite motto was the humanist credo 'Nothing human is alien to me.' Against this, Baudrillard seems to be suggesting that nothing inhuman is alien to him, and that nothing human is worthy of much respect. In a revealing passage in 'The Child in the Bubble,' Baudrillard states:

> It is not unreasonable to say that the extermination of men begins by the extermination of germs. For man, as he is, with his moods, his passions, his laughter, his secretions, is himself none other than a dirty little irrational virus that troubles the universe of transparency. When all is expurgated, when we have put an end to viral processes, to all social and bacilliform contamination, then there will remain only viral sadness, in a universe of deadly cleanliness and sophistication.[12]

Nietzsche's lament 'Human All-Too-Human!' becomes for Baudrillard '*Viva l'inhumain!*' Hatred of the human thus seems to be part of the background to Baudrillard's apotheosis of the object over the subject. But can we do without the categories of subject and the human? And how else might we characterize subject–object relations?

The Return of the Subject?

Baudrillard's science fiction and pataphysics are no doubt entertaining; but one might envisage alternative endings and different ways of story telling. Might not the subject profit from the profusion and hyperization of objects? Might the object not provide new pleasures, possibilities, networks and connections that might – just might – produce a new subject, who might in turn produce a freer, happier, better world? In fact, might not a new subject be to some extent an effect of precisely some of the developments described by Baudrillard, developments which might well augment, not diminish, subjectivity? Such is the thesis of Rudolf Bahro in *The Alternative in Eastern Europe* a thesis which was taken up by Herbert Marcuse in his last published article.[13] Bahro saw contemporary postindustrial socialist societies as producing surplus consciousness (that is, more imagination, creativity, technical knowledge, desires for a more fulfilling life and so on), which might serve as a motor for progressive social transformation if it could intervene more significantly in social life. Marcuse envisaged a similar situation and similar potentials in the capitalist countries.

There are surely problems with Marcuse's and Bahro's positions.[14] But do they not point to potentially increasing struggles between better developed and advanced subjects and a proliferating object world? The truth of Baudrillard's reveries is that human beings have been losing control of their objects and the object world, which have been taking on a life of their own (this was part of the classic theory of reification), thereby threatening the subject with loss of power, sovereignty and so on. But Baudrillard refuses to see any significant subject-object dialectic, and refuses mediation and all claims of the subject. This refusal completely undermines his position, however and allows us to delineate a quite different way of looking at the momentous clash of subject and object in the contemporary world.

At the outset, it seems impossible to separate subject and object in the ways that Baudrillard proposes. The subject is in some ways an effect of objects; but at the same time the object is in some ways an effect of subjects. Yet Baudrillard either does not see this or refuses to even consider the quite persuasive Kantian and neo-Kantian arguments that can easily be turned against his own views. Thus it is impossible to envisage a world of objects without human subjectivity, because it is impossible to gain access to objects or to perceive or conceive of them apart from our subjective modes of perception and cognition. T. W. Adorno, in an article entitled 'Subject/ Object,' argues as follows:

> The separation of subject and object is both real and illusory. True, because in the cognitive realm it serves to express the real separation, the dichotomy of the human condition, a coercive development. False, because the resulting separation must not be hypostasized, not magically transformed into an invariant. . . . Though they cannot be thought away, as separated, the *pseudos* of the separation is manifested in their being mutually mediated – the object by the subject and even more, in different ways, the subject by the object. The separation is no sooner established directly, without mediation, than it becomes ideology, which is indeed its normal form.[15]

Baudrillard sharply and illicitly separates subject and object, presupposing a (false and ideological) dichotomy between them. In addition, he presupposes an eternal relation of struggle and conflict, with the object eventually winning out. Adorno, by contrast, posits the possibility of peace and reconciliation (while rejecting ideals of absolute harmony, identity and so on). Seen within the context of the narrative of Hegelian Marxism, Baudrillard brings the problematic of reification to a bizarre conclusion. While Hegel and Lukács, among others, posited an ideal of unity and identity between subject and object as the goal of the overcoming of reification, by contrast with Adorno and the Frankfurt School, who merely wanted to preserve subjectivity and individuality in the face of its potential demise in the totally administered society, Baudrillard goes over to the other side, and proclaims the triumph of reification as a *fait accompli* with the triumph of the object over the subject.

This raises the question of *why* Baudrillard decided to go over to the side of the object. Is Baudrillard a traitor to the categories of the subject and the human simply out of opportunism, out of a belief that, since the object now reigns supreme, one is better off taking its side? Or does he believe that the subject is the great historical disaster that Marxists ascribe to capital and feminists to patriarchy? Or does he simply hold subjectivity in contempt and opprobrium? Moreover, one wonders which objects and ruses of the object world Baudrillard would suggest our studying and identifying with. Should we learn to be like cancer cells, and multiply and mutate until we have gained control of our environment and killed off phenomena that we dislike? Or should we learn the ruses and laws of computers so as to improve our mental capacities? Or could we become semiurgical demiurges like the media, and seduce and fascinate those around us? Or should we study the habits of birds and squirrels, and become more like our feathered and furry little friends? Or all – or none – of the above?

One cannot help but wonder what it was that led Baudrillard to conclude that objects now reign supreme, and that we should submit to their dictates and laws. Was his word processor (if he has one) taking over his thought processes? Or was his television set controlling his imagination? Did his car, as on an episode of the old *Twilight Zone* television series, start driving him one day? Did some incurable disease convince him that the subject was weak and feeble compared with the more powerful object world? Or did he simply attain a privileged mode of perception which enabled him to see for the first time the duel between subject and object, without the mediations that confuse the perceptions of the rest of us?

Yet Baudrillard's capitulation to reification is highly problematical and his metaphysics is impossible to confirm or verify. In fact, the very notion of domination by subject or object is much more problematical than has previously been indicated. For we may well ask whether the subject ever ruled the object world, and whether the object world could ever completely rule the subject. Are not such metaphysical fantasies of sovereignty – from either side – impossible to verify, and ultimately either narcissistic projections of supremacy or paranoid projections of domination? Is it not better to try to discern the complex interaction of subject and object in our experience? Should we not, like Adorno, learn to discern the ways in which subjects produce objects, and are in turn dominated by objects (and vice-vera)?[16]

Against Baudrillard, I would therefore argue that other perspectives on the subject-object relation are possible, as well as preferable, to his scenario.[17] I will appraise Baudrillard's metaphysics in more detail in 6.4 below. Let us first, however, accompany him on his trip to the United States, and see what metaphysical lessons he learned from his travels.

6.2 *AMERICA*

The postmodern carnival puts on its most spectacular and revealing shows in the United States. Baudrillard begins *America* with the warning (in English): 'Caution: objects in this mirror may be closer than they appear!' (*A*, p. 9). I suspect he means by this that the processes which he is describing from his observations of the United States will soon be manifest in France and much of the rest of the world.[18] Indeed, throughout *America*, Baudrillard takes the United States as the model for the new, emerging society of the future. For instance, he has experiences there of the end of a previous world (*A*, p. 62) and the morning of a new world (*A*, p. 51). In an extended analysis he compares Europe with the United States, and concludes that the latter was born into modernity, that it is a supra- or ultramodernity, and is really the only genuinely modern society, and so provides a model for the rest of the world (*A*, pp. 149ff.). Consistent with this view, throughout the book, he characterizes America as 'the center of the world' (*A*, pp. 50, 56, 153, *passim*).

 America consists of six studies, presumably written during or after his various trips to the United States in the 1970s and 1980s. The first study, 'Vanishing Point,' sets the stage for the rest. Although Baudrillard does not signal this, the title may refer to *Vanishing Point*, a 1971 Hollywood film directed by Richard Sarafian which has become a cult classic.[19] Like the film, Baudrillard's simulation of de Tocqueville's account of his trip to America concerns the metaphysics of speed, the desert and life in the United States today. Yet the title 'Vanishing Point' also refers to those grand referents of modernity – the social, political, meaning, truth and so on – which Baudrillard sees as vanishing in the contemporary world; and he sees the United States as the privileged site of their disappearance, the vanishing point of the icons of modernity. Thus he intersperses reflections on his travels with social commentary on the contemporary age, theorized as a metaphysics of America. Eschewing standard tourist sites (though he visited many), Baudrillard tells us:

> I looked for *sidereal* America, the America of the futile and absolute liberty of freeways, never the one of the social and cultural – the one of desert-like speed, of motels and mineral surfaces, never the 'deep' America of mores and mentalities. I searched in the speed of the trip's scenario, in the indifferent reflex of television, in the film of the days and nights across an empty space, in the marvellously affectless succession of signs, images, faces, ritual acts of the road, for what is closest to this nuclear and enucleated universe – a universe which is virtually ours even as far as the European-style thatched cottages'. (*A*, p. 16)

Baudrillard's metaphysical journal reflects on his experiences of the desert and the landscape, of speed and time, and of the specific urban, social, political and cultural features observed. Interpreting the United States through his metaphysical imaginary, Baudrillard chooses the desert and the primitive as his primary categories for reading the text of America. In his pursuit of 'the aesthetics of disappearance' (Virilio)[20] in speeding through the land and cityscapes of America, the country took on a desertlike aura, in which vestiges of 'real life' disappeared, leaving only dead images as after-effects – much as the desert contains dead crystalizations of a former existence. In terms of the metaphysical imaginary of *Les stratégies fatales*, Baudrillard apparently discovers in the dead forms of the desert the secret of a society governed by dead models, by nuclear forms. The desert reveals a landscape governed by the whims and indifference of the object, in which the human subject is an alien intruder. 'The desert: the luminous network and fossil of an inhuman intelligence, of a radical indifference – not only that of the sky, but that of geological movements where only the metaphysical passions of space and of time are crystallized' (*A*, p. 19). The dryness of the desert is the opposite of the lubricious viscosity of 'our civilized humors,' and its silence is almost visual, emanating an emptiness and desolation appropriate to a mutated, fossilized landscape which bears witness to the possibility of upheaval and catastrophe, in which one perhaps finds signs of our future.

Baudrillard's 'analysis' culminates in the conclusion that America is the 'realized utopia,' and by comparison with 'old' Europe represents fully triumphant modernity. Yet unable to resist the (hyper-European?) play of metaphor, Baudrillard reverts back to his images of the desert and the primitive to characterize America – a savagery reflected in the extermination of the Indians and the dissemination of this primal violence throughout society. 'Their towns have taken on the structure and color of the desert,' and in the 'savage mind' of the American people there is no longer any universal nature, any transcendence of the human or nature; nor is there history or any real culture (as it is conceived by Europeans). Rather, life in America is cinema, and its culture is its space, speed, technology and parodic excess (*A*, pp. 198–208).

In conclusion, Baudrillard provides some reflections entitled 'Desert For Ever.'[21] A symptomatic reading of this melancholy and disappointing conclusion might suggest that Baudrillard's failure to provide a more interesting analysis or conclusions points to a theoretical defeat of the subject (Baudrillard) by the object (America). Seen in this light, the concluding remarks perhaps point to the splendor, supreme indifference, impenetrability, mystery and impossibility of capturing the object – personified in the desert, which has frequently stood as a figure for the nonhuman or the anti-human. In turn, the desert stands as a figure for America itself, for its landscapes, cities, highways, (non)culture and way of life. Such a figure is obviously the creation of a European subject, in this case Baudrillard, for whom America represents the liquidation of a multi-dimensional and critical (European) culture, the desertification or one-dimensionalization of the social in the wasteland of the indifferent.

Although America – on this view – is without depth, meaning, aesthetic charm or seduction, it exerts 'an absolute fascination, that of the disappearance of all aesthetic and critical forms of life, in the irradiation without desire. That of Los Angeles: insane movement without desire. End of aesthetics' (*A*, p. 242). Baudrillard sees the desert of America as replacing the European 'system of seduction, of taste, of charm, of theatre, but also of contradictions, of violence always reappropriated by speech, by games, by distance, by artifice' (*A*, p. 243). In America there is a 'vertiginous absence of affect and character in the faces and the bodies' (*A*, p. 243). The disconnected bodies circulate on freeways and plug into computers, media, cars, nature, and the city itself; its fascination is that 'of dryness and sterility. Desert, not desire' (*A*, p. 245).

Baudrillard suggests at the beginning of his study that one should read America as a fiction (*A*, p. 59). But one could well read Baudrillard's own study as a fiction about America, as pataphysical projection of his own fantasies about America. More uncharitably, one could read the book as a whole as symptomatic of the decline of Baudrillard's theoretical powers and the collapse of social analysis and critique – as well as politics – in favor of highly uneven social observation and metaphysical ruminations. While some of the earlier parts of the book (especially pp. 55–126) contain some acute observations and while the project of analyzing the signs and constellations of America is certainly fascinating, Baudrillard fails to pull it off.

In fact, the same basic limitation in Baudrillard's metaphysics is apparent in his analysis of America: his subject matter is undertheorized, and his attempts at theory are uneven and problematical. Novel and original ideas cohabit promiscuously with banal stereotypes (America as a desert, as primitive). The problem with using these concepts as expressive of the very essence of America is that his treatment falls prey to a dull essentialism. Moreover, it is not just the pejorative and condescending tone of his particular concepts, but the very status of the key concepts themselves that is problematical. As Lyotard argued long ago, the very concept of 'the primitive' is an ideological construct with racist and imperialist overtones.[22] And 'the desert' is a rather stereotyped European cliché for modernity (see Antonioni's film *Red Desert*) or for the emptiness of the soul in a fallen world. Not much is gained by resurrecting such worn-out concepts.

Yet Baudrillard links 'the primitive' and 'the desert' in his analysis of America, and tries to give both these metaphors positive inflections. However, his uses of these concepts often border on the condescending, if not worse. Meditating on the 'primitive' splendor of Death Valley, rather primitive thoughts – no doubt leavened with the whiskey frequently alluded to in his metaphysical travelogue – seethed through his thought terminal and later computed as the following revery: 'Death Valley is always this grand and mysterious. Fire, heat, light, all the elements of sacrifice. One must always take something to sacrifice in the desert and offer it up as victim. A woman. If something ought to disappear there, something equal to the beauty of the desert, why not a woman?' (*A*, p. 132).

Regressive metaphysics is connected all too often with retrograde social attitudes. Never passing up an opportunity to raise the hackles of feminists, Baudrillard revels in ecstatic chauvinism. There is also a new obsession with race in *America* which sometimes borders on racist thinking. His distinctions between American and European *mentalités* are contestable, and he exhibits a proclivity for racial stereotypes. In addition, there is constant reference to the mixture of races in the United States as a defining feature of the country, and while he sees this as positive by comparison with the petty racism in France (*A*, p. 166), his reflections on race in the United States are highly superficial. Furthermore, by idealizing the alleged competition between racial and ethnic groups (*A*, pp. 188ff.), Baudrillard downplays the virulent racism that has characterized and continues to characterize American society and the domination by white males (and thus capitalist patriarchy) from the beginning to the present.

Is there a connection between metaphysics and sexist and racist thinking? The trend toward binary thinking (subject versus object, Europe versus America and so on) that typifies Baudrillard's metaphysics permeates his analysis, and much of his binary conceptualization is stereotypical and superficial (for example, his essentialist differentiation of masculine and feminine, or contestable distinctions between Europeans and Americans). Binary metaphysics would thus seem to produce stereotypical thought which exaggerates differences (between sexes, races, nations and so forth) while covering over or erasing similarities. Insufficiently deconstructive, Baudrillard's forays into metaphysics thus reveal all the traps and dangers of metaphysical thought and all its limitations.

Or it could be that the limitations of Baudrillard's analysis of America derive from his lack of social theory and from his primarily metaphysical focus? Metaphysics is a form of tunnel vision that is frequently connected – and this is certainly true in Baudrillard's case – with idealist sign fetishism, with obsessive focus on certain distinctive signs of 'the Real,' with an accompanying lack of focus on certain material underpinnings or less fascinating signs. So, for example, Baudrillard comes to California and discovers a 'realized utopia.' Santa Barbara is a utopia, Santa Cruz is a utopia, California is paradise, thus America is the realized utopia (*A*, pp. 61, 89ff., 149ff.). But for whom? one might ask. Baudrillard comes to California, and he sees the natural splendor of the desert and the eccentricities of its joggers, intellectuals, yuppies and freeway and media culture. His California is lily-white, Reaganized and yuppified. There are no migrant farm-workers, no Chicano barrios, no Central American refugees, no Vietnamese refugees or Asians, not even any blacks. Baudrillard hears that mental asylums have released some of their patients and sees some of them wandering in the streets; he does not, however, see the homeless, the hopeless underclass, so evident in the Reagan era, and does not mention that it is very specific political policies that have produced this suffering in the interest of a specific class of individuals.

Indeed, when Baudrillard looks at Reagan and Reaganism, all he sees is Reagan's smile – more evidence of his sign fetishism. He claims that the American propensity to smile signifies

'This country is good, I am good, we are the best.' It is also the smile of Reagan where the self-satisfaction of the entire nation culminates and which is in the process of becoming the sole principle of government. A self-prophetic smile, as all the advertising signs: smile and someone will smile on you. Smile to show your transparency, your candour. Smile if you have nothing to say, especially do not hide that you have nothing to say, or that you are indifferent to others. Allow that emptiness to show transparently, put on display that profound indifference of your smile and *make a gift* to others of that emptiness and that indifference; illuminate your face with the zero degree of joy and of pleasure and smile, smile. (*A*, p. 68)

Baudrillard suggests that Reagan's smile is at the root of (what was perceived as) his popularity, that it allowed him to obtain 'a consensus significantly superior to that obtained by any Kennedy through reason or political intelligence. The appeal to pure animal or infantile self-congratulation succeeds much better and all Americans converge on that toothpaste effect. Never has a single idea, not even the basic national values, produced such an effect. The credibility of Reagan is at the exact measure of the transparency and nullity of his smile' (*A*, pp. 68–9). This passage points to both the charm and the limitations of Baudrillard's reflections on America. It is true that there is something striking and sometimes unsettling in the way that Americans smile at strangers, at anyone and everyone, like the village idiot blessing the world with his tragic emptiness. It is also probable that Reagan's smile has something to do with his popularity; and Baudrillard's reflections on this conjuncture provide insights into both phenomena. Yet to reduce Reaganism to dentifical effects is to miss many aspects of this complex phenomenon. (I will return below and in chapter 7 to Baudrillard's metamorphosis of political analysis into a transpolitical fetishism of signs.) For Reagan's 'popularity' was also a result of public relations, image politics and the continued power· of capital in American politics. Yet there is no capital or political economy in Baudrillard's America beyond a couple of ludicrous comments to the effect that capital never caught on in the United States, and that it does not play much of a role in this supposedly capitalist country.[23] I would submit that it is precisely Baudrillard's metaphysical imaginary which is responsible for the limitations of his texts in recent years. Yet before elaborating further my critique of Baudrillard's metaphysics in 6.4, I will examine some mid/1980s texts which attempt to present and develop his metaphysical imaginary.

6.3 'FORGET BAUDRILLARD' AND *L'AUTRE PAR LUI-MÊME*

Various texts and interviews from the 1980s put on display Baudrillard's metaphysical imaginary, and elaborate his key concepts and positions. These texts exhibit some of the weaknesses of his simulation of metaphysics – in particular, the diminution of social theory and the absence of politics. His 1980s texts can be read as a type of the simulation machines that so fascinated him. In 'Forget Baudrillard' he simulates a dialogue, while in *L'autre par lui-même*, he simulates theory itself. In both texts, social theory and political analysis again evaporate, and Baudrillard's theoretical performance parodies itself in exhibition and display of his favorite categories and ideas.

In a series of interviews in Paris and Rome with Sylvère Lotringer in 1984–5, Baudrillard allows his metaphysical imaginary to hang out, and, provoked by Sylvère, produces a string of *bon mots* which exhibit his main concepts and ideas.[24] Uneasy with Sylvère's allegation that his thought represents the liquidation of Western culture in his theories of the end of production, history, the political and so on, Baudrillard distances himself from the very concept of 'the end of,' which he claims remains embedded in a linear view of history and states:

> I would prefer to begin, even if it sounds a little like science fiction, with a quotation from *Die Provinz des Menschen* (*The Human Provence*), a recent book by Elias Canetti. It is possible, he says – and he finds the idea rather painful – that starting from a precise moment in time the human race has dropped out of history. Without even being conscious of the change, we suddenly left reality behind. What we have to do now, continues Canetti, would be to find that critical point, that blind spot in time. Otherwise, we just continue on with our self-destructive ways. This hypothesis appeals to me because Canetti doesn't envisage an end, but rather what I would call an 'ecstasy', in the primal sense of that word – a passage at the same time into the dissolution and the transcendence of a form. (*FB*, pp. 67–8).

Baudrillard continues to describe the end of history in terms of a transformation of history into a state of simulation, a body kept in a state of hibernation, a series of special effects or a toy (*FB*, pp. 68ff., 134). He claims that history is not dead, in the way that it was once claimed that God is dead. Rather, 'Suddenly, there is a curve in the road, a turning point. Somewhere, the real scene has been lost, the scene where you had rules for the game and some solid stakes that everybody could rely on' (*FB*, p. 69). In other words, everything has changed, we are in a new situation, the grand referents of our previous theories have disappeared and we need new theories and concepts.

Yet Baudrillard resists providing a historical account of this rupture, or break, because he rejects the very concept of linear history and historical narrative, arguing that we are now in a new post-historical situation where the very concepts of history are no longer relevant. 'What interests me instead (but can you still call this history?) is the possibility of a pure event, an event that can no longer be manipulated, interpreted, or deciphered by any historical subjectivity' (*FB*, p. 70). (It is never clear in Baudrillard's writing what a 'pure event' would be, but we will pass this by for the moment.) Furthermore, Baudrillard interprets the fall out of history metaphysically – how else? – as a reversal of sovereignty between subject and object, as the end of the reign and problematic of the subject, in a world in which the object now reigns supreme. The dissolution of the subject brings to an end the reign of representation, of the belief that our concepts, theories, art and so forth represent the world (more naive fantasies of the subject to conquer the object). Thus Baudrillard is interpreting the end of history in terms of a metaphysical scenario concerning the triumph of the object, rather than in terms of a social or historical theory of a transition from one stage of society to another. Although the victory of the object brings along a time of nihilism, in that all the values of the old, pathetic subject are destroyed, Baudrillard does not see this as necessarily depressing. 'We can't avoid going a long way with negativity, with nihilism and all. But then don't you think a more exciting world opens up? Not a more reassuring world, but certainly more thrilling, a world where the name of the game remains secret. A world ruled by reversibility and indetermination' (*FB*, p. 71).

Such novelty and indetermination bring with them the now familiar Baudrillardian experiences of giddiness and vertigo and a rejection of previous views, including his own, which failed to take into account the novelty of the situation (*FB*, pp. 71–4). Rejecting desire as the motor of action and events, Baudrillard claims that, instead, one should look at seduction:

> Things make events all by themselves, without any mediation, by a sort of instant communication. There is no longer any metaphor, rather metamorphosis. Metamorphosis abolishes metaphor, which is the mode of language, the possibility of communicating meaning. Metamorphosis is at the radical point of the system, the point where

there is no longer any law or symbolic order. It is a process without any subject, without death, beyond any desire, in which only the rules of the game of forms are involved. (*FB*, pp. 74–5)

Metamorphosis is now Baudrillard's passion, his primal enchantment. Things 'metamorphosize' from one state of being into another. What if, Baudrillard fantasizes, we could metamorphosize ourselves, 'becoming-animal, becoming woman.' What if we could become objects beyond death and the limitations of being human, that pathetic state which should be overcome and left behind. There are (rather appalling and frightening) hints of such metamorphosis in 'metastasis – the proliferation of bodies, obesity, cancer – there again, unfortunately, the subject no longer exists' (*FB*, p. 75). Baudrillard thus fantasizes a world without the subject, a world of radical metamorphosis, a world in which objects make things happen, objects rule (the 'pure event': an event without the mediation of a subject?). The subject is disappearing, he claims, through mechanical contrivances such as cloning (see 4.1), through hyperrealization, massification, and through a game, an art of disappearance, in which subjects presumably become like objects. The disappearance of the subject and the triumph of the object might create dizziness or even panic, Baudrillard warns, but who knows, there may be new pleasures and modes of being awaiting us as we de-subjectify and progressively objectify ourselves, now disappearing in the ecstasies of objectification.

Later in the interview, Baudrillard elaborates further on his latest positions, and most of the ideas put forward should be familiar to those who have read this far in my study. Before forgetting this interview, however, I would like to raise the question of why Baudrillard titled his performance 'Forget Baudrillard.' Obviously, one answer concerns its juxtaposition with his earlier study 'Forget Foucault' in the *Semiotext(e) Foreign Agents* collection. Yet the title might be intended to convey additional messages. Perhaps Baudrillard is telling us to forget him as a subjectivity with a trajectory and a history, because he is now demanding our fascination with the object named Jean Baudrillard! Perhaps he is telling us to forget Baudrillard because all his earlier work is now out of date, and that whatever he says in the interview will also be passé by the time the text has found its way into the reader's hands. Or perhaps he is telling us to forget Baudrillard precisely to seduce us into – remembering Baudrillard?

In his 1987 text *L'autre par lui-même* (translated in 1988 as *The Ecstasy of Communication*), Baudrillard provides one of the first simulated texts, a pastiche of key moments of his earlier work with some new elaboration and development. The title refers to French collections of texts like *Sartre par lui-même*, which excerpted some key passages from previous publications, and which is reminiscent of Barthes's attempt to write a text about himself in the series, the book published as *Barthes by Barthes*.[25] Outdoing Barthes,

Baudrillard presents simulation models of some of his key earlier texts, accompanied by a couple of new ones. The collection is subtitled 'Habilitation' and was intended as a presentation of his work as a whole to the Sorbonne for a doctoral degree, as a type of the 'Habilitation' dissertation necessary for promotion in certain European countries.

Baudrillard begins by noting the paradox involved in providing a panoramic retrospective on work that never wanted perspective and is not yet finished: 'Yet this is an exercise of simulation which may be resonant with one of the principle themes of the whole: to pretend that this work were accomplished, that it developed in a coherent manner and has always existed. I do not see any other fashion in talking about it than in terms of simulation, much in the same manner that Borges reconstitutes a lost civilization through the fragments in a library' (*ALM*, pp. 9–10; *EC*, pp. 9–10).

The text contains six short studies, including a republication of the English text 'The Ecstasy of Communication' which we have already examined, 'Rituals of Transparency,' 'Metamorphosis, Metaphor, Metastasis,' 'Seduction or the Superficial Abyss,' 'From the System of Objects to the Destiny of the Object,' and 'Why Theory?' I will examine the last two studies here, having already drawn on some of the earlier ones in previous sections. Reflecting on his theoretical itinerary, Baudrillard notes how he passed from an analysis of *Le système des objets* rooted in the standpoint of a subject alienated and oppressed by objects and by reification (see 1.1) to a theory of the destiny of the object, proclaiming the triumph of the object (*ALM*, pp. 67ff.; *EC*, pp. 77ff.). A 'double spiral' took him, he now claims, from the system of objects to fatal strategies. The first spiral concerns a veering from symbolic exchange to seduction, which continued to pose an opposite, an other, to the system of production, of the code, of simulation. Baudrillard tells how he eventually surrendered the dream of a transgression through symbolic exchange, which he now perceives as the strategy of a declining and disappearing subject. For simulation itself has passed to the stage of transparency and ecstasy, in which every attempt to oppose it itself appeared as a simulation. Then, in a second spiral, Baudrillard veered to the side of the object, because '*it is the object itself which takes the initiative of reversibility*' (*ALM*, p. 69; *EC* p. 80). He concluded that seduction is best conceived not as a strategy of the subject, but as the very being of objects, of their seductive fascination: 'The desire of the subject is no longer at the center of the world, it is the destiny of the object' (ibid.).

Baudrillard thus proclaims the end of the era (and philosophy) of subjectivity, of the values and ends of the subject. Against the pious dreams of the subject to rule and transform the world, Baudrillard contrasts a 'radical exoterism, the reflection of the exteriority of the object.' Against all the interiorities celebrated by philosophers from Descartes and Pascal to Sartre, Baudrillard contrasts 'that externality, that exterior power which, beyond the principle of finality of the subject, sketches the fatal reversibility of the object' (*ALM*, p. 71 *EC*, p. 82). Baudrillard appeals to current social developments to legitimate this reversal of the metaphysical tradition. Things have surpassed their essence, their definition, he claims; they have become extreme, ecstatic, out of control, surpassing subjective attempts at definition or control. There are no more potentialities to realize: the objects themselves have surpassed all potentialities ascribed to them; there are no more transcendent goals to reach, for the objects have already gone beyond them. There are no limitations to transgress: all limitations have been put aside in a condition of *hypertelia*, in which objects surpass all ends ascribed, all potentialities, all limits.

Critical Theory measured existing beings and states of affairs in terms of their higher potentialities, and criticized all restrictions or limitations that kept individuals and societies from reaching a higher state. In place of such surpassed critical theories, Baudrillard recommends 'a fatal theory, perfecting that objective irony of the world' (*ALM*, p. 72; *EC*, p. 83). He thus denies that any potentialities remain to be realized in what he sees as a fully realized world: utopia is here and there are no more dreams to be realized or goals to strive for. Metaphysics has thus replaced social theory, which in Baudrillard's imaginary no longer has any objects or goals. What can we say in conclusion about Baudrillard's metaphysical turn and the surprising developments in his 1980s texts?

6.4   BAUDRILLARD AND THE RETURN OF METAPHYSICS

Martin Heidegger once wrote that Nietzsche was the last metaphysician, the last thinker to provide an interpretation of reality in terms of metaphysical categories, and it is true that the past two decades have seen powerful assaults on the metaphysical imaginary by deconstruction and other versions of poststructuralism.[26] Against the universalizing and essentialist discourses of metaphysics, Foucault and others have tried to show how discourses are historically constructed and are secretly constituted by rules of discourse, conceptual frameworks, and relations of power and domination which deflate metaphysical pretensions to grasp the universal and essential. Against the metaphysics of representation and reality, many poststructuralists argued that metaphysics is a construction of the real, rather than its mirror or translucent representation. Against claims that metaphysics presents a primal or primary reality, Derrida and others have argued that metaphysics is simply a form of binary thinking which takes one term of a series of binary oppositions and illicitly privileges it as primal, grounding, fundamental and so on, whereas a deconstructive analysis can show that it is really derivative of – even inferior to – its opposite, and that no metaphysical system is really stable or well grounded.

In light of these assaults on metaphysics, it is curious to see Baudrillard, supposedly the most ultra-hip and avant-garde thinker, reverting to a mode of thought supposedly surpassed. In this chapter I have been suggesting that Baudrillard falls into all the metaphysical traps depicted by contemporary philosophy, and at this point I wish to show how his new metaphysics reveals the limitations of metaphysics itself.

Deconstruct Baudrillard!

To begin, I believe that Baudrillard's turn to metaphysics is motivated by his sign fetishism. For what more satisfying fetishism could one indulge in than taking one's signs of the real for the real itself, especially if these signs are one's own special, privileged constructs and representations? Baudrillard's self-presentation of theory indicates further reasons for turning to metaphysics. First, he believes that theory itself is simulation, a projection of models of the real as the real, the creation of simulations of reality which attempt to capture the reality of simulation (*ALM*, pp. 84ff.; *EC*, pp. 97ff.). Second, he sees theory as an attempt 'to seduce, to draw things from their condition, to force them to a superexistence incompatible with the real' (ibid.). That is, in this view, theory is a challenge to reality to become itself, to become as the theory challenges it to be. In this (pataphysical) mode, Baudrillard thus sees theory as an imaginary construct which tries to seduce the world to become as the theory wants it to be, to follow the scenario scripted in the theory.

Now Baudrillard's script has become increasingly essentialist and binary in structure – precisely the features of traditional metaphysics attacked by poststructuralism. In fact, almost all his writings are marked by sharp binary distinctions between different social orders and different sorts of fundamentally opposed activities and object domains. His early writings contrast symbolic societies with productivist societies and symbolic exchange with exchange value and use value, in which the symbolic is valorized over the productivism, utility and other values associated with contemporary capitalist (and contemporary Communist) societies. Later he contrasts production with seduction, with the latter privileged over the utilitarian, rationalistic values of both political economy and libidinal economy (see 5.3).

And his 1980s metaphysics is marked by a series of binary oppositions between seduction and production, fatal and banal strategies, the subject and the object, and countless binary subcategories. In each case, Baudrillard privileges one side of the binary opposition, and denigrates the other side. Such binary thinking and conceptualization is highly problematical, however, and should be deconstructed. It is curious that Baudrillard, at one time a thoroughgoing deconstructionist, is not more deconstructive himself. In *L'échange symbolique et la mort*, his most deconstructive text, he cites several key points of the deconstructive critique of binary metaphysics (see

ES, pp. 193ff., *passim* and my discussion in 4.2). Yet a pervasive set of binary oppositions pervades his own thought, and takes it over almost completely in the 1980s texts, which feature constant battles and oppositions between subject and object, masculine and feminine, Europe and America, and so on, in which one of the binaries is claimed to be superior or preferable to the other.

Baudrillard's Fundamental Binaries

Subject	Object
Production	Seduction (earlier: Symbolic Exchange)
Masculine	Feminine
Depth (reality)	Surface (appearance)
Appearance	Disappearance
Sense (meaning)	Non-sense
Interpretation	Charm
Scene	The Obscene
Potentiality	Ecstasy
Law	Game
The True	The False
Good	Evil
Discourse	The Look
Irreversibility	Reversibility
Banal Strategy	Fatal Strategy

I have already contested and taken apart his rigid subject-object dichotomy in 6.1, and want to proceed here from reflections on Baudrillard's metaphysics to the deconstruction of metaphysics itself. My analysis has suggested that metaphysics is a supremely projective imaginary, in which the metaphysician projects his or her imaginary on the world, interpreting the world in terms of its *subjective* categories, fantasies, hopes and fears. Baudrillard arguably does the same thing, projecting his subjectivity on the object itself, ascribing his own privileged subjective experiences to the being of the object world itself in a typical imaginary of idealism. On this reading, Baudrillard comes off as the Walt Disney of contemporary metaphysics, anthropomorphizing objects in imaginary (ideological) projection in the same way in which Disney anthropomorphized animals and things, thereby turning animals and the object world into the simulacra of small-town America as envisaged in his conservative imaginary. Baudrillard's metaphysical world, however, is more malefic than Disneyland, for its objects seduce and revenge themselves on hapless subjects, with no guarantee of a happy ending.

A close scrutiny of the essential features which Baudrillard ascribes to objects suggests that he is indeed projecting his secret fantasies and primal desires on those fascinating objects which he has been monitoring. Desiring to seduce and to be seduced, he projects seduction onto the being of objects. Desiring sovereignty, he projects sovereignty onto objects. Desiring revenge, he projects revenge onto objects. Supremely ironic, Baudrillard projects objective irony onto objects. Desiring to become a destiny and fatality himself – recall Nietzsche for the psychological roots of this peculiar lust[27] – he ascribes destiny and fatality to objects, and conjures up a fatal universe. Increasingly indifferent to the fate of society and his fellow human beings, Baudrillard ascribes indifference to that supreme object of objects, the masses. Himself impatient, he ascribes impatience to the masses and to the object world. Losing critical energy and growing apathetic himself, he ascribes apathy and inertia to the universe. Imploding into entropy, Baudrillard attributes implosion and entropy to the experience of (post) modernity.

Like all metaphysicians, Baudrillard has thus constituted a world to his own measure and taste. His metaphysics is a subjective construct, a projective machine which projects favorite categories onto the being of the world. It is thus able to wield a will to power over the complexity and confusion of experience. Baudrillard's metaphysics, like all metaphysical imaginaries, is fetishistic: enthraled like Narcissus gazing at his image in a pool of water, the metaphysician is fascinated to see his concepts staring back at him from the face of the world. Fixated at the mirror stage, the metaphysician derives narcissistic gratification from seeing his concepts reflected in the world around him.

I argued earlier that Baudrillard is best interpreted as a sign fetishist who ascribes more reality to signs than to things, and I would now propose that his metaphysical imaginary be read as an example of sign fetishism, of a fetishizing of the signs of his metaphysical imagination into 'objective' realities and being itself. Indeed, is not metaphysics itself a form of sign fetishism and projection, a taking of the subjective constructions of signs 'the real' to be *reality itself*? Is not the metaphysical imaginary itself a form of *narcissism* and sign fetishism that reads into the real the signs that it has projected there?

Put in slightly different terms, is not metaphysics itself a form of pataphysics? Is not the metaphysical imaginary precisely this: an imaginary construction, a projection of the subject's categories into the real, and a subsequent reading of these categories as indexes of reality, signs of the really real? Is there not something slightly ridiculous and absurd – that is, completely imaginary and pataphysical – in thinking that one can construct a mirror of the real, or capture in concepts the order of things? Between psychopathology and pataphysics, the metaphysical imaginary thus reveals itself as a particularly problematical mode of discourse that is both regressive and illusory.

I would also propose that although Baudrillard wants to present himself as the voice and advocate of the object, he is really a double agent, secretly representing the subject as he anthropomorphizes the object world in an amazing creative display that out-Disneys Disney. For it is clear that, ultimately, he is projecting the categories of subjectivity, as well as his own subjective imagination, into the domain of objects (ascribing to them as objective features his subjective projections such as revenge, indifference and so on), thus secretly continuing in a different form the very philosophy of subjectivity that he pretends to combat.

Yet Baudrillard should be taken seriously as a double agent, for he has at least tried to go over to the side of the object, motivated by a not so secret yearning to become an object himself. Several times Baudrillard claims that there is a desire in all subjects to become objects, and one passage in *L'autre par lui-même* points to a deep admiration for objects and a yearning to cross over, to metamorphosize: 'How could the subject even be able to dream of jumping over its shadow and of falling into the silence and the perfect destiny of stones, animals, masks and stars? It cannot rid itself of language and desire, or of its own image, because the object only exists in that it is designated and desired by the subject' (*ALM*, p. 77; *EC*, p. 90).

Part of the pathos of the Baudrillardian universe is the impossibility of the world becoming subject or the subject becoming an object (ibid.), though I have suggested that by projecting his own metaphysical imaginary onto the world, onto the object, a sign fetishist like Baudrillard can make the world like himself. But it is more tricky to become like an object oneself, to divest oneself of one's pesty subjectivity; and though Baudrillard's celebration of metamorphosis points to the secret dream of becoming an object, so far, at least, it is just a dream, and poor old Baudrillard must continue to live in the hostile, menacing world of objects condemned to subjectivity and finitude. Indeed, perhaps the ultimate boon for a subject-metamorphosis into objecthood is immortality, the ultimate reward and perhaps secret telos of Baudrillardian metaphysics.

Metaphysics, Sexism and Racism

Baudrillard's turn toward metaphysics is accompanied by a reversion to the traditional accompaniments of the metaphysical imaginary: sexism and racism. I argued earlier that metaphysical thinking operates with binary oppositions in which one category is held to be superior to another category, which is posited as its inferior 'other.' In general, in sexist and racist and metaphysical thinking the 'other' is the projection and construct of the individual subject. In particular, for white male subjects 'the other' is usually women and other races. Such thinking is rooted in discriminations which attempt to establish fixed boundaries between various phenomena and a hierarchy of categories – precisely the imaginary of metaphysics seeking to erect stable, fixed boundaries for categories and to provide an ordered discrimination of values. But suddenly, in the 1980s, Baudrillard begins polemicizing against promiscuity, against an indiscriminate mixing of categories, races and objects. Following Nietzsche's call for discriminations and hierarchy (*Rangordnung*: a revealing term) for an aristocratic code of values, Baudrillard intensifies his polemic against promiscuity, and exhibits an aristocratic disdain for suffering, oppressed races and women.[28] I have pointed to some examples of an intensified, transparent sexism and racism in *America*, and a close reading of a truly loathsome 1980s essay, 'What Are You Doing After the Orgy?,' will show how his neo-aristocratic, neo-Nietzschean metaphysical imaginary falls prey to some of the most virulent features of the conservative imaginary – racism and sexism.[29]

The title of the article appears in his analysis of California in *America*, where he poses the question, 'What Are You Doing After the Orgy?' He then elaborates: 'What do you do when everything is accessible – sex, flowers, the stereotypes of life and of death? This is the problem of America and, from there, it has become that of the entire world' (*A*, p. 61). A bit later he writes:

> Santa Cruz, as in many other aspects of contemporary America, is *the universe after the orgy*, after the convulsions of sociality and of sexuality. The survivors of the orgy – sex, political violence, the Vietnam war, the crusade of Woodstock, but also the ethnic and anticapitalist struggles and at the same time the passion of money, the passion of success, the hard technologies – the survivors are all there, jogging in tribalism, neighbors of the electronic tribalism of the Silicon Valley. (*A*, p. 92)

Baudrillard thus establishes the domain of his current theory as the situation of advanced capitalist societies after the 'orgy' of the 1960s and the 1970s. He begins his article 'What Are You Doing After the Orgy?' by repeating his analysis of obscenity as a key category for describing the present age, and finds instantiations of contemporary 'cold obscenity' in a hyperrealist exhibition at Beaubourg (his aesthetic *bête noire*), in the computerized assemblage and analysis of the remains of the victims of a DC-10 plane wreck, of Issei Sagawa's murder and cannibalism of 'Renée, "white and soft-skinned Occidental,"' of *Playboy* pictures, of male strippers and female mud wrestling (pp. 43–4). This performance suggests that the metaphysician is not only a fetishist who makes a fetish of his or her conceptual productions, but is a hysteric, seeing his or her categories everywhere, repeating his or her obsessions endlessly, letting subjectivity vent itself to the full in paroxysms of excess. Indeed, in a little metaphysical vignette entitled 'The Obscenario,' Baudrillard displays his aristocratic 'discriminations':

> One day, in a seminar on seduction regularly attended by a physically and verbally handicapped man who nevertheless spoke constantly and

specifically about seduction, thereby causing a chill to permeate the auditorium with every interjection, a beautiful and feminist young woman arrived to wage war against seduction, which to her is a sexist ideology. She sat down next to the handicapped man and throughout her (aggressive) argument leaned tenderly toward him, slipping a lit cigarette in and out of his mouth to enable him to smoke. With the rhythm of someone tending a pipe, she had him suck his butt as though she were a nursing mother, for this poor wreck of a male, who served as crutch and alibi, as she vituperated against males who think only of seduction. Beautiful, provocative girl doling out her little revenge through a poor, impotent polio case. And him glowing painfully with the pleasure of this unexpected rape.

Ah yes, the roles should have been reversed, but in what sense? She was making me 'smoke' too with the naughty pleasure that she was getting out of this scene and that I found echoed in the self-contained joy of the bland cripple who hated me from the start and from whom I had never been able to conceal my revulsion – but this new revulsion was still worse because I found myself identifying with him as he underwent the girl's symbolic caresses; she was soliciting me as she practically masturbated him before my eyes, she was saying to me: 'Look, if you were a mongoloid, an impotent, you would have the right to my favors, I am raping you through him and there's nothing you can do about it.' (Later, when I ran into her by chance at a party, she started to cruise me shamelessly – but I would have preferred, for a seminar, to have been that cripple between those lips she placed the cigarette).

She did not know him at all. It was a stroke of genius to place herself next to him and to use him as a foil. It was obscene, but it had genius. Without him she would have been just a ridiculous type of feminist. (pp. 44–5)

Baudrillard lets it all hang out – shamelessly, unrepentently, good Nietzschean aristocrat to the core. No compassion for the suffering or willingness to engage in dialogue with feminism: aristocratic disdain to the nth degree. He follows this pathetic story with his umpteenth discussion of the metaphysical differences between the masculine and the feminine (pp. 45ff.; see also *FB*, pp. 95–6). Such a metaphysical mode of thought essentializes differences which have evolved historically, and in Baudrillard's case produce peculiar metaphysical discriminations. It allows him to place women in a category of his own making, into any conceptual apparatus that he pleases: 'Women, children, animals – we must not be afraid of assimilations – do not just have a subject-consciousness, they have a kind of objective ironic presentiment that the category into which they have been placed does not exist' (*FB*, pp. 97–8). Yet Baudrillard continues to produce categories of women, and to engage in relentlessly sexist asides as it suits his (metaphysical?) purposes and whims.

In order to properly balance sexist and racist vignettes, Baudrillard offers some reflections on race in 'What Are You Doing After the Orgy?:

> Black is the embarrassment of White. The obscenity of blackness gambles and wins against the obscenity of whiteness.
>
> Marvelous Idi Amin Dada, who has himself carried triumphant by four English diplomats, whose ambassador is received by the Pope. Marvelous Emperor Jean-Bedel Bokassa, eating up little black babies, lavishing diamonds upon the Western dignitary! Nowhere else as in Africa does the concept of power undergo parody in as Ubu-esque a fashion. The West will be hard pressed to rid itself of this generation of simian and prosaic despots, born of the monstrous crossing of the jungle with the shining values of ideology.
>
> Let us remember the rulers, let us remember the lumpen-bureaucrats of the bush who go home at night to the forest to mime their leader, in epileptic and frothing trances, the white employee, the white chief of Abidgan, let us remember the locomotive! All of them Bokassas, all of them Amin Dadas. Incredible, no hope for that continent. All the Peace Corps and other charitable institutions will go under there. The power of scorn, Africa's contempt for its own authenticity. (p. 46)

This passage is shamelessly racist and chauvinist. Just as earlier in the article Baudrillard identified the (presumably Third World) Issei Sagawa's cannibalist ritual murder of 'Renée, "white and soft-skinned Occidental," ' with the savage barbarism of non-Western cultures, Africa is equated here with Idi Amin and Bokassa, and deemed hopeless. Is Europe to be condemned in toto because of Hitler and Stalin? Is the United States to be seen as hopeless because of Reagan and Bush? Baudrillard's metaphysical-(trans)political thinking is itself hopelessly clichéd and simplistic. The metaphysician eschews more detailed analysis, and replaces hard, difficult political analysis with metaphysical vignettes. How would Africa appear from the standpoint of analysis of Kwame Nkrumah, Seke Toure, Nelson Mandella and Steve Biko? And why make white and black metaphysical opposites?

In the context of Baudrillard's 1980s metaphysical turn, the passages that I have just cited suggest that such metaphysical 'discrimination' can lead to sexist and racist thinking, and to aristocratic contempt for those different from oneself, those others who are 'other' to the metaphysical subject. This analysis suggests that metaphysics is a form of regressive thinking, in that its fetishizing of categories reduces the world to its conceptual scheme and interprets everything in terms of its categorical projections and values. Metaphysics is thus an extreme form of conceptual imperialism and terrorism, of a sort that Baudrillard and his contemporaries sharply criticized in the 1960s and 1970s. The return of metaphysics in the 1980s is thus part and parcel of a turn to conservativism, to submission to a conservative imaginary which has long haunted and attracted Baudrillard, and to whose seductions he ultimately capitulates. Beware of metaphysics!

Baudrillard thus turns out to be a rather self-indulgent metaphysician, rather than an avant-garde social theorist. What began as a philosophy of the orgy, of the madcap machinations of the postmodern world, thus becomes an aristocratic metaphysics of the object world after the orgy, a neo-Nietzschean form of metaphysical 'discrimination'. Yet Baudrillard ultimately proves to be extremely weak in the realm of theory. He does not adequately theorize his best insights, so admitting: 'I am not really a philosopher in the sense where argumentation or terminology would interest me. It's not that they escape me, it's just that I don't depart from there. That's not what I attempted! It's like this. What interests me, is to depart from object-situations, or else strategies of the masses. These are events which are modern, or postmodern – I don't know which – but which are our thing.'[30]

Baudrillard fails to adequately mediate his metaphysics with his social analysis however, and does not adequately situate his metaphysical categories and analyses within the context of the present historical moment. Note also how in this passage he is uncertain as to whether our contemporary situation should be described as 'modern' or 'postmodern,' pointing to his lack of a coherent and well-developed theory of post-modernity. Although he occasionally produces a promising category, he has difficulty contextualizing his concepts in concrete phenomena, and has little patience for sustained research and analysis. While he might reply that the superficial abstraction in his theoretical works reproduces the superficial abstraction of the current social organization – and thus, as he wishes, imitates the machinations of the object – it is rather his surrender of radical social theory and politics which is responsible for his current theoretical impasse – a point I shall elaborate on in the next chapter.

7

Beyond Baudrillard

In the previous chapter I critically discussed Baudrillard's turn to a metaphysical imaginary. Closely connected with this metaphysical imaginary is what might be called a 'political imaginary.' Every individual sees and relates to the world through a political imaginary, through a political cognitive mapping and its accompanying values.[1] The political imaginary is a social construct which is part of the available repertoire of political vision and identification in one's social group and environment. In any society there are a limited number of political ideologies which offer interpretations of history, politics, economics, society and values. As ideologies become disseminated and incorporated in social groups, they crystalize into political imaginaries – that is, specific ways of seeing and interpreting the events and issues which individuals deal with in everyday life. While a coherent and specifiable metaphysical imaginary – one that articulates and allows living a specific, relatively coherent view of reality – is more esoteric, and is limited to small groups or sets of isolated individuals, a political imaginary is more widespread. It consists of the configurations of the most common representations, beliefs, ideals and so on shared by dominant social groups and classes in a particular society.

For example, many individuals in contemporary capitalist societies see the world through a conservative imaginary or a liberal imaginary, a fascist imaginary, a feminist imaginary, a Marxist imaginary, an anarchist imaginary and so on. Not everyone, to be sure, lives within a coherent, specifiable political imaginary of the sort that I have just named, but one can construct ideal types of the dominant political imaginaries in a given society. Indeed, one frequently encounters individuals who live a particular imaginary – say, liberalism, conservativism, or feminism – and this becomes more obvious as one becomes more familiar with him or her. A political imaginary is in a sense a person's political unconscious, his or her deeply held political attitudes and beliefs. For one is generally not aware that one's political vision is a social construct, an arbitrary position that one has unconsciously incorporated through one's experiences and life history. Rather, a political imaginary is lived as common sense, as the way things are, as the way of the world.

Theorists, too, inhabit various political imaginaries constituted by their theoretical and political views. I suggested in previous chapters that while the explicit imaginary of Baudrillard's early writings was a neo-Marxian one combining the semiological imaginary with Marxian revolutionary perspectives, there were also elements of the capitalist imaginary in his view of the consumer society, which articulated capitalist views of consumption, commodities and the consumer society itself (see 1.4). For, using the semiological imaginary to interpret contemporary society as a cornucopia of signs, the product of an always proliferating semiurgy, he posited the omnipotence of signs, codes and the consumer society which came to fascinate and dominate individuals caught up in the thrall of conspicuous consumption and the passion of sign value – precisely as viewed by capitalists themselves.

Yet as an alternative vision to the consumer society, Baudrillard continued to project various 'revolutionary' perspectives, though sometime around 1970, he exchanged his neo-Marxian imaginary for what might be called a 'primitive communist imaginary' which valorized symbolic exchange over socialism, production, liberation or any of the other great signs of the radical imaginaries of the period (see 2.2). As he turned to his analyses of simulations and simulacra, his vision came to be dominated by the semiological imaginary (and, briefly, a cybernetic imaginary – see 3.2), with politics itself bursting into a play and display of signs. But in *De la séduction* (1979) Baudrillard traded his primitive communist imaginary for what might be called an 'aristocratic aesthetic imaginary' in which seduction replaced symbolic exchange as the privileged locus of value and preferred alternative to the wretched imaginaries and ways of life which he rejected in our contemporary societies (see 5.3, and note that Baudrillard's imaginaries are becoming more and more peculiar). Although one could interpret seduction as a mode of symbolic exchange, as a play with signs consistent with the sign fetishism that runs through his work, it is clear that he divested this ideal of the primitive communist inflection that it had received especially in *L'échange symbolique et la mort*, which valorized tribal modes of incorporating death into life through symbolic exchange and even valorized their initiation rituals, circulation of women and cannibalism. Baudrillard no doubt recognized that such valorizations opened him to charges of nostalgia, retrogression and worse, and he divested his theoretical project of idealizations of past societies by limiting his theoretical ideal to the preferred mode of aristocratic aestheticism, namely, 'seduction'.

And finally, in the 1980s, Baudrillard included 'fatal strategies' among his political positions, which would push ideas or processes to their outer extremities, beyond their limits, either to help bring about collapse or reversal or simply to imitate the ruses of objects, which were themselves supposedly surpassing their own limits and boundaries in the brave new world of excess, ecstasy and excrescence (see 6.1). The theory of 'fatal strategies' situates him in a French aestheticist-modernist tradition which depended on shock, scandal and going to extremes and beyond all previous boundaries for their effects. During the 1980s, Baudrillard distances himself even further from radical politics and social theory, and engages in ever more frequent metaphysical ruminations and aesthetic analysis. Yet in many of his 1980s texts, he continues to address political issues and to give political critiques – though it is not always clear what his own standpoint is.

With hindsight, one thus sees a series of surprising developments marking Baudrillard's progression from a critique of the political economy of the sign to theories of simulations and simulacra, seduction, pataphysical metaphysics and fatal strategies. His work has become increasingly esoteric, metaphysical and idiosyncratic. Yet I believe that a semiological imaginary traverses his work, focusing on the life of signs in contemporary society. This is the common motif in his social analysis, political posturing and metaphysical games. The value and limitations of his work thus ultimately consist – at least up to the present point in his unfinished theoretical itinerary – in his tracking the increasingly fundamental role of signs and images in our life. We have noted that he increasingly falls into a semiological idealism, abstracting signs from their material underpinnings and, indeed, erasing materiality from his theory (see 6.2). He also abstracts signs from sign systems (codes, structures, cybernetic organization), suggesting that they take on a life of their own in ever more aleatory combinations and permutations.

This obsession with signs connects him with a certain French aestheticist tradition (Baudelaire, Bataille, Barthes and so on), and marks Baudrillard as a semiological dandy, as an avatar of the sign as the mark of the real. Such a position increasingly divorces him from contemporary politics, and inscribes him within an apolitical aestheticism. Yet this does not prevent him from continuing to take political positions, and I will begin my final summing up of Baudrillard's contributions and limitations with a discussion of *La gauche divine* and other essays which provide access to his critique of contemporary politics – though we will see that almost all his political critique focuses on the Left, raising the question of the actual political effects of his new theoretical undertakings (7.1). I will then undertake a systematic critique of Baudrillard's 1980s works as a whole, in a final confrontation with his most recent theoretical and political endeavors (7.2). I conclude with a brief defense of radical social theory and politics against Baudrillard's critique, while sketching some alternative perspectives on contemporary society and politics (7.3).

7.1 THE DIVINE LEFT

During the 1970s Baudrillard began to conclude that the strategies for social transformation adopted by the Left were fatally flawed in light of the new social conditions which he had been describing and of the fatal limitations and illusions of the various Left political groupings and imaginaries. At this time he published some explicit polemics against the Left in books, pamphlets and newspaper and journal articles.[2] It might appear that Baudrillard is an example of a one-time radical intellectual who goes so far to the Left that he ends up on the Right. Instead, I would maintain that he ends up in a position between apolitical aestheticism and aristoratic, conservative individualism, which I would see as a logical consequence of his metaphysical turn and his keen nose for current cultural trends during an era (the 1980s) in which many people became tired of all existing political parties and options.

Baudrillard's *La gauche divine* (*The Divine Left*) was published in 1985 and contains a series of political studies sketched out between 1977 and 1984. The first section provides a sharp and spirited critique of the French Communist Party written in 1977 and 1978 (see 2.3 above). The second section, 'The State of Grace,' contains studies of 'The Ecstasy of Socialism' and 'The Divine Left,' written respectively in 1981, after the French Socialists had won an electoral majority and were the governing party, and in 1983 when disillusionment with the Socialists was becoming more widespread. The third section, 'Euphoria with Infusion,' was written in September 1984, after what seemed to be the collapse of the Socialist government with the resignation of key ministers and the Communist Party cabinet members.

His studies of the 1980s in *La gauche divine* expend much more energy explicating for the nth time the divine Baudrillard's social theory, rather than carrying out detailed political analysis. The extreme poverty of specifically political analysis and critique thus parallels his extremely superficial analysis of the American political situation and Reaganism in *America* which appeared a year later (see 6.2). His 'thesis' is that the French Socialist Party is an 'ecstatic' form of a pure model of socialism, which is in 'a state of grace by virtue of the exorbitant assumption of a model which has lost its truth en route' (*GD*, p. 70). The ecstasy of socialism thus refers to attempts to realize a model of socialism whereby socialism will go outside and beyond itself as a model, and become incarnated in 'the real.' Several times Baudrillard remarks that the turmoil of May 1968 retarded the advent of French socialism by a decade or so, but that the model was slumbering like a hidden child in the womb of French society for some time: 'It germinates, it incubates, it explodes and it invades everything all at once. It's exactly as in [the film] *Alien*. The Left, it's the monster of *Alien*. And the event in its ensemble reveals itself as a gigantic special effect – very successful besides – in short, a brief ecstasy in the morose course of our popular destiny' (*GD*, p. 71).

Note the use of film metaphors and cinematic terms like 'special effects.' Baudrillard will attempt to interpret the advent of French socialism in terms of his own categories and theories as part of an effort to simulate a Socialist politics, to simulate change, to simulate continuity with the French Revolution, French history and the tradition of socialism, as well as to simulate a politics of virtue, honesty and transparency: 'The model, as all models, is made in order to realize itself in a total resemblance to itself, thus it is made in order to hyperrealize itself. This is why I say that it is ecstatic: the hyperreal is the ecstasy of the real congealed in its own resemblance, expurgated from the imaginary and congealed in its model (even if this model is that of change)' (*GD*, p. 73).

What is particularly interesting in Baudrillard's analysis, however, is not his attempt to explain French socialism in terms of his categories, but rather his discomfort in confronting a political phenomenon and challenge which rejects his entire set of values and ideas and, instead, represents another set of values in which he once believed but now sees as having disappeared. He writes: 'Lately, however, here is what is happening to us: the assumption of a socialist alternative, the materialization under the sign of political power of the entire conceptual system of values (progress, morality of history, rationality of politics, creative imagination and *last but not least*: virtue transfigured by intelligence in power) – in short, the entire Platonic ideal which is fundamentally that of the intellectual class even if it denounces it' (*GD*, pp. 74–5).

Baudrillard is especially skeptical of Socialist claims to shape the march of history with a voluntaristic, coherent project, to realize the political will of the people, to provide genuine democracy and produce a rational and open free society. Now his skepticism might be justified in the face of the history of socialism – or of contemporary politics *tout court* for that matter. But it is revealing that those aspects of the French Socialist project which Baudrillard specifies and criticizes are precisely the *ideologies* of socialism, the *signs* of French socialism. That is, he neglects to analyze the Socialists' actual political programs, their material demands, their challenge to capital and the French ruling classes – that is, their early demands for a 35-hour week, nationalization plans, rationalization of the state, a more centralized and rationalized economy, and a democratized society. It could be argued that the French Socialists had difficulty realizing these demands either because of the resistance of capital or because of their own failures and limitations; but it is indicative that Baudrillard focuses his critique from the beginning on the level of the signs of French socialism, and never considers the material-historical conditions under which French socialism operated or the material constraints which led to its failure.

Instead, he merely mocks the Socialists' demands for the intellectuals to participate in the new government, which he fears would compromise their very being, which he claims depends on the power of negation and critique (*GD*, p. 78). His argument is that French socialism is itself a simulation, and that therefore the intellectuals are being summoned to 'participate as if it were a first-hand, real event,' whereas it is really 'a second-hand unreal event' (*GD*, p. 81). As Baudrillard's analysis unfolds, it is clear that he believes that the Socialists have no understanding whatsoever of either the role of simulations in contemporary media societies or of 'the rules of the political game.' Baudrillard claims that the Socialists naively believe that politics concerns solidarity, the common good, instituting public virtue, being honest and transparent, promoting education, health, culture and other social goods – in short, that it is a moral enterprise geared toward the public good and realizing certain social values.

For Baudrillard, on the contrary, politics, as Mandeville suggested in his *Fable of the Bees*, is properly centered on private vices rather than public virtue, and is thus a game played with individuals' baser instincts, which are primarily immoral (*GD*, p. 82). The French Revolution did not change the rules of the political game, he insists; and the Socialists, believing in another kind of politics of virtue, themselves completely fail to understand what politics is all about – namely, Baudrillard's favorite games of spectacle, seduction, ritual and an immoral play of signs (something well understood, incidentally, by Reagan's and Bush's media advisors).

This critique shows the distance which Baudrillard has traveled from 'straight' socialism and the Left liberal political ideals which he had previously shared with his generation, however tenuously. The above critique was written in 1981, during a general euphoria on the Left over the Socialist victory. Baudrillard presumably withdrew, ignored Socialist requests for progressive intellectuals to participate, and wrote his metaphysical treatise *Les stratégies fatales*, which we discussed in the last chapter. After its completion, Baudrillard seems to have returned to political analysis of the contemporary scene in September 1983 to carry out an analysis of 'the Divine Left' (*GD*, pp. 85–104). This analysis makes use of the metaphysical categories which we have already discussed, and would probably appear quite strange to a reader unfamiliar with Baudrillard's peculiar categories.

He begins by claiming that French socialism has engendered a corruption of French intellectuals, because 'it presents itself as an absolution of every contradiction, as a realized utopia, as reconciliation of theory and practice, as well-being, as benediction' (*GD*, p. 85). This robs the intellectuals of their oppositional standing, of their power of negativity, and thus

of the proper passion of the intellectual. For it does not suffice to demand of intellectuals to be a critical conscience of their time, or a moral caution. Yet, it is still necessary that intellectuals proceed from their own passion: with Gide, it was sincerity, with Sartre, it's lucidity, with the situationists and others it's radicality – afterwards, however, it's finished, there is no longer political-intellectual virtue. Afterwards, it's irony, the fascination of a world dominated by aleatory processes, microscopic developments – transhistory of which the crossing is as dangerous as that of a mine field. (*GD*, p. 86)

Note that Baudrillard proposes his irony as the logical successor to Gide, Sartre and 1960s radicalism. In short, this is what Baudrillard believes is missing in the French Socialists, and he proceeds to lecture them on the objective irony and immorality of things (this is the theme of *Les stratégies fatales*), and gives the hot tip that the Socialists should develop a 'new immorality' in their politics to correspond to this situation, rather than just advocating the old superseded morality (*GD*, p. 88). Later he is pleased to announce that the French Socialists have finally picked up some cynicism and immorality; but presumably it is a bit late to do them any good. Besides it is doubtful that they could be cynical or immoral enough to please the divine Baudrillard.

The other lecture which Baudrillard offers concerns a rehash of his theories of the social, the political, the media and simulations (*GD*, pp. 88ff.). Interestingly, his text omits completely any discussion of the economy. Nor does he share his no doubt fascinating ideas on culture and art with a Socialist government which was probably one of the few governments of the world at the time to be genuinely interested in promoting a progressive cultural politics. Furthermore, Baudrillard makes what might be taken as excessive demands on a government that was not even able to shorten the work week to 35 hours, complaining that socialism has failed 'to produce a new history, an original history' (*GD*, p. 92), and thus to provide a really revolutionary break with history – though Baudrillard fears that history is coming to an end due to other processes (see 7.2 below). Indeed, he suggests that French socialism is probably accelerating the processes which he has been analyzing concerning the end of the social and the end of history (*GD*, pp. 95ff., 107ff., *passim*).

At bottom, Baudrillard appears angry that the Socialists do not share his values, and in response he defiantly affirms his most extreme positions in the face of calls to join the Socialist project in France. He complains that the Socialists do not understand Bataille's concept of 'the accursed share' (*la part maudite*), of the role of immorality in politics, both of which disappear in the calls for solidarity and reconciliation.[3] In addition, 'The idea of an aestheticism of the world disappears. The idea of antagonism, of an ambiguity, of a reversibility, the idea of an arbitrariness, an irony, or an ineluctable cruelty in the order of things and in the order of characters disappears. The idea of any other collective passion disappears in the dull and homeostatic equilibrium of the discourse on social change' (*GD*, p. 95).

In short, the Socialists do not share Baudrillard's Nietzschean aristocratic aestheticism or his pataphysical metaphysics. Further – and this passage is the best expression of the reasons for his distancing himself from the Socialists – they have no idea of the role of simulation and signs:

> Socialism does not like signs and simulacra, it only likes values. It wants to be profoundly moral and for it simulacra and simulation could only be that of a previous period, which the historical truth of socialism is going to efface. All revolutions, even those which fail, share this desire for the purification of signs, of dissimulation and of moralization of the contents of history. The historical task of socialism is to exterminate simulacra, to exterminate every specious seduction and to reestablish all things in the moral luster of their history. This can only be confounded with the political will of a restoration of the hypothetical authenticity of the social. This renders the socialists profoundly blind to every actual reality which is – thank God – more subtle and more perverse. All the hypotheses concerning a field of distortion of signs, the evil genius of signs, the perverse effects of information, of signification in the social – and thus of a fundamental ambiguity that is not only political – of media and of culture and of many other things: such [Baudrillardian] views are insupportable and inconceivable, and this misrecognition becomes tragic for them [the socialists] as well. (*GD*, pp. 97–8)

Baudrillard claims that for the Socialists (and for morality) 'the sign is the principle of evil' (*GD*, p. 98). For Baudrillard, by contrast, it is the principle of the way of the world *tout court*. But once again, note how Baudrillard formulates the being of socialism in fundamental relation to signs, rather than to other economic, political or social conditions. He might be right that socialism – or any other kind of government – might not be able to defeat the reign of signs in contemporary society, to reverse the process of semiurgy. But in fact that is not really a fundamental part of the French Socialist program, which involved more modest demands to improve health, education, welfare, income distribution, culture, the quality of life and so on – all of which are ignored in Baudrillard's metaphysical ruminations and critiques, which reveal once again the extent to which he is a thoroughgoing sign fetishist, obsessed with signs as the fundamental reality and the only phenomenon really worth one's time.

Thus his critique centers on the claim that 'it seems that the socialist era has definitively lost the analytic of signs, the ironic power of the sign in the games of society. The recognition of a dimension of illusion, of irony, of perversion . . . is excluded in the perspective of the edification of the social' (*GD*, p. 98). Therefore the Socialists must self-destruct politically, because they cannot escape 'the objective irony' of the process of things rebelling against their masters, of the decomposition of energies of human contact, power and 'the vanity which strikes all enterprises of reconciliation' (*GD*, pp. 99–100). (Curiously enough, as I write this in January 1988, I see television reports of the avant-garde use of signs and slogans in the French Socialist Party electoral campaigns, and I ask, Did the French Socialists read Baudrillard, or did they simply realize some of his ideas in an aleatory fashion, in a *Zeitgeist* effect?)

La gauche divine is interesting because, more clearly than most of his other books, it lays bare the *essentialist* views of politics, human beings and reality that support and underlie Baudrillard's positions. Politics *an sich* for Baudrillard concerns signs, simulations and simulated power, and Mandeville and Machiavelli are his master thinkers, his keys to the essence of the political. I noted his citation of Mandeville's notion of the mobilization of private vices as part of the essence of the political. Later he cites Machiavelli's *The Prince* as another authority:

To make use of and to make work evil, vice, the interests, the passions, to count on evil, that is to say on the intelligence of the secret detour of things and not to ever count on good, that is to say upon their rectitude, was the only possible way of existing for the political – but also for us today because it is the sole strategic rule of survival – and it is by these stakes alone that the social itself can exist. This evidence is not cynical – it is simply the rules of a game. To deny this evidence, to deny this rule, is equivalent completely to a total absence of political sense. It is that which renders hypothetical the project of the socialists and it is that which produces the hypocrisy and the weakness of all their discourses. (*GD*, p. 101).

For Baudrillard, there are thus 'rules of the game' in the nature of things, rules which he grasps but the Socialists ignore. Moreover, the political essence is deeply rooted in an anthropological essence which is also accessible to Baudrillard's intuitions:

This rule of the game, this fundamental immorality, must remain hidden – it is part of that accursed share that no social reason can ever grasp. It is only at rare moments that a society gives itself the spectacle of its immorality. . . . That which resists the social lies in the fact that each of us carries in itself the phantasm of a secret society in which the most small privilege becomes the initiary sign. The privilege, literally, is to have our own law, our own rule, our sovereignty. That is almost the same thing, etymologically, as autonomy, although it has surreptitiously taken on the meaning of placing oneself under the law. But the people do not allow themselves to be fooled. They have no profound desire for autonomy, but for privilege. (*GD*, pp. 101–2)

Baudrillard's aristocratic values and vision of human beings here reproduces the discourses of a conservative-individualist tradition to which he now attaches himself. Human beings are basically irrational, asocial, resistant to the social, fixated on their own privileges, contemptuous of freedom and so on – a typical conservative aristocratic view of human nature. Baudrillard also attaches himself in the 1980s to the sign of a neo-Nietzschean, neo-aristocratic anthropology and ethic of privilege, just as he earlier attached himself to a Bataillean anthropology of waste, expenditure, luxury and the like. During the 1980s he explicitly grounds his positions in the cynical, conservative, individualist tradition, frequently citing Mandeville, Machiavelli, Nietzsche and Canetti.[4] All Baudrillard's political and rhetorical posturing rests, as I have been arguing, on the presumption of an essentialist metaphysics of human being, the social and the political, upon which his entire project now rests. Baudrillard is truly one of the last metaphysicians who has forgotten or ignored the critique of metaphysics carried out during the 1960s and 1970s.

Baudrillard continues his assault on the divine Left by claiming that French society (all societies?) was sick from political leukemia, and that the French Socialists were trying to inject homeopathic doses of the political and the social into the deeply sick patient. Using this metaphor, Baudrillard analyzes the ways in which the French Socialists attempted to infuse an artificial, simulated euphoria of progress, rationality, morality and so on into the French political scene, and why this project was doomed to fail because of their neglect of the indifference, cynicism, apathy and the rest of the masses and the inertia of the social.

Yet Baudrillard suggests that the Left might actually remain in power indefinitely, precisely because its simulations of the social and the political are themselves carrying out 'the sole task which remains to the political class: to administer the end of representation' (*GD*, p. 107). The (alleged) decline of real differences between Left and Right and the (alleged) indifference of the masses to politics will also help the Left to maintain power, Baudrillard suggests (though within two years of his writing this, the Left lost majority representation in France – although it regained a precarious majority in 1988). His crucial point, however, is that the Left is the beneficiary of the end of genuine political representation in a new situation in which anyone and any party can gain power through chance alone. This transformation is produced not merely by 'the professionalism of the political class' and the role of the media in politics, but also by the collapse of poles between representatives and the represented, which brings to a close the very space of political representation, due to 'the acceleration of a flux which has burned the circuits. . . . Better: the people literally do not have any more opinion, as they literally do not have any political will any longer. These have become aleatory and do no more than respond to solicitation and to the artificial movement of polls and electoral consultations which have become innumerable and permanent by the force of things, that of forcing the aleatory to nonetheless signify something' (GD, p. 111).

Elections, polls and political debates are themselves only simulations of politics. Politics is thus reduced to special effects. The sphere of the political is thus inherently unstable and 'this could continue eternally' (GD, pp. 112–3). In this situation, it is not accidental that someone like the French actor Yves Montand could rise in the public's eye as a political authority, or that Ronald Reagan could be elected president in the United States. In a media society, rather than philosopher-kings or even technocratic experts being summoned to political power, it is media specialists and professionals who have the edge. Baudrillard sarcastically comments that after Reagan, it would not be surprising to see 'a cosmonaut trying to become President. We are perhaps going toward the republic of crooners, of speakers, of sprinters, of animators. Why not? In Rome, they had crowned a horse emperor' (GD, p. 114).

Baudrillard's clever sarcasm is followed by a rather vicious cynicism, which has come to characterize his 1980s texts: 'Effectively, it is more joyful that for once one at least escapes the boredom and the philistinism of our political leaders. Isn't it more amusing to see Reagan smile without complex than to see Mitterrand smile under perfusion. To the indifference of the people corresponds the smile of their leader. And, if at bottom, our society is a society of simulation, isn't it better if our leaders are grand simulators, professionals of simulation?' (ibid.). Baudrillard concludes that today politics is intrinsically equivalent to advertising, publicity, sports, fashion and special effects, and that this is in part the revenge of the masses, who demand such entertainment from the political class. The result, of course, is the end of the political, the end of representation, the end of history and so on (GD, pp. 115ff.).[5]

The rest of the book focuses on Baudrillard's analysis of the current social system, and makes very few references to French socialism and 'the divine Left.' Some passages are quite interesting, and I will discuss them in the next section. In general, *La gauche divine* is symptomatic of Baudrillard's own political alienation and uncertainty. Although he repeatedly claims, à la McLuhan, that the end of the era of alienation has already occurred in a media and consumer society in which everyone is plugged in, it is clear that he is totally alienated from the political scene in France and elsewhere. Baudrillard's political dilemma is evident in an interview entitled 'Intellectuals, Commitment and Political Power,' published in *Thesis Eleven* in Australia.[6] Baudrillard readily admits the exhaustion of his political energy, his disconnection, political retreat, disaffection and marginality. He then states that being on the margins is 'the true position of the intellectual,' and that 'intellectuals are carriers of negativity' who are much more suited to opposition than to being in power (p. 169). When asked if intellectuals cannot also 'create positivity' – that is, positive alternatives or effects – at the same time, he denies this possibility because of the ubiquity of the media:

> There is an over circulation of ideas, of the most contradictory ideas, all in the same flux of ideas. What happens is that their specific impact is wiped out. I mean their negativity is wiped out. Mass-media and all that, are not vehicles for negativity. They carry a kind of neutralising positivity. That's why some intellectuals don't trust the mass-media. They want to preserve their purity. We also have the very real fact of how any kind of analysis becomes ready for reception because it has been mediated by the media. But this analysis is too ready for reception. What I mean by that is that it can go anywhere and be accepted anywhere, all over the place. The problem is that in a society of mass-media, the difference between positivity and negativity is pretty well wiped out by this absolute positivity, which, at that point, is no longer positivity but becomes a media-tape winding forward. (p. 170)

Once again Baudrillard uses the media's neutralizing force as an alibi to refrain from political intervention. A fundamental contradiction in his political position also emerges at this point. On the one hand, he presents intellectuals as barriers of negativity and even of an (impossible) utopia (p. 173); yet he himself focuses critical negativity only on the Left (especially the French Left) in the 1980s, calling the United States a 'realized utopia' (see 6.2), and even providing an ironic 'legitimation' of Soviet-style Communist societies as realized 'bureaucratic utopias' (*GD*, pp. 150ff.). When describing social developments, on the other hand, Baudrillard tends to shed himself of negativity, and provide 'ecstatic' descriptions of simulations and objects, renouncing social critique and constructing utopian alternatives completely, and even providing what might be called a theory of the conditions for their impossibility.

The question thus arises as to whether Baudrillard has gone over to the Right? Has Baudrillard secretly become a Rightist – despite himself or perhaps even from personal choice? Can Baudrillard be read as part of the conservative turn in France and elsewhere during the 1980s? Answering this question – or any other concerning Baudrillard – is highly complex. In the English-speaking world, Baudrillard is no doubt read as a Leftist radical, as a hyperradical more radical than radical and more leftist than Left. This is due in part to the texts that his English-language promoters have chosen to translate, and in part perhaps to lack of knowledge of the debates and vicissitudes of the Left in France. In fact, Baudrillard has published several of his 1980s books in a series edited by 'new philosopher' entrepreneur

Bernard-Henri Levi, who helped lead the cavalry of the New Right against the Left in attacks on Marxism and the Left which were held responsible for the Gulag and other political atrocities. The 'new philosophers' became the darlings of the media in France in the late 1970s and early 1980s, and carried out a sustained polemic against Marxism and the Left.

But Baudrillard never really joined the 'new philosophers,' and has occasionally distanced himself from them. In the *Thesis Eleven* interview, for instance, he wrote: 'The business of the "new philosopher" is a complicated business. Are they on the Right? Are they reactionary? You know that I did not defend them and don't think their critique is really significant. Or rather, it was too opportunistic; it was too well placed at the time given. Then, they used and abused the media. It is more this last aspect which disqualifies them in my eyes, (p. 171).[7] Yet despite this distancing of himself from the 'new philosophers,' Baudrillard chose to publish in their series, though he has another argument as to why such a move should not be judged politically incorrect:

> As for saying Left/Right, I don't know. I only want to judge people on new things. The criterion Left/Right leads us into dividing people into good and bad. I can no longer function according to this criterion. If we had new criteria, if we had something else, I would not be averse to taking up some kind of political will. But I would have to have different bases. I refuse to make any pronouncements on these old bases, on this tired political play. (ibid.)

Baudrillard thus presents his thought as a flight into a new theoretical space beyond all the categories of the old politics; thus he does not want to be judged in their terms. Yet it remains the case that his critique in the 1980s is primarily of the Left, of the 'divine' socialist Left in France, and his writings from the later 1970s to the present are replete with attacks on feminism, the peace and anti-nuclear movement, the ecology movement and other political tendencies generally deemed 'progressive.' Moreover, what he writes of Reaganism, America, yuppies and so on lacks the sharp satirical and critical bite of his attacks on the Left, although he offers a few critical comments on the Right in France in *La gauche divine*. Nonetheless, one could easily argue that his critiques on the whole benefit the Right more than the Left.

At bottom, however, the Baudrillard of the 1980s is best read as 'transpolitical,' and as difficult to categorize in terms of traditional political models. I have suggested that Baudrillard's imaginary is more of a metaphysical imaginary than a political imaginary, and that his fundamental passion is signs, not politics – though I have pointed to some curious intersections between Baudrillard's metaphysical imaginary and the conservative political imaginary, and will elaborate this critique below. From this position, Baudrillard's political imaginary is that of a neo-aristocratic sign fetishist. Yes, Baudrillard is beyond Left and Right and traditional political determinations. Nevertheless, his political asides have the pungent flavor of a neo-Nietzschean aristocratic aestheticism, which is hardly unknown to French culture and is indeed quite a typical imaginary for French cynical aesthetes who stand, as does Baudrillard, in the tradition of Baudelaire and aesthetic modernism.[8] This might explain why Baudrillard has trouble crossing the divide to postmodernism à la Arthur Kroker and others, for Baudrillard may be unable to give up or go beyond the sort of modernist aestheticism of Baudelaire, Jarry and the French tradition of aristocratic aestheticism.

In the final analysis, Baudrillard thus presents us with the poignant dilemma of what a sign fetishist is to do in a society of simulations. The signs beloved and fetishized by aristocratic aesthetes are hyperrealized and banalized in the society of simulations. A sign fetishist is thus perhaps torn – and one sees this in Baudrillard – between fascination and melancholy in the face of the disappearance of deep signs, the big signs of modernity like the real or art, and the advent of 'obscene' signs (flat, one-dimensional, fully explicit) in the society of simulations. Baudrillard's writings thus exhibit alternating psychotropism, moving from fascination to melancholy in response to the disappearance of the big signs, and to nostalgia for their resurrection or return. Curiously, one mood missing in his current psychotropic repertoire is a dreaming of the new, the next stage of history or another realm of signs – a dream that one rarely if ever finds in Baudrillard, who fails to project any positive alternatives to the current society of simulations.

We see, then, that Baudrillard's sign fetishism serves as his theoretical and political imaginary. In fact, it is difficult for a sign fetishist to commit him or herself to specific political positions (since signs are more divine than messy politics or smelly economics). In any case, Baudrillard's sign fetishism, his metaphysical imaginary and perhaps his political exhaustion have taken him beyond politics and the political imaginaries of our time, into a thought in orbit, which moves in its own theoretical sphere. In the next two sections, I will make some final critical comments on Baudrillard's thought games, as I examine some of his latest works.

7.2 THE ECSTASY OF BAUDRILLARD

In 'The Ecstasy of Communication' Baudrillard describes a society without secrets, inhibitions, repressions or depth which is rendered totally visible, explicit, overt, manifest and 'obscene' in the ominipresent and ubiquitous mass media of communication. In a study of 'The Ecstasy of Socialism' in *La gauche divine*, Baudrillard writes:

Ecstasy characterizes the passage to a pure state, in its pure form, in a form without content and without passion. . . .

Thus one could speak of an ecstasy of the state. Dispassioned, disincarnated, disaffected but all powerful in its transparency, the state accedes to its ecstatic form which is that of the transpolitical. At the same time no one believes it and there is a kind of total oblation, of total recourse, of universal solicitation toward that unique figure which has itself disappeared, or is on the way to disappearing from the point of view of politics: the state. (*GD*, p. 70)

This is, I submit, a perfect description of the ecstasy of Baudrillard himself and his disappearance in a pure state of simulation and the hyperreal. Like his description of French socialism, Baudrillard has passed from a theoretical model of Baudrillard into an ecstasy of Baudrillardian texts. Like the State he describes above, Baudrillard himself is transpolitical, transparent in his biases, assumptions and positions, which are endlessly repeated and recycled, without much political energy, passion or direction. In the 1980s, therefore, along with the ecstasy of socialism (and of conservatism in the United States, England and elsewhere), we have the ecstasy of Baudrillard.

Baudrillard has thus passed beyond himself into a pure model of himself. His simulations of theory are more and more hyperreal, more Baudrillardian than Baudrillard. Over and over, he takes his analyses to the limit, repeating incessantly his positions on the ecstasy of communication, the end of history, the silence of the masses and so on. His books and essays of the 1980s read and feel like simulations of a pure Baudrillardian model, with each text citing previous references and the same stories to re-present the same ideas in an attempt to drive them to the superlative, to the nth degree, to the point of simulation and parody.

In the 1980s, Baudrillard ecstatically uses theoretical texts (*Les stratégies fatales*), quasi-political treatises (*La gauche divine*), travelogues (*America*), simulated pastiches of his major works (*The Ecstasy of Communication*), memoirs (*Cool Memories*) and frequent articles and interviews to present his theoretical position. In these ecstasies Baudrillard constantly attempts to go beyond himself, to go further with his (same) ideas, to hyperrealize himself.

Indeed, many of the same critiques which Baudrillard makes of a society of simulations can be made of his own work. Baudrillard speaks of contemporary societies becoming more leukemic and losing their immune systems (*GD*, p. 119). But is Baudrillard's critique losing vigor and energy in the eternal simulation of the same? Is he losing his political-ideological immune system in letting sexism, racism, conservatism and other viral ideological infections run rampant? He speaks of intellectual critique passing from the position 'of herald of negativity and becoming the buffoon of dissidence' (*GD*, p. 132). But is Baudrillard becoming the buffoon of dissidence, the court jester of the societies on which he has chosen to comment? He concludes *La gauche divine* with the question: 'After the ecstasy, the hysteria of socialism?' (*GD*, p. 162). Yet are not Baudrillard's own oft-repeated prophecies and ecstasies increasingly hysterical themselves?

The ecstasy of Baudrillard is evident in his 1987 book, *Cool Memories.*[9] This glaciated collection of some of his travelogues, diaries and sexual and textual ecstasies of the years 1980–5 gather together a black mass of many of his greatest hits, his most theoretically acute and confessional passages, some of which I have discussed. (The entirety of 'What Are You Doing After the Orgy?', for instance, is here). It is not clear from the collection, however, whether it consists of his notebooks, which chronologically exhibit the laboratory of his thought and writings of the 1980s, or whether he has simply collected a potpourri of his most tasty delicacies of the decade, for his fans to admire and so as to seduce new readers into Baudrillardamania. His mania for simulation, however, leads one to suspect that it is a carefully calculated selection of texts aimed at seducing the maximum number of buyers. Indeed, the text has been his biggest sensation and best seller to date, allegedly seducing him to entrust his hitherto pure and virginal electrons to the fractal networks of the French broadcast media for the first time.

In addition, for the first time, Baudrillard opens his personal life to rather detailed inspection, and in a quasi-confessional mode (preparing himself for the Last Judgment?), tells us of his birth (*CM*, p. 180), confesses episodes of self-abuse while describing the ablutions of his toilet bowl (*CM*, p. 188), describes his sexual ecstasies with Thai prostitutes (*CM*, pp. 209–10) and (*auf Deutsch*) with a moist-lipped German woman ('Ich kam mir vor wie Arthur Miller in den Armen Marylin Monroes') (*CM*, p. 242), and in general gives a glimpse into his everyday life usually suppressed in his more semiological and metaphysical texts. But most interestingly, the book puts on display his cultural opportunism, his playing to the trends of the 1980s. In the 1980s there was a turn to the Right; and Baudrillard obliges with his critique of French socialism. In the 1980s, particularly in France, there was also a return to philosophy; and Baudrillard obliges with a metaphysical turn and in *Cool Memories* with groups of philosophical aphorisms à la Nietzsche or Adorno's *Minima Moralia* (with which Baudrillard's text could interestingly be compared – though I suspect that his immediate inspiration was Canetti's *The Human Provence*).[10] In the 1980s too, one aspect of the yuppie phenomenon involved hypernarcissistic concern with self and material pleasures; so Baudrillard obliges with self-confession, frequent references to travel, money, material goods and the upper-class concerns ecstatically celebrated in the 1980s.

The orgy is over, but Baudrillard hyperrealizes himself and implodes in ecstasy. *Cool Memories* is Baudrillard's ecstasy, his triumphant accession to pure commodification and self-fetishism. As a pure commodity the text sells itself as more Baudrillardian than Baudrillard: hyper-Baudrillard. The text is a triumph of marketing and packaging. Baudrillard hawks his wares with clever aphorisms, tantalizing morsels from his major 1980s texts and revealing personal asides which promote Baudrillard himself as a personality, as a seductive and fascinating object. *Cool Memories* glaciates Baudrillard's theory as slogans, repeating for the hundredth time his favorite *bon mots*: the Left is Divine; Reagan's smile is good; America is a realized utopia; society today is obscene, hyperreal, cynical and ecstatic; history is over and the year 2,000 won't happen. Fetishized into slogans, Baudrillard's thought becomes increasingly repetitive, obsessive and predictable.

So it appears that Baudrillard himself has become more and more like the object of his critique. I noted the beginning of this process earlier in the book where I claimed that Baudrillard's critique of advertising and the consumer society was becoming more and more like the object of the critique in its use of slogans, its hard-sell rhetoric and its attacks on competitors' products (1.4 and 5.4). Likewise, I believe that sometime around the period of *Les stratégies fatales*, Baudrillard chose to become ecstatic, hyperreal and a (hopefully seductive) simulation model himself – or he simply became this as a consequence of his particular mode of thought. Thereafter, he became a special effect, an ecstatic object, hyperreal. He also became a fetish object, an object of admiration and emulation, a sign of something new and exciting.[11] To conclude, citing Arthur Kroker:

> In his recent schizo-biography, Jean Baudrillard said this about the invasion of the body, under the double signs of the pleasure of catastrophe and the terror of the simulacrum, by the logic of exterminism – that is, the implosion of the postmodern body into an indifferent sign-slide between the hermetic self and the schizoid ego:
> 'And if reality under our eyes would suddenly dissolve? Not into nothingness, but into a real which is more than real (the triumph of simulation?). If the modern universe of communication, the space of hypercommunication through which we are plunging, not in forget-fulness, but with an enormous saturation of our senses, would consume us in its success – without trickery, without secrets, without distance? If all this mutation did not emanate, as some believe, from the manipulation of subjects and opinion, but from a logic without a subject where opinion vanishes into fascination? If it would no longer be correct to oppose truth to illusion, but to perceive generalized illusion as truer than truth? And if no other behavior was possible than that of learning ironically how to disappear? If there were no longer any fractures, lines of flight or ruptures, but a surface full and continuous, without depth, uninterrupted? And if all of this was neither a matter of enthusiasm nor despair, but fatal?'[12]

After the ecstasy of Baudrillard, hysteria?

No doubt. The question now arises: To what extent can Baudrillard's work even be considered as social theory? Or is it something altogether different?

Science Fiction or Social Theory?

In the introduction to *The Left Hand of Darkness*, Ursula Le Guin writes: 'Science fiction is often described and even defined, as extrapolative. The science fiction writer is supposed to take a trend or phenomenon of the here-and-now, purify and intensify it for dramatic effect and extend it into the future. "If this goes on, this is what will happen." '[13]

From this perspective, I would suggest that while Baudrillard's texts are arguably quite good science fiction, they are rather problematical as models of social theory. Like a good science fiction writer, Baudrillard often illuminates aspects of reality frequently overlooked, by utilizing the vantage point of a future intensification of present social trends. He provides a new way of looking and an imaginative vision of a hypermodern society mutating and metamorphosing so rapidly that social theory must be constantly on the run to keep up with current developments and rapid change. Probably Baudrillard is at his most useful in illuminating trends of social development which may be actualized in the near future, or perhaps sooner.

One can thus read Baudrillard as providing some great dystopic fiction, in the tradition of *1984* and *Brave New World*, which takes current trends to possible conclusions, and provides instructive warnings about certain social tendencies and phenomena. Yet – and this is why he is a problematical social theorist – *Baudrillard takes current trends and possibilities as finalities, treating tendencies as realized states*. Moreover, his futuristic theory overlooks and neglects many aspects of our current social experience. I have already noted the omissions in his media theory (3.2) and his erasure of materiality (noted throughout these studies). Consequently his thought is too futuristic to capture many aspects of our current social situation – namely, the continued hegemony of capital, the political hegemony of the New Right and so on.

Although occasionally Baudrillard himself uses the term 'science fiction' to describe his works, and, quite accurately identifies his theory as pataphysics in the tradition of Alfred Jarry (see 6.1), he also claims to be articulating the fundamental social processes of the day, to be providing an account of what is really going on, an accurate description of the present age. Over and over again, one encounters such 'realist' passages and claims in his texts, as when he claims in 'Forget Baudrillard' that his analysis of the hyperreality and ecstasies of politics today 'does after all correspond more to the way things are evolving nowadays.'[14] In 'Nuclear Implosion' he makes a similar claim, arguing that 'This logic seems more interesting to me because it corresponds more to the evolution of things today.'[15] In the article 'The

Year 2000 Has Already Happened,' he admits that his text is a simulation model, and then adds: 'I am no longer in a state of "reflecting" something, I can only myself push hypotheses to their limit, to extract them from their critical zone of reference, to make them cross a point of no return. I am thus making theory also pass into the hyperspace of simulation in which it loses all objective reality but perhaps gains in coherence – that is to say *in a real affinity with the system that surrounds us.*[16]

Further, *La gauche divine* is full of claims that he is providing a true, accurate account of actual changes taking place in today's society that are missed by conventional social theory. He writes, for instance: 'Many things have changed. There are no more children destined to obey, there are no more women destined to be possessed, there are no more objects destined to be analyzed in science [remember: they are now in permanent rebellion], there are even no more masses or people destined to be represented' (*GD*, p. 110). Thus Baudrillard consistently makes 'realist' claims about what is going on in society, and even offers vast historical panoramas and totalizing representations of entire historical periods.[17]

Furthermore, Baudrillard claims ever more frequently to speak for the masses, and assumes that he knows exactly what 'they' want. Frequently he includes himself in their category, and uses the term 'we' to express their supposedly common refusal of demands by society or the political class, claiming, for instance, in the face of demands to participate in the information and computer society, that 'we are fatigued in advance and perplexed' (*GD*, p. 121). In fact like everyone else, Baudrillard speaks solely for himself. Yet with ever more frequency and audacity, he claims to speak for the masses, for the way things are, for the march (or end) of history itself. Taking over a Hegelian position as the scribe for the *Zeitgeist*, Baudrillard purports to be giving tips for hot investments into the current social and political trajectory. Over and over, he proclaims the end of something and the beginning of a new era, though his mode of presentation is generally in terms of an apodictic declaration rather than a historical description or narrative.

In *La gauche divine*, for example, he announces the end of the consumer society and its replacement by the information society. While the consumer society offered a grand spectacle of commodities ('a sweet folly of objects and needs' and the 'discrete charm of alienation'), accompanied by an exciting political scene,

> the new society promises to function in a quite different glacial and non-spectacular manner. Operationality has replaced usage, the contact, the networking and the promiscuity of information replace the prestiges of transcendence (of which theoretical and critical analysis was part). Absolute and excessive promiscuity. The simultaneity of all points of space, of time, of people under the sign of the

instantaneity of light: no more language. No more surface (ah, was not
the surface beautiful in the time of depth!), no more distance (wasn't
proximity beautiful in the time of distance!), no more appearance, no
more dimensions [but rather] interface and transparency. One speaks
of the closeness (*proxemique*) of human relations. It is better instead to
speak of the *procuring (proxenetique) of information*, of flux, of
circuits, which institute a proximity of all places, of all human beings
related to each other, the circularity of questions and of responses, of
problems and of their solutions. The scatology of information:
the dream of an absolute conductability can only be excremental.
(*GD*, p. 145)

Note once again how Baudrillard is implicitly claiming to provide insight
into actual changes taking place in society, thus presenting his work as a
theory of contemporary society, rather than a science fiction projection of a
possible future. Note also how he steadfastly refuses to countenance the
possibility that there may be something liberating in these new networks and
apparatuses of information, seeing only 'a fantastic promise and a derisory
result' (*GD*, p. 144). Or worse:

information, the excess of information upon us is a sort of electro-
cution. It produces a sort of continual short-circuit where the
individual burns its circuits and loses its defenses. The deep immunity
of a being resides in its non-transitivity, in its non-conductability in
the multiple fluxes which surround it, in its secret and the ignorance
where it is of its own secret – it is not by chance that today everywhere
the loss of immune defenses coincides with the excess of information.
(*GD*, pp. 145–6)

Let us reflect a bit on this passage. Note the negative evaluation of the
implementation of high-tech information technologies and the excessive
claims concerning their effects. As is so often the case, Baudrillard takes
trends and possibilities and presents them as actualities – usually frightening
ones. Note too the use of medical analogies to describe technological
processes, and the implicit assumption that such technologies are unhealthy
for one's body (one's immune system), as well as for one's mode of life (one
loses one's secret; and it appears that the possibility of having secrets is
becoming a particularly central value for Baudrillard's metaphysical universe).
As social theory, such description and evaluation are highly dubious. Yet,
taken as science fiction or pataphysics, Baudrillard's thought provides useful
warnings concerning what might be taking place and what might happen in
the future – though Baudrillard is short on prescriptions for how to prevent
the worst.

For example, after expressing his (exaggerated? groundless?) fear of
immune system burnout in information circuits and the loss of space for

secrets, Baudrillard suggests some of the ways in which the 'fatality' of information networks might bring about new demands and anxieties for those new human terminals who are being plugged into the information society. While 'that marvelous information and cybernetic culture' – note the sarcasm – might provide new opportunities for play, happiness and life, it requires that individuals learn how to survive in a new aleatory society in which everything is always changing. This

> game is supremely exciting for the privileged strata of the infoculture, but not necessarily for the rest, for the mass of others, who risk quite simply finding themselves thrown into a computerized Third World, which will exhaust itself trying to find an ideal autonomy in the management of its own affairs – for that is the form of 'liberty' in an indeterminate universe. This modern, or 'postmodern', form of liberty is eventually unacceptable. The responsibility of each individual before the probabilistic management of their own life, before their own permanent recycling, is eventually unacceptable. (*GD*, pp. 146–7)

No doubt full development of the information society – if, indeed, it does become fully realized – will create new anxieties, challenges, resistance and intense changes; but Baudrillard is projecting a possible social development as an actuality, and is claiming to speak for the masses in declaring that the whole project is 'unacceptable.' Yet his account is completely undialectical, and fails to uncover anything very useful, progressive or beneficial in the new technologies and the impact they are having. In a sense Baudrillard thus provides the inverse of McLuhan's theory of the media and of theories of the post-industrial society. While McLuhan and the ideologues of the post-industrial society celebrate the new media and information technologies as purely progressive forces, with purely (or largely) beneficial results, Baudrillard sees them as producing predominantly, if not completely, baleful results.

In *La gauche divine*, Baudrillard also tells the story of the end of bureaucracy, the end of the State, which he says everyone will be happy to see go, but then he goes on to say that this will be 'without doubt in the profit of another abomination – that of change, of communication, of information and performance at all costs' (*GD*, pp. 147–8). While on the one hand, Baudrillard seems to be naively proclaiming the end of the state and bureaucracy; on the other hand, he seems unjustifiably pessimistic in assuming that the allegedly new information society will be an 'abomination' just as wretched as the previous consumer or bureaucratic society. In fact, it is not yet certain if an information society will emerge, what form it will take, and what its benefits and costs will be. Yet Baudrillard claims that it is already here, and that the outcome is suffocation, a new mood which appears to add itself to his psychotropic repertoire of giddiness, vertigo, anxiety and the rest. As we approach the year 2,000, he claims, exhaustion and indifference are intensifying:

> The euphoria of the new information society does not succeed in masking that mental recession in indifference, that slowing down of time. . . . It is as if we are, as in [the novel/film] *2001*, voyagers in space at rest in a coma, under the surveillance of a master computer. The information, the communication, maintains the social body in a state of survival, all the vital functions continue – circulation, respiration, metabolism, cardiac tonus, regeneration of cells – exactly as for the biophysical functions of the passengers in a vessel. But life is simply not there anymore. In our societies in a way, life is no longer there either but information and the vital functions continue. . . . It's true: our societies are changing. It is no longer so much the police atmosphere which weighs on us, nor the servitude of work, it is the performative atmosphere which we are getting fed up with, *qui nous pompe l'air*. Literally, the euphoria, the dumping, the acceleration, absorb all ambient oxygen and leave us without respiration, as fish on the beach. It's not hope, liberty, or objectives that are missing, but air. (*GD*, pp. 160–1).

When the chips are down and Baudrillard is trying to play his best hand, he uses a Nietzschean category, this time, *life* to trump the information society. We are being robbed of life and air; Baudrillard is forced to revert to a biophysical metaphor for his critical position. For an ecological theory, such a standpoint would make perfect sense, but Baudrillard constantly rejects and makes fun of ecological theories and politics, and is thus forced to revert to an image of himself choking to death in asphyxiation to win sympathy and support for his theories. Poor Baudrillard! The theorist of the new order ends up suffocating just when he is about to reveal the trajectory to and beyond the year 2,000!

The point that I am trying to make is that Baudrillard actually – and frequently – claims that his theory *does* provide an account of present-day social conditions, that it is more than mere science fiction or amusing pataphysics. Moreover, he also claims to provide metaphysical insights into the very order of things. We have noted frequently his assumption of a Bataillean anthropology and Mandevillean-Machiavellian metaphysics of the political grounded in a certain conservative theory of human nature, and in the last chapter we analyzed his curious subject-object metaphysics (agonistics). Indeed, the only fundamental domains of contemporary life which he does not essentialize are the economic sphere, which he simply ignores, because he thinks that nothing important happens there, and the social, because it has disappeared and perhaps never existed. (He thus robs his academic discipline of sociology of its subject matter. No doubt this is

Baudrillard's revenge on his discipline, and his 'gift' and 'challenge' to his fellow sociologists.)

Baudrillard thus wavers between a skeptical epistemology which denies the very possibility of access to the real – let alone a metatheory of how this might be possible – and declarative revelations and ecstasies which supposedly cue us in to what is really happening in the world today. In general, Baudrillard's texts of the 1980s become increasingly exaggerated, metaphysical and hyperbolic in the ubiquitous and fantastic roles that he assigns to the media, information and semiurgy in the society of simulations. He repeats incessantly his main ideas, trying to drive them further, beyond themselves, but ends up simply becoming increasingly tiresome. It appears, therefore, that Baudrillard's thought has reached an impasse, and it is this impasse that I shall attempt to describe in the next section.

Ennui and Fin de Siècle Exhaustion

In his 1980s writings, Baudrillard becomes increasingly obsessed with the up coming end of the century, with the approach of the year 2,000.[18] As the end of the century draws nearer he seems to be becoming more cynical, more exhausted, more iconoclastic and more burned-out. This disposition – quite widespread today – is reminiscent of fin de siècle exhaustion at the end of the nineteenth century, then associated with a period of cultural exhaustion, decadence and ennui.[19] In attaching himself to a tradition of French aestheticism, Baudrillard thus draws on – that is, hyperrealizes – an all too familiar cultural trope, which he tries to resurrect for its effects and exchange value.

Baudrillard's fin-de-siècle exhaustion and theoretical impasse is clearly revealed in two 1980s texts: the article 'The Year 2000 Has Already Happened' and the book *Cool Memories*.[20] In the article, Baudrillard writes once again of his fascination with Canetti's notion of the end of history, and proposes three different interpretations as to how this might have occurred. His first hypothesis derives from astrophysics, and has to do with the possibility that the increasing speed with which the universe is expanding will accelerate the movement of history to such an extent that it will eventually vanish 'into a hyperspace where it loses all meaning' (p. 36). His second hypothesis also derives from the physical sciences, but the scenario proposed is the inverse of the first. Drawing on the concept of entropy, Baudrillard suggests that if society, the masses, reach a state of absolute passivity, boredom and so on, history will implode into a state of inertia (pp. 37ff.). His third hypothesis derives from technology, and suggests that in a situation of technological perfection, entities will cease being what they were previously. Thus music, as we presently know it could conceivably disappear as stereophonic perfection increases. Other phenomena could similarly disappear as they become perfected. As a result, we would enter a qualitatively new field of experience, as we left the realm of history for that of simulation (p. 40).

Baudrillard then suggests that history may always have been a simulation, that it never really existed, and that we face a new, futureless future in which no decisive event can await us, because all is finished, perfected and doomed to infinite repetition: the eternal recurrence of the same as the fate of the West. He suggests that frenetic attempts to gather and circulate information and to record historical events are simply symptomatic of a desperate awareness that there is no more history to come, that we are frozen in a glacial present in which time is annihilated (p. 43). He concludes: 'It remains for us to accommodate ourselves to the time left to us, which is seemingly emptied of sense by this reversal. The end of this century is before us like an empty beach' (p. 44).

The article 'The Year 2000' thus reveals Baudrillard's thought as being frozen in static images of the end of history, obsessively fixated on a vision of stasis, entropy and sterile repetition: precisely the modality of his own work of the 1980s so far. The last several pages of *Cool Memories* also clearly reveal his theoretical impasse, although they offer some faint hope that he might be considering some new theoretical directions and developments. In the midst of his reflections on such things as Rome, the ideal woman and seduction, Baudrillard offers some reflections on the end of the world: 'End of the Roman Empire, end of the Middle Ages. The ambiance of the end of the world, the millennial ambiance frenetically brings together the sexes or irremediably distances them' (*CM*, p. 284). The passage was written during 1985, at the time of 'The End of the World' conference in New York, which reportedly found Baudrillard in a particularly funky mood of gloom and doom. He reports on the conference in his journal:

> Small tribal ceremony among intellectuals, on Fifth Avenue, to speak of the end of the world. The idea might seem marvelous to speak of it precisely in New York, which is the epicenter of the world. Yet upon reflection, this makes no sense, for New York is already the end of the world and it makes no sense to reflect it in miniature within a scenario strikingly inferior to its model. Except, precisely the demand to save *the idea* of the end of the world from the real event – this is the habitual work of intellectuals. (*CM*, p. 286)

Baudrillard next reflects on the Challenger disaster and Chernobyl, and then suggests that contemporary disasters are mere holograms or simulacra (ibid.). He recounts a dream of being in a mysterious asylum and of being mad in a previous lifetime, and then provides what might be taken as a poetic expression of his current state of mind:

Rire de la femelle
Spectre du rire rale de la femelle
rire intermittent d'une spectatrice albinos
Sexe transparent d'une spectatrice femelle
Fin du monde dans la Cinquième Avenue
prurit du collapse
collapse du prurit
Fistules ontologiques   Billevesées
Lèvres impures   lèvres expures
Ethique de l'agonie. (*CM*, p. 287)

This verse reflects the despair and sense of collapse and hopelessness which have come to pervade Baudrillard's works, and the three passages which follow indicate that he has definitely come to the end of a theoretical trajectory and is uncertain where to go next. He tells of how he has just completed a cycle of projects, and for the first time in ten or twenty years has nothing to do (*CM*, p. 288). Then he writes: 'There are things of which one can no longer speak or not yet speak of again: Marxism? There are other things of which one cannot speak yet, or can speak no longer, because their phantom runs already through the streets, their shadow precedes them. Information, communication?' (*CM*, p. 289). Another prose poem follows this passage, and its conclusion reveals Baudrillard's quandary: 'Where to go? Berlin? Vancouver? Samarkande?' (*CM*, p. 290).

The text thus ends with a question suggesting boredom with previous trajectories and terrains, and uncertainty as to his directions. But the collapse of Baudrillard's theoretical enterprise also points to possibilities for new openings and developments. Baudrillard has shown himself to be theoretically resilient and capable of surprising new ventures. Thus it is possible that he will emerge from his current ennui and malaise, and produce some exciting new theoretical perspectives.[21] Baudrillard's project is still open and unfinished and it is to be hoped that he will have some new surprises for us.

7.3   FOR RADICAL SOCIAL THEORY AND POLITICS

Les stratégies fatales is Baudrillard's last serious theoretical work. His succeeding works either repeat or even pastiche previous positions (*La gauche divine* and *L'Autre par lui-même*) or abandon the form of theoretical argumentation altogether in favor of the genres of travel reports (*America*) or memoirs (*Cool Memories*) which revel in random asides, personal observations and aphoristic insights. Those readers who journey through Baudrillard's writings encounter the same theory-scape, first set forth in his metaphysical ob-scenario *Les stratégies fatales* and then replayed and recycled in succeeding interviews, travelogues, notebooks and essays. His writings thus take on a 'postmodern' style which pastiches previous texts (his own), mixes together various subject matters, and eventually provides a frozen, glaciated hyperrealization of texts increasingly more Baudrillardian than Baudrillard, in which he provides his own model which is endlessly reproduced.

Baudrillard's articles after *Cool Memories* tend to be eccentric commentaries on issues of current interest, such as Heidegger and the Nazis, drugs, the 1986 French student movement, the 1987 stock market crash and contemporary art. These articles combine some acute sociological insight with clichéd commonplaces, repetitions of his pet ideas, and downright distortions and sophistries. For instance, in reflections on the 1986 French student movement which forced Jacques Chirac to abandon some proposed 'reforms' (that is, cutbacks), Baudrillard opens with the accurate – albeit obvious – observation that this new movement is primarily 'positive' and 'soft,' and abandons the negativity and radicalism of past student movements. These 'children of advertising, the media generation,' speak the language of advertising and media, and this informs their 'politics.' So far, so good; but then Baudrillard comments: 'In advertising, there are no negatives; even when irony's involved, everything is positive and affirmative. In present-day society, as in the images that bind it together, the negative is absent.'[22]

Such an interpretation of advertising is completely false, however. Much advertising plays on – even creates – negative fears, and also frequently presents competitors' products as negative (the famous advertising wars which were highly visible in the United States in the 1980s). Political advertising, too, often uses 'negative advertising,' which was claimed to be the decisive force in the American presidential election of 1988, in which Bush used viciously negative advertising against Dukakis. Indeed, negative fears have been a predominant feature of United States politics in the 1980s, ranging from the highly trumpeted fears of communism and terrorism which defined the foreign policy of the Reagan administration at least until 1987, to fear of welfare cheats, governmental regulation, AIDS, illegal immigrants and countless other 'negative' phenomena utilized by the conservative government. Liberals and Democrats, by contrast, often played on fears of unemployment, of a worsening economy, of loss of civil liberties, and of a decline in the middle- and working-class standard of living under the conservative hegemony. So, at least as far as the United States is concerned, Baudrillard's comments on advertising, politics and positivity are completely off the wall.

This is symptomatic of Baudrillard's work of the late 1980s, which combines some incisive observation with repetition of pet ideas and sheer nonsense. He does not provide any significant new perspectives or ideas; nor does he adequately develop his observations into a fully developed theory of the contemporary stage of neo-capitalism. There are several important reasons why Baudrillard is unable to provide an adequate theory of the contours of contemporary society or of the alleged transition to post-modernity. First, his embrace of the thesis of the 'end of history' makes it difficult – perhaps theoretically impossible – to provide a historical narrative of such an epochal transformation (though I have suggested that in fact he is not averse to providing such narratives, at least for the previous period of modernity).[23] Doctrines of the 'end of history' rule out in advance the possibility of either historical contextualization, further historical development or rupture (of the sort presupposed by theories of social progress or revolution), and historical determination and causality. All these traditional features of history and historical consciousness disappear in Baudrillard's aleatory, vertiginous, indeterminate postmodern world of simulations, codes, hyperreality and so on.

Interestingly, such postmodern theories of the end of history share a lineage with certain conservative, postindustrial theories which make similar claims. As Claus Offe points out, theories of *'post-historie,'* such as those of the conservative German sociologists Gehlen and Schelsky, rule out the possibility of future global alternatives, or of examining developments of the 'technological society' which these theorists, along with Baudrillard, see as the fate of the West.[24] These theories utilize a model of a self-reproducing, perfected apparatus of control and functionality similar to that maintained by celebrants of the technological or cybernetic society and Baudrillard. In this way, the 'radical' Baudrillard aligns himself with a conservative tradition of critique of 'mass' or 'technological' society.

I have indicated that Elias Canetti is Baudrillard's most frequently cited source for the theory of the end of history, and in fact, Baudrillard's theory is coming to resemble Canetti's position more and more. Baudrillard shares with Canetti and a conservative tradition a cynical, metaphysical view of human nature, society and politics, which focuses on the selfish, 'evil' and unchanging features of human beings and society. Like Canetti and the conservative tradition of theories of mass society, he sees society as a chaotic conjunction of 'masses' and 'crowds' – although he presents a more volatilized and pulverized theory of power (see 5.2) than Canetti whose theory is more structured, centered and determinate.[25] Like Canetti and the tradition of conservative individualism, Baudrillard's own thought and writing are becoming ever more idiosyncratic, blending some traditional conservative positions with Jarry's pataphysics and the cynical, amoral nihilism of a French aesthetic and bohemian tradition that includes Sade, Baudelaire, Artaud and French Nietzscheans like Bataille.

Thus Baudrillard replays some traditional conservative positions with his own peculiar metaphysical twists and high-tech glosses. But can radical social theory and politics do without a theory of history? Is 'history' in fact something that can come to an end, that the human race can escape? Or is history that realm of necessity, materiality, the force of circumstances, institutions, power, events and developments that we cannot evade? Can one do social theory without historical contextualization and analysis to provide perspective and illumination of contemporary events? Is social theory not intrinsically historical and are not the categories of social theory intrinsically historical?[26] Further, is not history the terrain of radical politics, of projects of change and transformation?

Radical social theory and politics thus seem intrinsically bound with history as their context and conditions of possibility. Radical social theory also requires empirical research into conditions, tendencies and developments of the present age, and here too Baudrillard's work is deficient, becoming ever more sketchy and incomplete. If he had engaged in more patient description of the media and popular culture, cybernetics, architecture and social planning, design and semiosis, he could have developed a more powerful theory of social and cultural hegemony in the present age (although this would have to be supplemented by accounts of opposition, conflict and emancipation if it were to be genuinely progressive and useful for radical theory and politics today). I would also see his later writings as weakened through neglect of the dynamics of commodities and consumption, to which he paid attention in his earlier work; for, as we have seen, he explicitly claims that the era of the consumer society is over (one of his most problematical allegations). This rejection of the problematic of the consumer society is strange, given that one of Baudrillard's major contributions is his study of the life of signs in society. His earlier notion of a critique of the political economy of signs is extremely important, as is his notion of the importance of sign value as a constitutive of the commodity, which takes on fundamental importance in the consumer society. Yet when he turned to his study of the society of simulations, he immediately dropped his studies of the consumer society; and in *La gauche divine* he states that the era of the consumer society is over, and that we are now in a new social order altogether. This is a highly doubtful allegation, and it seems to me that one of the major flaws in Baudrillard's trajectory is the rupture between his critique of the political economy of the sign and his later theory of simulations which proclaims – prematurely, one would think – the end of the era of production and the end of political economy.

Instead, it would seem preferable to theorize the ways in which simulation and commodification, media and political economy, technology and capital, the information society and the consumer society are inextricably inter-connected in our current social constellation.[27]

Baudrillard, by contrast, abstracts from political economy and concrete, empirical, historical reality which he claims have all disappeared in the mutation into a postmodern society. For example, in his reflections on the 1987 stock market crash, Baudrillard argues that there cannot be a '*real* catastrophe' of the economy because the economy today is purely 'fictional' and 'virtual catastrophe,' a blip in the circuit of imaginary, fictive capital. Once again, he repeats his slogans concerning the end of political economy, claiming that: 'Political economy now expires before our very own eyes, disappeared by its own self-mutation into a speculative transeconomy which undermines its productivist logic . . . and which no longer has anything to do with either the economic or the political – a pure game of floating and arbitrary rules.'[28] Baudrillard claims that: 'For us, this is the real state of things, this is the only reality we can be *objectively* concerned with: an unbridled orbital round of capital which, even if it crashes, doesn't produce any substantial disequilibrium in the real economy (contrary to the crash of '29, where the disconnection of the fictive economy and the real economy was far from being accomplished; and where, therefore, one catastrophe had serious repercussions for the other)' (ibid). Note here how he claims to be both giving insights into the 'real' state of affairs of contemporary society and how he claims that there is an absolute rupture between the current situation and the previous stage of society and that this rupture involves the 'end of political economy.'

Equally problematical is his rejection of Debord's notion of the society of the spectacle in a society which continues to thrive on commodity, media and political spectacles. Baudrillard claims that there are no more scenes, spectacles or secrets in the obscene society of information. Once again he is reading a future possibility and social development into the present, and is overlooking the extent to which spectacle continues to play a crucial role in politics, the media and social life, in a society in which our ruling classes, as well as private individuals, continue to have and protect their 'secrets.' Baudrillard to the contrary, there are arguably spectacles, scenes and secrets that continue to constitute our contemporary societies.[29]

Consequently it appears at this point that Baudrillard's radical critique of the categories of political economy, Marxism, sociology and so on has ended up in a cul-de-sac from which he seems to deny the very possibility of social theory or social transformation. 'Implosion' collapses social phenomena into one another, in such a way that it is impossible to distinguish between media and reality, classes and masses, simulations and realities, forces and relations of production, and so forth. Moreover, in such a totally cyberneticized, rationalized society, resistance and revolt are a 'mirage,' and social transformation is an 'illusion' (two of Baudrillard's favorite terms). Thus, consistent with this bleak picture, Baudrillard no longer poses *any* social alternative, resistance, struggle or refusal.

What is most distressing with regard to Baudrillard's current excursions into transpolitics and pataphysics is that, now, more than ever, critical, reconstructive intervention into the field of radical social theory and politics is needed. The social movements and theoretical efforts of the last two decades have not achieved the goals set by the radical movements of the 1960s, though I, for one, am not ready to throw in the towel and declare that our projects were illusions and not worthwhile. Nevertheless, we have learned – and here Baudrillard has something to teach us – that much established social theory and politics of the last two decades is highly flawed, and fails to conceptualize the new social conditions and experiences of our epoch. In other words, we need new theories, ideas and politics to get us out of the morass of the present (of which Baudrillard is an instructive symptom) into a better future. If it is true, as many people are now coming to believe, that we are living in an era of transition from one epoch to another, in which previous boundaries in our theories and social worlds no longer hold, then we need new maps of the social world and new political strategies to produce a better world.

Baudrillard is of some help here, but I fear that he may well turn out to be an impediment, because his map points to a future world that may never arrive and fails to account for too many aspects of the old order which are still around – in particular, capital, the Right and a conservative academy unwilling to question its beliefs and practices and to surrender its privileges. It is striking that Baudrillard has spent much effort attacking the Left in recent years, but has not to my knowledge expended much, if any, energy in attacking the Right. This constitutes a major failure and aporia of his project, since the Right has been hegemonic in the United States, Britain and many other countries over the past decade, including his own France, despite the French Socialists' efforts, which Baudrillard totally scorns, without offering any insight into the difficulties entailed in constructing socialism in neo-capitalist countries. Against Baudrillard's indifference and cynicism, I would suggest that a major task for critical social theory today is a critique of conservative ideology and politics in order to prepare the way for a renewal of the Left. To be sure, the Left has labored under many illusions in the past – including a revolutionary proletariat, the certainty of socialism and a belief that socialism will automatically produce disalienation. But it seems too early to surrender belief in the socialist project and the Left – which effectively means surrender to the hegemony of the Right until the day when another, better alternative arrives.

In political terms, this is what I believe Baudrillard's project comes down to ultimately: capitulation to the hegemony of the Right and a secret complicity with aristocratic conservativism. Of course, Baudrillard would retort that the very categories of Left and Right no longer mean anything, and that politics has been undermined and contorted by media simulations. This view may be comforting to a critical critic in his Paris apartment who no longer wants to go out and do battle in the public sphere, but it will not help the millions being harmed, even killed, as a result of the domestic and foreign policies of the Reagans, Bushes, Thatchers, Bothas and Pinochets of the world.

From the perspective of those of us who want to leave behind the era of conservativism inflicted upon us for the past decade, Baudrillard's earlier attempts at the reconstruction of political economy, social theory, Marxism and social struggle and resistance have ended in a questionable and arguably reactionary attempt to demolish social theory, political economy and radical politics altogether. Unlike Critical Theorists such as Marcuse or Habermas or some of Baudrillard's French contemporaries who attempt to criticize the productivist version of radical social theory and to reconstruct radical social theory and politics in the contemporary era, Baudrillard wildly attacks all radical social theory and politics as his transpolitical pataphysics flies ever higher into orbit. Now there may be problems with the various radical critiques and politics of the last two decades, but this attitude of wholesale dismissal does not seem to be a helpful or appropriate response to limitations of the radical tradition.

Since Baudrillard is distancing himself from the radical tradition anyway, it may seem inappropriate to criticize him in terms of that tradition; but the fact is that Baudrillard is still read and received as a political radical, and those who are becoming increasingly attracted to his thought generally perceive themselves as 'radicals' of some sort. Seen within the context of the radical tradition, I have suggested that Baudrillard is the latest example of critical criticism which criticizes everything, but rarely affirms anything of much danger to the status quo. Ultimately Baudrillard is both safe and harmless. A court jester of the society he mocks, he safely simulates criticism, advertises his wares and proceeds to enjoy the follies of the consumer and media society.

Finally, I would conclude that Baudrillard's project is vitiated by the absence of a theory of agency and mediation. His theory has always bordered on, and sometimes affirmed, social determinism, whereby the code, social engineering and control or objects come to dominate the thought and behavior of subjects, who might have illusions about their sovereignty over the object world, but who are really its slaves. However, a *political* theory – a theory of struggle and political change – depends critically on a theory of political agency; yet the impossibility of any sort of agent of political change becomes a central position within Baudrillard's theorizing.

Likewise, he denies the reality or significance of mediation. Against this, I would argue for the centrality of dialectics and mediation in both radical social theory and politics. Critical social theory has traditionally analyzed the mediations between the economic base and the entire infrastructure. But for Baudrillard in a curious fashion, all these mediations disappear in an amorphous play of simulations and implosion, and then in the metaphysical triumph of the object over the subject.

While it is too early to sum up definitively the contributions and deficiencies of a work still in process, at present it appears to me that Baudrillard's work points to the failure of a type of French ultra-radicalism typical of the late 1960s to bring about significant social change and to its subsequent disillusionment and turn to either the Right or apolitical cynicism. Now Baudrillard might get out of his current malaise, and produce something of value for radical theory and politics. Yet I fear that he has fantasized himself into a repetitive metaphysical orbit with no apparent exit, and that, unless a dramatic reversal appears, his work will become ever more bizarre, trivial, reactionary and pataphysical.

Nonetheless, the appeal of Baudrillard's thinking might suggest that we *are* living in a transitional situation whereby new social conditions are putting into question the old orthodoxies and boundaries. Baudrillard is most valuable at this point, at least as a provocateur who forces us to question conventional wisdom and to rethink contemporary radical social theory and politics in the light of current, new, constantly changing sociohistorical conditions. But though I am willing to concede that we are living in an age of transition and dramatic change, I am not sure that we have now transcended and left behind modernity, class politics, labor and production, imperialism, fascism and the phenomena described by classical and neo-Marxism, as well as by other political and social theories which Baudrillard rejects out of hand. From this vantage point, Baudrillard can be criticized as part of the tradition of 'postindustrial society' which exaggerates the extent to which we have entered a Brave New World in ways that cover over the continued existence of the bad old one. Consequently, I would propose that we go beyond Baudrillard and the fashions of new-wave postmodernism and recognize the limitations of these modes of thought and action and the need for more creative syntheses of the old and the new which will help us to create a better future, rather than to fall into the abyss which lies ahead of us and to the right.

Notes

1 See inter alia, Arthur Kroker and Charles Levin, 'Baudrillard's Challenge,' *Canadian Journal of Political and Social Theory*, 8, nos.1–2 (1984), p. 6. On the Australian reception of Baudrillard, see Alan Frankovits, ed., *Seduced and Abandoned: The Baudrillard Scene* (Glebe, Australia: Stonemoss, 1984); and for the German reception, see the discussions between Baudrillard and a group of Germans in *Der Tod der Moderne*, ed. Heidrun Hesse (Tübingen: Konkursbuch-verlag, 1983).

2 Up to the present, Baudrillard has been seriously neglected in the major works which survey the contemporary French intellectual scene – and in particular the vicissitudes of Marxism, structuralism, semiotics and poststructuralism. For instance, in the following books on contemporary French thought which deal with his cohorts, Baudrillard is barely mentioned, if at all: Mark Poster, *Existential Marxism in Postwar France* (Princeton: Princeton University Press, 1975); Dick Howard, *The Marxian Legacy* (New York: Urizen, 1977); Rosalind Coward and John Ellis, *Language and Materialism* (London: Routledge & Kegan Paul, 1977); Edith Kurzweil, *The Age of Structuralism* (New York: Columbia University Press, 1980); Arthur Hirsch, *The French New Left* (Boston: South End Press, 1981); Perry Anderson, *In the Tracks of Historical Materialism* (London: New Left Books, 1983); Luc Ferry and Alain Renaut, *La Pensée 68. Essai sur L'anti-humanisme contemporain* (Paris: Gallimard, 1985), and Peter Dews, *Logics of Disintegration* (London: New Left Books, 1987). And when Baudrillard *is* mentioned, he is often characterized in extremely misleading ways: Poster refers to his work as an attempt to synthesize Sartrean existential phenomenoloy with structural Marxism (*Existential Marxism*, p. 360), while Kurzweil in her only reference labels him a ' "Hegelian" sociologist.' But there is little that is 'Hegelian' (even in quotes), Sartrean or structuralist Marxist about Baudrillard's writing; indeed, he contests all these currents.

Furthermore, as of this writing, I have found almost no comprehensive critiques of Baudrillard's work. The introductions to the English translations of *The Mirror of Production* and *For A Critique of the Political Economy of the Sign* tend to be laudatory in nature, and there has been little critical discussion of

Baudrillard's work in the many articles on him in English that I have examined. Perhaps this is because there has been little presentation of his challenges to Marxism, classical political economy and sociology, psychoanalysis, semiology, and so forth, and not much in the way of sustained response to his criticisms of the established positions in these areas. Likewise, there have been no critiques of his use – or misuse – of semiology, anthropology, Bataille, Nietzsche and others.

3 See Poster, *Existential Marxism*; Hirsch, *French New Left*; and Coward and Ellis, *Language and Materialism*.

4 John Ardagh, *The New French Revolution* (New York: Harper and Row, 1968).

5 Ardagh, *New French Revolution*; Poster, *Existential Marxism*; Henri Lefebvre, who published various volumes and editions of his multivolume *La vie quotidienne dans le monde moderne* in 1947, 1958, 1961 and 1968, a text that was translated into English as *Everyday Life in the Modern World* (New York: Harper and Row, 1971).

6 Roland Barthes, *Mythologies* (New York: Hill and Wang, 1962; orig. 1957), p. 9.

7 On the new theories of language and discourse, see Fredric Jameson, *The Prison House of Language* (Princeton: Princeton University Press, 1972), and Coward and Ellis, *Language and Materialism*.

8 Lefebvre, *Everyday Life*.

9 On Lefebvre's political interventions, see Poster, *Existential Marxism*.

10 See Lefebvre's critique of structuralism in *Au-delà du structuralisme* (Paris: Anthropos, 1971).

11 See Guy Debord, *The Society of the Spectacle* (Detroit: Black and Red, 1976), discussed in Poster, *Existential Marxism*; Hirsch, *French New Left*; and Steven Best, 'The Commodification of Reality and the Reality of Commodification: Baudrillard and Postmodernism,' *Critical Perspectives in Social Theory*, 9, (forthcoming, 1989).

12 Baudrillard's translations from the 1960s include Peter Weiss's *Marat/Sade*, *Discourse on Vietnam* and other plays such as Brecht's *Dialogues d'exilés* and a text on messianic theories of Third World revolution: Wilhelm E. Muhlmann, *Messianismes révolutionnaires du tiers monde* (Paris: Gallimard, 1968). He also edited a photography collection published as *Les Allemands: photographies de Réne Burri* (Paris: Delpire, 1963).

13 See Henri Lefebvre, *The Explosion* (New York: Monthly Review Press, 1969), and the discussion of the political context in George Ross, *Workers and Communists in France* (Berkeley: University of California Press, 1982).

14 Charles Levin, 'Baudrillard, Critical Theory and Psychoanalysis,' *Canadian Journal of Political and Social Theory*, 7, nos. 1–2 (1984), p. 36.

CHAPTER I   COMMODITIES, NEEDS AND CONSUMPTION IN THE
CONSUMER SOCIETY

1 Jean Baudrillard, *Le système des objets* (Paris: Denoel-Gonthier, 1968); *La société de consommation* (Paris: Gallimard, 1970); and *Pour une critique de l'économie politique du signe* (Paris: Gallimard, 1972); translated as *For a Critique of the Political Economy of the Sign* (St Louis: Telos, 1981). Selections from these texts are translated and collected in Jean Baudrillard, *Selected Writings*, ed. Mark Poster (Cambridge: Polity Press, 1988) (hereafter *SW*).

2   Fredric Jameson, 'Reification and Utopia in Mass Culture,' *Social Text*, 1 (1981), p. 139.

3   On the Lukácsian problematic of the commodification and reification of the totality of life under contemporary capitalism, see Georg Lukács, *History and Class Consciousness* (Cambridge, Mass.: MIT Press, 1971), p. 83, where he writes:

> It is no accident that Marx should have begun with an analysis of commodities when, in the two great works of his mature period, he set out to portray capitalist society in its totality and to lay bare its fundamental structures. For at this stage in the history of mankind there is no problem that does not ultimately lead back to that question and there is no solution that could not be found in the solution to the riddle of commodity-*structure*. Of course the problem can only be discussed with this degree of generality if it achieves the depth and breadth to be found in Marx's own analyses. That is to say, the problem of commodities must not be considered in isolation or even regarded as the central problem in economics but as the central, structural problem of capitalist society in all its aspects. Only in this case can the structure of commodity-relations be made to yield a model of all the objective forms of bourgeois society together with all the subjective forms corresponding to them.

The Frankfurt School had also discerned the importance of commodities and consumption in the reproduction of capitalist societies; but although the starting point and perception are similar, Baudrillard's work eventually differed from that of his predecessors because of his use of the categories of semiology to explore the commodity world. On the Frankfurt School analyses of commodification and the consumer society, see Douglas Kellner, *Critical Theory, Marxism and Modernity* (Cambridge and Baltimore: Polity Press and Johns Hopkins University Press, 1989).

4   Theories of the technological society predominant in France at the time include that of Gilbert Simondon, *Du mode d'existence des objets techniques* (Paris: Aubier, 1958), which Baudrillard cites. Other theories include those of Jacques Ellul, *The Technological Society* (New York: Vintage, 1964; orig. 1954); and those expounded in texts produced by the *Arguments* group (see Poster, *Existential Marxism*).

5   On the historical background of the consumer society, see Stuart and Elizabeth Ewen, *Channels of Desire* (New York: McGraw-Hill, 1982).

6   See Douglas Kellner, 'Critical Theory, Commodities and the Consumer Society,' *Theory, Culture and Society*, 1, 3 (1983), pp. 66–83, and idem, *Herbert Marcuse and the Crisis of Marxism* (London and Berkeley: Macmillan and University of California Press, 1984).

7   See Lukács, *Class Consciousness*.

8   Karl Marx, *The Poverty of Philosophy*, in Marx-Engels, *Collected Works*, vol. 6 (New York: International Publishers, 1976), p. 113; quoted in Baudrillard, *The Mirror of Production* (St Louis: Telos, 1975; orig. 1973) (hereafter *MoP*), p. 119.

9   See Karl Marx, *Capital* (New York: International Publishers, 1967), ch. 1.

10 Marx, *Capital*, ch. 1, sec. 4, and the commentary in Sut Jhally, *The Codes of Advertising: Fetishism and the Political Economy of Meaning in Consumer Society* (New York: St Martin's, 1987).

11 Roland Barthes, *The Fashion System* (New York: Hill and Wang, 1983; orig. 1967).

12 See Karl Marx, *Economic and Philosophic Manuscripts of 1844*, in Marx-Engels, *Collected Works*, vol. 3 (New York: International Publishers, 1975), where he writes: 'The meaning of private property . . . is the *existence of essential objects* for man, both as objects of enjoyment and as objects of activity' (p. 322). I am suggesting that Marx's notion of commodities as at least potential objects of enjoyment and activity should be part of a critical theory of the commodity.

13 Michel de Certeau, *The Practice of Everyday Life* (Berkeley: University of California Press, 1984); sections are translated in *Tabloid*, 3 (1981), and *Social Text*, 3 (1982). Similar studies of how individuals resist homogenization in the consumer society and produce their own styles, taste cultures and practices are found in Pierre Bourdieu's *Distinction* (London: Routledge & Kegan Paul, 1984).

14 Certeau, *Everyday Life*, pp. 24ff.

15 Ibid.

16 The term 'imaginary' is borrowed from Lacan, and I am using it here to refer to the mind-set, or ways of perceiving and interpreting the world, peculiar to a specific group, with its inevitable limitations, distortions, one-sidedness and so on. In this sense, there could be a capitalist imaginary, a feminist imaginary, a Marxist imaginary, etc.

17 Andrew Wernick, 'Sign and Commodity: Aspects of the Cultural Dynamic of Advanced Capitalism,' *Canadian Journal of Political and Social Theory*, 8, nos. 1–2 (Winter–Spring 1984), pp. 17–34.

18 See Harry Cleaver, *Reading Capital Politically* (Austin: University of Texas Press, 1977), and Antonio Negri, *Marx Beyond Marxism* (South Hadley, Mass.: Bergin, 1980). A fuller discussion of self-valorization, which would go beyond the boundaries of this text, would address the question of how self-valorization could be part of a revolutionary strategy as formulated by 'autonomous Marxism.' See, e.g., Cleaver, 'Marginality and Self-Valorization' (unpublished manuscript) p. 4, where he writes:

> People's struggle against valorization involves the refusal of the subordination of life to work and amounts to the effort to cease being 'working class,' to cease having their lives unidimensionally defined by work. Self-valorization is the process of developing self-defined goals and ways of being which are not compatible with capitalist organization. N.B.: the term *self*-valorization is not meant to refer just to individuals' struggles, but more generally to the autonomous projects of social groups, communities and peoples which both undermine [capital] accumulation and develop ways of being not based on endless work. Both success in the struggle against work, in the reduction of the amount of time and energy that has to be given up to capitalist valorization and success in the battles to appropriate land or buildings or 'rooms of their own' expands the times and spaces for self-valorization. The fewer hours people can be forced to be workers, the more time and energy they have to pursue their diverse paths of self-determination. The more space which is subtracted from capitalist control, the greater the room for autonomous projects.

19 For similar critiques of the ahistorical and vague nature of Baudrillard's concept of the code, see Wernick, 'Signs and Commodity,' and Robert Goldman, 'Marketing Fragrances: Advertising and the Production of Commodity Signs,' *Theory, Culture, & Society*, 4, no. 4 (Nov. 1987), pp. 691–726. As an alternative

to Baudrillard's theory of codes and signs, Goldman offers a model of commodity signs to interpret advertising and the phantasmagoria of the consumer society.

20 For a theory of language as code, see Ferdinand de Saussure, *Course in General Linguistics* (New York: McGraw-Hill, 1966; orig. 1916). One might compare this model of semiology with that of Roland Barthes, *Elements of Semiology* (Boston: Beacon Press, 1967; orig. 1964), and especially his *S/Z* (New York: Hill and Wang, 1974; orig. 1970), in which he explicates a plurality of codes that constitute classical narrative literature. In fact, there are a plurality of semiological concepts of 'code,' ranging from rather monolithic and often rigidly defined concepts, analogous to language as a master code, to more pluralistic and more loosely defined notions, such as that found in Barthes's *S/Z*. I would suggest that in social semiology, more pluralistic, conventionalist and open notions are more useful than the unitary, monolithic notion of 'the code,' as found in Baudrillard's work.

CHAPTER 2   BEYOND MARXISM

1 See Jean Baudrillard, *The Mirror of Production*, and idem, *L'échange symbolique et la mort* (Paris: Gallimard, 1976) (hereafter *ES*).

2 Robert D'Amico, *Marx and Philosophy of Culture* (Gainesville: University of Florida Press, 1981), p. 51. Jhally, *The Codes of Advertising*, also defends Marx against Baudrillard's polemics.

3 Marx and Engels, *The German Ideology*, in Marx-Engels, *Collected Works*, vol. 5 (New York: International Publishers, 1976), p. 42; Marx, cited in D'Amico, *Marx and Philosophy of Culture*, pp. 51–2; Marx, cited in Jhally, *Codes of Advertising*, p. 42; and Marx, *Capital*, ch. 1, sec. 2, and ch. 15.

4 In *Economic and Philosophic Manuscripts of 1844*, p. 306, Marx writes:

> Under private property . . . every person speculates on creating a *new* need in another, so as to drive him to fresh sacrifice, to place him in a new dependence and to seduce him into a new mode of *enjoyment* and therefore economic ruin. Each tries to establish over the other an *alien* power, so as thereby to find satisfaction of his own selfish need. The increase in the quantity of objects is therefore accompanied by an extension of the realm of the alien powers to which man is subjected and every new product represents a new *potentiality* of mutual swindling and mutual plundering. Man becomes ever poorer as man, his need for *money* becomes ever greater if he wants to master the hostile power. The power of his *money* declines in inverse proportion to the increase in the volume of production: that is, his neediness grows as the *power* of money increases.

5 This position is close to that of the Frankfurt School. See my presentation, critique and reconstruction in *Critical Theory, Marxism and Modernity* and 'Consumer Society'.

6 I am building here on the work of Certeau, in *The Practice of Everyday Life*, and the tradition of 'autonomous Marxism' (Negri, Cleaver, etc.), as well as on my own previous work cited in n. 5 above.

7   On the two sides of use value in Marx's analysis, see Harry Cleaver, *Reading Capital Politically*.

8   Lacan, *Écrits* (New York: Norton, 1977).

9   Jürgen Habermas, *Theory and Practice* (Boston: Beacon Press, 1972).

10 The following passages in *The Marx-Engels Reader*, ed. Robert Tucker (New York: Norton, 1978), document Marx's position: on the realm of freedom, pp. 439ff.; on the 'free association,' pp. 490, 518; on the possibility of a life beyond socially imposed labor in a society of automation, pp. 278ff.; and on democratization and the Paris Commune, pp. 618ff. Baudrillard consistently ignores these and many other aspects of Marxism which would put in question his thesis that Marx merely reflects capitalist society, is merely a 'mirror of production.'

11 Jean Baudrillard, 'When Bataille Attacked the Metaphysical Principle of Economy,' (orig. 1976), translated in *Canadian Journal of Political and Social Theory*, 11, no. 3 (1987), pp. 57–62; subsequent page references cited in text. Several key works of Bataille have been translated into English; see *Visions of Excess* (Minneapolis: University of Minnesota Press, 1985), the journals *Semiotext(e)*, 5 (1976) and *October*, 36 (Spring 1986); and *The Accursed Share* (New York: Zone Books, 1988).

12 Marcel Mauss, *The Gift* (New York: Norton, 1967; orig. 1925).

13 Baudrillard seems to have had a keen interest in anthropology at the time and the American anthropologist Marshall Sahlins remembers Baudrillard in the late 1960s and early 1970s as a 'very serious' person with an earnest interest in anthropology and sociology (taped interview with Marshall Sahlins by Steve Best, Chicago, 1987).

14 Bataille, *Visions of Excess*; idem, *Accursed Share*.

15 See Jacques Derrida, *Margins of Philosophy* (Chicago: University of Chicago Press, 1981), which has been used to legitimate a politics of 'marginal groups.' The notion of the politics of 'difference' is associated with Michel Foucault.

16 The key texts in the micropolitics of desire at the time were perhaps Gilles Deleuze and Felix Guattari, *Anti-Oedipus* (New York: Viking, 1977; orig. 1972), and Jean-Francois Lyotard, *Économie libidinale* (Paris: Minuit, 1974). At this point, Baudrillard was opposing all 'productivist' models (of which those of Deleuze and Guattari and of Lyotard would be prime examples); later he would break completely with 'the micropolitics of desire' and all Freudian theories (see 5.1 and 5.2). Interestingly, in *Économie libidinale* Lyotard presents both Deleuze and Guattari and Baudrillard as 'brother' critiques, maintaining that his own theory is both 'synchronized and copolarized' with Baudrillard (p. 128); even if he reproaches Baudrillard for still believing in a 'truth' which is presumably forgotten or repressed by Marxism.

17 See Alvin Gouldner, *The Two Marxisms* (New York: Seabury, 1980), who distinguishes between 'scientific Marxism' and 'critical Marxism,' arguing that Marxism has given rise to quite different interpretations and can be put to quite different uses. 'Scientific Marxism' refers to theories like Leninism or Althusser's 'structuralist Marxism,' which portray Marxism as a science and tend to privilege the party, which supposedly has knowledge of the laws of history, as the preferred instrument of social change. 'Critical Marxism' refers to more Hegelian versions, which tend to present Marxism as a hermeneutic of

society and history which is primarily a vehicle of social critique and practice. This version emphasizes the importance of practice, and is less deterministic and apodictic than the 'scientific' variety. Obviously, these models refer to ideal types; but my point in introducing this distinction is to suggest that, while many of Baudrillard's polemics provide a devastating critique of 'scientific Marxism,' his arguments are often less devastating vis-à-vis other versions of Marxism.

18 This position is argued in detail in my *Critical Theory, Marxism and Modernity*.

19 See Walter Adamson, *Marx and the Disillusionment of Marxism* (Berkeley: University of California Press, 1984).

20 On the Young Hegelians and their 'critical criticism,' see Karl Marx and Friedrich Engels, *The Holy Family* and *The German Ideology*, in Marx-Engels, *Collected Works*, vols 4 and 5 (New York: International Publishers, 1975 and 1976).

21 Jean Baudrillard, translation of Peter Weiss, *Discours sur la genèse et le déroulement de la très longue guerre de libération du Vietnam: illustrant la nécessité de la lutte armée des opprimés contre leurs oppresseurs* (Paris: Ains, 1968). See too, his translation of Wilhelm E. Muhlmann, *Messainismes révolutionnaires du tiers monde*.

22 'Conversation à bâtons (in-)interrompus avec Jean Baudrillard,' *Dérive*, 5–6 (1977), p. 78.

23 Jean Baudrillard, *Le P.C. ou les paradis artificiels du politique* (Foutenay-Sous-Bois: Cahiers d'Utopie, 1978; collected in *La gauche divine* (Paris: Grasset, 1985) (hereafter *GD*).

24 For an excellent account of the situation of the French Communist Party on the eve of the 1978 elections, see George Ross, *Workers and Communists in France*.

25 A similar vision of capitalism is advanced in Deleuze and Guattari, *Anti-Oedipus*, which stresses the deterritorialization inherent in the relentless circulation of capital at all costs. In effect, Deleuze and Guattari argue that capitalism is by nature 'insane' and 'cruel'; thus Baudrillard is here repeating their critique.

26 Reprinted in Louis Althusser, *Ce qui ne peut plus durer au PCF* (Paris: Maspero, 1978).

27 The 'new philosophers' include André Glucksmann, Bernard-Henri Levi and others who undertook an aggressive polemic aganist Marxism in the mid- to late 1970s and received much media attention for their (ideological) services. In fact, these polemics are not 'new'; nor are they 'philosophy' in the sense of providing systematic perspectives on human beings, society and history. Rather their work is best read as a rather old, often recycled anti-Communist ideology. On the 'new philosophers,' see Peter Dews, 'The "New Philosophers" and the end of Leftism,' in *Radical Philosophy Reader*, ed. Roy Edgeley and Richard Osborne (London: New Left Books, 1985), pp. 361–84, and the dossier of materials published in *Telos*, 33 (Fall 1977), pp. 93–122.

CHAPTER 3   MEDIA, SIMULATIONS AND THE END OF THE SOCIAL

1 Jean Baudrillard, *L'échange symbolique et la mort*, ibid. Selections of this text, on which I will draw in this chapter, are translated in *Selected Writings* and *Simulations* (New York: Semiotext(e), 1983).

2 Marshall McLuhan, *Understanding Media* (New York: McGraw-Hill, 1964). See further discussion of the concept of implosion in 3.3.

3 Baudrillard presents a rather extreme variant of a negative model of the media which sees mass media and culture simply as instruments of domination, manipulation and social control, and which fails to develop theories of radical media or cultural politics. He thus shares a certain theoretical terrain with the Frankfurt School, many Althusserians and other French radicals, and those who see electronic media, broadcasting and mass culture simply as a terrain of domination. For my critique of the Frankfurt School media theory, see *Critical Theory, Marxism and Modernity*.

4 Baudrillard, review of Marshall McLuhan, *Understanding Media*, in *L'Homme et la Société*, no. 5 (1967), pp. 227ff.

5 See Jürgen Habermas, *Theory and Practice*, and the critique in Rick Roderick, *Habermas and the Foundations of Critical Theory* (London: Macmillan, 1986).

6 Hans-Magnus Enzensberger, 'Constituents of a Theory of the Media,' in *The Consciousness Industry* (New York: Seabury, 1974).

7 McLuhan, *Understanding Media*. Scott Lash proposes use of the term 'de-differentiation' as a defining feature of postmodernity, in 'Discourse or Figure? Postmodernism as a "Regime of Signification,"' *Theory, Culture & Society*, 5, nos. 2–3 (June 1988).

8 In *In the Shadow of the Silent Majorities* (New York: Semiotext(e), 1983; orig. 1978, (hereafter *SSM*).

9 Jean Baudrillard, *De la séduction* (Paris: Donoel-Gonthier, 1979) (hereafter *SED*).

10 On McLuhan's Catholicism, see John Fekete, 'McLuhancy: Counterrevolution in Cultural Theory,' *Telos*, 15 (Spring 1973), and Arthur Kroker, *Technology and the Canadian Mind* (Montreal: New World Press, 1984).

11 Fekete, 'McLuhancy,' criticizes the technological reductionism and devaluation of human practice in McLuhan's privileging of the eye and the brain over the hand and the other senses, a privileging which appears in an even more extreme form in Baudrillard.

12 In Hal Foster, ed., *The Anti-Aesthetic* (Port Washington, N.Y.: Bay Press, 1983); subsequent page references in text.

13 Baudrillard's tendency to essentialize media like film or television is evident in *The Evil Demon of Images* (Annandale, Australia: Power Institute Publications, 1984), pp. 3–50. The text brings together several studies in *Simulacres et simulation* (Paris: Editions Galilée, 1981), and claims that while cinema is being 'contaminated' by television, and is itself moving toward increased hyperrealism, it continues to be predominantly a vehicle of image, myth and an imaginary, whereas television is conceptualized purely in terms of information processing (pp. 24ff.).

14 See Steven Best, 'After the Catastrophe: Postmodernism and Hermeneutics,' *Canadian Journal of Political and Social Theory*, 12, no. 3 (1988), pp. 87–100, for an elaboration of this position.

15 Baudrillard celebrates graffiti art as a form of cultural revolution in 'Kool Killer' (*ES*, pp. 118ff.). For some reason, the translation of 'The Orders of Simulacra' in the English edition of *Simulations* omitted this section, perhaps because

Baudrillard was in the process of abandoning all theories of cultural resistance and struggle.

16 This argument is elaborated in Douglas Kellner, 'Public Access Television: *Alternative Views*,' *Radical Science Journal*, 16, *Making Waves* (1985), pp. 79–92, and Steven Best and Douglas Kellner, 'Watching Television: Critical Reflections on Television and Postmodernism,' *Science as Culture*, 4 (1989). I point to some of the limitations of Baudrillard's media theory with regard to analysis of contemporary politics in my 'Baudrillard, Semiurgy and Death,' *Theory, Culture & Society*, 4 (1987), pp. 125–46. A more appreciative reading of Baudrillard's media and social theory, which uses his concepts to interpret contemporary social and cultural phenomena, is found in my 'Boundaries and Borderlines: Reflections on Baudrillard and Critical Theory,' *Current Perspectives in Social Theory*, 9 (forthcoming, 1989).

17 Jeremy Shapiro, 'One-Dimensionality: A Universal Semiotic of Technological Experience,' in *Critical Interruptions*, ed. Paul Breines (New York: Seabury, 1972).

18 Compare Herbert Marcuse, *One-Dimensional Man* (Boston: Beacon, 1964).

19 Jean Baudrillard, *L'échange symbolique*; translated in *Simulations* (New York: Semiotext(e), 1983) (hereafter *SIM*).

20 Compare Michel Foucault, *The Order of Things* (New York: Random House, 1970; orig. 1966).

21 Michel Foucault, *Discipline and Punish* (New York: Vintage, 1977; orig. 1975). I discuss Baudrillard's critique of Foucault's theory of power in 5.2.

22 Sometimes Baudrillard even refers to a cybernetic attempt to totally organize society into 'perfected systems' of deterrence or control. See, e.g., 'The Child in the Bubble,' *Impulse*, 11, no. 4 (1985), p. 13, and *Les stratégies fatales* (Paris: Grasset, 1983), which I will discuss in ch. 6.

23 Jean Baudrillard, *In the Shadow of the Silent Majorities*.

24 Jean Baudrillard, 'The Beaubourg-Effect: Implosion and Deterrence, *October*, 20 (Spring 1982), pp. 3–13.

25 This analysis is a key to Arthur Kroker and David Cook's *The Postmodern Scene* (New York: St Martin's, 1986), which takes Baudrillard's concept of 'excremental culture' as a hermeneutical key to interpreting the current 'postmodern' social situation.

26 This is the position advocated by Guy Debord and the situationists. See Debord, *Society of the Spectacle* and Steven Best's Debordian critique of Baudrillard, 'Commodification.'

27 In the 'Ecstasy of Communication,' Baudrillard makes negative remarks about both the radio and alternative media (pp. 131–2), and generally puts down alternative cultural practices.

28 Paul Piccone, 'The Crisis of One-Dimensionality,' *Telos*, 35 (Spring 1978), pp. 43–54.

29 Baudrillard would justify this position in terms of a 'double refusal' of the social and historical subjecthood or agency. See Kroker and Levin, 'Baudrillard's Challenge,' which concludes:

> Against the emancipatory claims of historical subjecthood, Baudrillard proposes the more radical alternative of 'resistance-as-object' as the line of political resistance most appropriate to the simulacrum. . . . Baudrillard thus valorizes the

position of the 'punk generation': this new generation of rebels which signals its knowledge of its certain doom by a *hyperconformist simulation* (in fashion, language and lifestyle) which represents just that moment of refraction where the simulational logic of the system is turned, ironically and neutrally, back against the system. Baudrillard is a *new wave* political theorist just because he, more than most, has understood that in a system 'whose imperative is the over-production and regeneration of meaning and speech,' all the social movements which 'bet on liberation, emancipation, the resurrection of the subject of history, of the group, of speech as a rasing of consciousness, indeed of a 'seizure of the unconscious' of subjects of the masses' *are acting fully in accordance with the political logic of the system.* (p. 15)

Yet Baudrillard's followers seem to fail to see that on this analysis those who continue to bet on liberation and those 'new wavers' who practice hyper-conformist simulation are both following what Baudrillard claims is the logic of the system, and that there is no reason to believe that – even on Baudrillard's (problematical) theory – one practice is any more 'radical' than the other.

30 On the turn from structuralism to poststructuralism, see Coward and Ellis, *Language and Materialism*.

31 Derrida, *Of Grammatology* (Baltimore: Johns Hopkins University Press, 1976).

32 Michael Ryan, *Marxism and Deconstruction* (Baltimore: Johns Hopkins University Press, 1982), and Gayatri Spivak, *In Other Worlds, Essays in Cultural Politics* (New York: Methuen, 1987).

33 On Nietzsche and poststructuralism, see *The New Nietzsche*, ed. David Allison (New York: Dell, 1977). For an impassioned critique of New French Theory and its German ideological roots, see Jürgen Habermas, *The Philosophical Discourse of Modernity* (Cambridge, Mass.: MIT Press, 1987).

34 See Jean Baudrillard, 'Le cristal se venge,' p. 28, where he writes: 'It is certain that there is an echo, if not a reference to Nietzsche. I had read him passionately, but that was a long time ago and since then I have not reread him.'

35 On Nietzsche's philosophical positions, see *The New Nietzsche*, and Arthur Danto, *Nietzsche as Philosopher* (New York: Macmillan, 1975).

36 See Jean Baudrillard, 'On Nihilism,' *On the Beach*, 6, (Spring 1984; Orig. 1980), pp. 38–9 and Arthur Kroker, 'Baudrillard's Marx,' *Theory, Culture & Society*, 2, no. 3 (1985), pp. 69–84.

37 On distinctions between modernity and postmodernity see Douglas Kellner, 'Postmodernism as Social Theory: Some Challenges and Problems,' *Theory, Culture & Society*, 5, nos. 2–3 (June 1988).

CHAPTER 4   THE POSTMODERN CARNIVAL

1 Parts of the studies contained in *L'échange symbolique et la mort* which I will examine in this chapter have been translated. Sections are found in *The Structuralist Allegory*, ed. John Fekete (Minneapolis: University of Minnesota Press, 1984), and *Selected Writings*; most of 'The Order of Simulacra' is found in *Simulations*; and part of the sixth study, 'The Extermination of the Name of God,' has been translated in *Discourse*, 3 (1981), pp. 60–87, with the title 'Beyond the Unconscious: The Symbolic.' In the Semiotext(e) collections and in

almost all the translations of Baudrillard's articles, the French source is not noted; nor are there indications as to when the texts translated have been cut or are incomplete. I would hope that in the future, Baudrillard's English translators and publishers would indicate where the translations have been taken from. Otherwise Baudrillard's texts are removed from their historical context and from their textual underpinnings. I would also hope that *L'échange symbolique* would be translated in its entirety, for it is a key text in Baudrillard's oeuvre. It is one of his most complex texts, and requires a more systematic explication of its project than I am able to carry out here. Hence, for the purposes of this book, I have split my discussion among several different topics instead of discussing the text as a whole – in part because Baudrillard abandons the ambitious project systematized in the book.

2   On the 'carnivalesque,' see Mikhail Bakhtin, *Rabelais and His World* (Cambridge, Mass.: Harvard University Press, 1968), and the discussions in *Bakhtin: Essays and Dialogues on His Work*, ed. Gary Saul Morson (Chicago: University of Chicago Press, 1986).

3   On theories of postmodernism, see Douglas Kellner, 'Postmodernism as Social Theory'.

4   See Jean-Paul Sartre, *Being and Nothingness* (New York: Philosophical Library, 1956; orig. 1943), and Maurice Merleau-Ponty, *The Phenomenology of Perception* (New York: 1962) For theories of the body that build on these and other theories, see John O'Neill, *Five Bodies* (Ithaca, N.Y.: Cornell University Press, 1985).

5   On the body in contemporary French theory and postmodern culture, see *Canadian Journal of Social and Political Theory, Body Digest*, 11, nos. 1–2 (Winter–Spring 1987). For the latest trials and tribulations of the postmodern body, see Arthur and Marilouise Kroker (eds), *Body Invaders* (New York and London: St Martin's and Macmillan, 1988).

6   For discussions of the body, fashion and sexuality which draw on Baudrillard and other New French Theorists, see the articles by Gail Faurschou, 'Fashion and the Cultural Logic of Postmodernity,' and Kim Sawchuk, 'A Tale of Inscription/Fashion Statements,' collected in both the sources cited in n. 5 above. For Foucault's theory of the disciplinary society and 'normalization' of the body, see *Discipline and Punish*.

7   Jean Baudrillard, 'Publicité absolue, publicité zero,' *S&S*, pp. 133–43.

8   It would be pleasant to imagine these studies of sexuality as exercises in what Baudrillard later described as an attempt to take categories as far as possible in order to destroy and explode them; but he continues to interpret sexuality in markedly Freudian categories in *De la séduction*, and continues in the 1980s to use castration and the phallus as privileged categories which supposedly articulate the truth about sex.

9   Baudrillard published his essay 'Clone Boy' in *Traverses*, 4; it was subsequently collected in *S&S*, and was translated in an issue of *Z/G*, 11 (1986), devoted to cloning. The text was recycled in *SED*, pp. 227ff.

10 In *ES*, pp. 193ff., Baudrillard draws on several of Foucault's major works, citing them as 'masterful analyses of the true history of our culture, the Genealogy of Discrimination' (p. 195). The entire book resonates with Foucaultian notions of the disciplinary society, the normalization of the body and so on, which makes it all

the more curious that Baudrillard will soon tell us to 'Forget Foucault' (see 5.2).

11 Once again we see how Baudrillard turns to Bataille at a crucial juncture in his argument; see 2.2.

12 In my research for an introduction to a republication of the first collection of photographs of mass warfare and death after World War I, I discovered that only after the war were photographs of its unprecedented death and carnage allowed to be published. Likewise, there was state censorship of photos during the US Civil War, the Crimean War in the 1850s and probably most other previous wars in the age of photoreal mechanical reproduction. See my introduction to Ernst Friedrich, *War Against War* (Seattle: Real Comet Press, 1987).

13 In a parallel argument, Baudrillard praises 'primitive' bodily multilations, tattooing, ornaments and so on as reflecting a natural mastery of the world of signs which is somehow superior to 'modern' renunciations of these procedures. These passages show how Baudrillard's sign fetishism bolsters a problematical primitivism beneath his sophisticated posturing and the ways in which he legitimates forms of oppression by means of philosophical argumentation.

14 On Nietzsche's philosophy of life, see articles in *The New Nietzsche*, especially that of Gilles Deleuze entitled 'Active and Reactive,' and Georg Lukács, *The Destruction of Reason* (Atlantic Highlands, N.J.: Humanities Press, 1980; orig. 1962).

15 Jean Baudrillard, *La société de consommation*. The study of pop art in the book was translated as 'Is Pop An Art of Consumption?' in *Tension*, 2 (1983), pp. 33–5; subsequent references to the translation cited in text.

16 References to art abound in Baudrillard's major texts. He has also written art catalogue introductions and monographs include studies of Jean Revol, Barbara Kruger and others.

17 Peter Halley, 'Essence and Model,' program notes to 'International with Monument' exhibit, New York, n.d.

18 Hal Foster, 'Signs Taken for Wonders,' *Art in America*, June 1986, pp. 80–91. Foster provides a survey and critique of current Baudrillardian trends in the art world.

19 Ibid., p. 139.

20 Grant Kester, 'The Rise and Fall? of Baudrillard,' *New Art Examiner*, Nov. 1987, pp. 20–3. Kester notes a Jan. 1987 'Anti-Baudrillard' exhibition, and provides some all too rare criticisms of his theories and influence on the art world.

21 Jean Baudrillard 'The Beaubourg-Effect: Implosion and Deterrence.' subsequent page references cited in text.

22 Jean Baudrillard 'Interview: Game with Vestiges,' *On the Beach*, 5 (Winter 1984), pp. 19–25.

23 For Baudrillard's most systematic discussion, see his article 'Modernity,' *Canadian Journal of Political and Social Theory*, 11, no. 3 (1987; orig. 1985), pp. 63–73.

24 Jean Baudrillard 'On Nihilism,' subsequent page references cited in text. 38–9; subsequent page references cited in text.

25 Kroker and Cook, *The Postmodern Scene*.

26 Baudrillard, 'Game with Vestiges.'

CHAPTER 5   PROVOCATIONS

1   Jean Baudrillard, *Forget Foucault* (New York: Semiotext(e), 1987; orig. 1977) (hereafter *FF*), and *De la séduction*.

2   Deleuze and Guattari, *Anti-Oedipus*; and Foucault, *Discipline and Punish*; and idem, *The History of Sexuality* (New York: Random House, 1978; orig. 1976).

3   On the shifting role of the intellectual in France, see, first, Jean-Paul Sartre, 'Pleas for Intellectuals,' in *Between Existentialism and Marxism* (New York: Pantheon, 1974), and idem, *On a raison de se révolter* (Paris: Gallimard, 1975), and my review of the latter in *Telos*, 22 (Winter 1974–75), pp. 188–201. For some current shifts, see Regis Debray, *Teachers, Writers, Celebrities. The Intellectuals of Modern France* (London: New Left Books, 1981).

4   As an example of Baudrillard's use of deconstruction, the English speaking reader might look into his article 'Fatality or Reversible Imminence: Beyond the Uncertainty Principle,' *Social Research*, 49, no. 2 (1981), pp. 272–93. Without using the term 'deconstruction,' Baudrillard in effect deconstructs the philosophical antinomy between chance and necessity, freedom and determinism, by arguing against the claims and grounds proffered by the proponents of both positions. But he also seems to posit a third position beyond both (see discussion in 6.1 below).

5   Jean Baudrillard, 'The Ecstasy of Communication,' pp. 126ff.

6   See Jean-François Lyotard, *Économie libidinale*.

7   See Lacan, *Écrits*, and the discussion in Coward and Ellis, *Language and Materialism*.

8   Deleuze and Guattari, *Anti-Oedipus*.

9   Jean Baudrillard, 'Beyond the Unconscious: The Symbolic,' *Discourse*, 3 (1981), pp. 60–87; subsequent page references given in text.

10 It appears that Baudrillard collapses Derrida's notion of dissemination into Bataille's notion of a general economy of expenditure, for Baudrillard wants dissemination to be a pure waste, discharge, expenditure or whatever. In Derrida, however, 'dissemination' refers to a special kind of textual productivity, the multiple effects produced by texts, using a productivist model which would be antithetical to Baudrillard's purposes. See Jacques Derrida, *Dissemination* (Chicago: University of Chicago Press, 1981). On Saussure's anagrams, see the special issue of *Semiotext(e)*, 11, no. 1 (1975).

11 The cunning of chance, reversibility: the English translation reads 'of any evolutionary analysis.' Baudrillard's French reads 'de toute analyse révolutionnaire' (*ES*, p. 342). What happened? A slip of the translator's pen or the printer's hand? An instruction to change the discourse by a writer who had decided to polemicize against the concept of revolution and revolutionary analysis? Who knows?

12 In the interview 'Le cristal se venge,' Baudrillard tells how he wanted to write 'a sort of *Mirror of Desire*' parallel to the *Mirror of Production*, and then decided that it was not worth the trouble because 'psychoanalysis found itself marginalized, almost useless' (p. 30). He often took the same position in other texts of the era.

13 *L'échange symbolique* (1976) is full of positive references to Foucault (see *ES*,

pp. 193ff., 217, *passim*), while *Forget Foucault*, originally published the following year, contains a broadside attack on him. Evidently theoretical loyalties of the period were shifting dramatically and rapidly.

14 Based on discussions with Mark Poster held in Austin Texas, in Oct. 1986. Another account, related to me by John Rajchman in Washington in Dec. 1988, maintains that Baudrillard and Foucault were planning to publish an exchange of views in *Les temps modernes*, and that when this appeared not to work out, Baudrillard published his polemic separately.

15 Michel Foucault, *Discipline and Punish*.

16 For development of this position, see some of the articles in *Body Invaders*.

17 Lyotard, *Économie libinidale*, and Deleuze and Guattari, *Anti-Oedipus*.

18 See Ernst Bloch, *Erbschaft dieser Zeit* (Frankfurt: Suhrkamp, 1977; orig. 1935), and the issue of *New German Critique*, 11 (1977), which has several discussions of the importance of Bloch's concept of nonsynchronicity.

19 Jürgen Habermas, *Philosophical Discourse of Modernity*.

20 Kim Sawchuk offers a feminist defense of fashion in 'Fashion Statements,' pointing to recent revisionist attempts to reverse the attacks on fashion which characterized an earlier stage of feminism.

21 See Søren Kierkegaard, 'The Diary of the Seducer,' in *Either/Or* (New York: Doubleday, 1959; orig. 1841).

22 The study of *De la séduction* by Louise Burchill, 'Peripeteia of an alternative in Jean Baudrillard's *De la séduction*,' in *Seduced and Abandoned. The Baudrillard Scene*, is rather uncritical, and cites a positive response by Luce Irigaray to Baudrillard's book (p. 43). For a critical study, see Jane Gallop, *Men in Feminism*, edited by Alice Jardine and Paul Smith (New York: Methuen, 1987), pp. 111–15.

23 Gallop, *Men in Feminism*, p. 113.

24 Apparently, either someone confronted Baudrillard with this objection or he anticipated it, because in *Les stratégies fatales* he provides an 'answer' to this critique, claiming that such an understanding of seduction is fatally flawed, and is but a form of 'vulgar seduction.' 'The vulgar seducer, he, understands nothing. He wants to become a subject and envisages the other as the victim of his strategy. He is as psychologically naive as those good souls who play the part of the victim. Neither the one nor the other see that all initiative, all power, comes from the other side, from the side of the object' (*SF*, p. 175). I shall examine Baudrillard's position on this topic further in 6.1; here it suffices to say that Baudrillard seems to believe that the male seducer who thinks he is seducing the woman is really being seduced by the woman's body as a sexual object. Nonetheless, one could still argue that no matter how brilliant one's insights into seduction, valorizing this activity in the current sexist, masculist world simply encourages activities which benefit neither men (who have the pressures and anxieties of the seducer-stud foisted upon them) nor women (who have the anxieties and indignities of the sexual object foisted upon them). Reconstruction of sexuality and sexual relations requires a much more radical, thoroughgoing effort than Baudrillard offers in his highly problematic theory of seduction.

25 Baudrillard reverses McLuhan here, since for the latter, film was a hot medium; see McLuhan, *Understanding Media*, pp. 248ff.

26 Herbert Marcuse, *Eros and Civilization* (Boston: Beacon, 1955).

27 Debray, *Teachers, Writers*.

28 Critiques of Baudrillard's early works and accompanying defenses of Marxism include D'Amico, *Marx and Philosophy of Culture; Jhally, The Codes of Advertising*; and the current study. I have found no defense of Marxism against Baudrillard in the French literature, which tends to ignore his critiques.

CHAPTER 6   THE METAPHYSICAL IMAGINARY

1 For some contemporary critiques of metaphysical thinking, see Jacques Derrida, *Of Grammatology*; Michel Foucault, *The Order of Things*; and Richard Rorty, *Philosophy and the Mirror of Nature* (Princeton: Princeton University Press, 1979). Despite these and other critiques of metaphysics in the last two decades, Baudrillard persists in this outmoded and nasty mode of thought.

2 For a fuller discussion, see Douglas Kellner, 'Postmodernism as Social Theory'.

3 'Forget Baudrillard: An Interview with Sylvère Lotringer,' in *Forget Foucault*, p. 84. In an interview with Ulysses Santamaria in *Cuadernos del Norte* 5, 26 (1984), Baudrillard responded: 'I am neither a philosopher nor a sociologist. I have neither followed the academic trajectory nor an institutional evolution in either of the two cases. In the University I figure as a sociologist but do not recognize myself in either sociology or in philosophy. A theorist, that's what I'd like to be; a metaphysician in the final analysis; perhaps a moralist' (p. 10). I might note that the thought of some of his contemporary French theorists like Lyotard and Castoriodus was also becoming increasingly metaphysical or, in the case of Deleuze, had already been highly metaphysical. Metaphysics, like the paraphernalia of bohemianism, is the perpetual temptation and addiction of the French intellectual.

4 Jean Baudrillard, 'Le cristal se venge,' p. 28. Baudrillard also presents himself as a metaphysician in discussions with a group of Germans in 1983, published as *Der Tod der Moderne*, pp. 70ff., *passim*.

5 Jean Baudrillard, *Les stratégies fatales* (Paris: Grasset, 1983) (hereafter *SF*). Several fragments of this curious book have been translated into English: 'Reversible Imminence,' 'The Ecstasy of Communication' and 'Fatal Strategies,' in *Selected Writings*. It is significant and perhaps revealing that Baudrillard is now publishing his books in Bernard-Henri Levy's 'New Philosophers' series, which signifies either an explicit allegiance to the new philosophers and the Right or that other publishers are not interested in his latest excursions into metaphysics.

6 Baudrillard, 'Reversible Imminence.' Baudrillard's argument is in part directed against the indeterminacy position represented, among other places, in Jean-François Lyotard, *The Postmodern Condition* (Minneapolis: University of Minnesota Press, 1984).

7 Alfred Jarry, 'What is Pataphysics?,' in *Evergreen*, no. 13, pp. 131ff. Baudrillard's references to Jarry and pataphysics first appear at the beginning of *L'échange symbolique*, where he uses the belly of Jarry's character Ubu as a metaphor – circular, all-absorbing and embracing – for the society of simulations, and seriously (or playfully?) proposes 'pataphysical' opposition to

the hyperrealist system (ibid., p. 58). By *Les stratégies fatales* Baudrillard is identifying with the 'pataphysics' of the absurd developed by Jarry in his *Ubu Roi* plays and theoretical writings. See Jarry, *Ubu Roi* (New York: Evergreen Press, 1968), and idem, *Selected Writings* (New York: Grove Press, 1960). Baudrillard cites Ubu Roi throughout *SF*, and frequently identifies his own position with pataphysics in his 1980s writing (see *SF*, pp. 19, 41–3, 102, 120, *passim*). His key interviews also affirm his allegiance to pataphysics, which suggests that he is serious about it.

8   Baudrillard, 'Reversible Imminence,' pp. 279, 286–7.

9   Ibid., p. 287. The whole affair is more humorous when one reads the English translation of the article in an issue of *Social Research* devoted to contemporary French theory, rather than in the context of the narrative of *Les stratégies fatales*. In the book, the 'theory' of 'reversible imminence' is an amusing part of his story of the triumph of the object; but without this framework I am not sure what a diligent English reader wanting to bone up on the latest French theory import would make of it.

10 This peculiar fatalism is also evident in Baudrillard's text *Please Follow Me*, which accompanies Sophie Calle's *Suite venitienne* (Seattle: Bay Press, 1988; orig. 1983).

11 On this issue, Baudrillard sides with the 'theoretical anti-humanism' advocated by Althusser, Foucault and others. This position is the target of a recent critique by Ferry and Renaut, *La Pensée 68*.

12 Baudrillard, 'The Child in the Bubble,' p. 13.

13 Rudolf Bahro, *The Alternative in Eastern Europe* (London: New Left Books, 1978), and the discussion by Herbert Marcuse, 'Protosocialism and Late Capitalism,' in *Rudolf Bahro: Critical Responses*, ed. Ulf Wolter (White Plains, N.Y.: M. E. Sharpe, 1980), discussed in Kellner, *Herbert Marcuse*, pp. 307ff.

14 Kellner, *Marcuse*, pp. 307ff.

15 One could also develop a deconstructive argument against Baudrillard. For it cannot be determined whether objects exist independently of the subject in the way in which we perceive them, or if the apparatus of the subject does not, at least to some extent, constitute objects as we perceive, experience and interact with them. Kant argued that there were a priori categories of perception and understanding whereby the subject organized his or her experience and gained access to objects, and Absolute Idealists like Berkeley argued that the object world is purely a creation of God and the subject. The counterposition to Berkeleyan or Kantian idealism is an equally questionable materialism according to which the subject simply mirrors or reflects objects that exist totally in their own right, in accordance with their own laws (Lenin in his materialist reflection theory of knowledge came close to this position). Against these traditional positions in the old idealism-materialism, subject-object debate, a contemporary deconstructive argument might maintain that it is undecidable what the subject contributes to the constitution of experience and the material world, and what contribution the object makes to the constitution of experience and subjectivity. This would imply that the most reasonable philosophical position involves focusing on and analyzing subject-object interaction and the ways in which the subject and objects interact in the constitution of experience, society, the external world and so on.

16 T. W. Adorno in his article 'Subject and Object,' in *The Essential Frankfurt School Reader*, ed. Andrew Arato and Eike Gebhardt (New York: Continuum, 1982), also claims that the object has gained supremacy over the subject in the contemporary world. Yet Adorno attempts to carry out a subject-object dialectic and to strengthen the powers of the subject in its (losing) battle with the object. In *Negative Dialectics* (London: Routledge and Kegan Paul, 1973), Adorno also supports a methodological priority to the object as a counter against the philosophy of subjectivity (pp. 183ff.).

17 Charles Levin, in 'Baudrillard, Critical Theory and Psychoanalysis,' *Canadian Journal of Political and Social Theory*, 8, nos. 1–2 (1984), pp. 35ff., argues that British and American object relations theory and Lacan's structural Freudian theory provide perspectives superior to that of Baudrillard for exploring the ways in which objects, objectification and differentiation of the relation to the objects of our inner and outer worlds function in our lives. For a good summary of this object relations theory, see Nancy Chodorow, *The Reproduction of Mothering* (Berkeley: University of California Press, 1978), and idem, 'Beyond Drive Theory,' *Theory and Society*, 14 (1985), pp. 271–319.

18 Jean Baudrillard, *Amérique* (Paris: Grasset, 1986); (London and New York: trans. Verso, 1988) (hereafter *A*). Pagination in my text refers to the French edition. Marx made a similar claim in the Preface to *Capital*, where he wrote that the story which he was narrating about the development of capital in England would soon be about other scenes as well: *'De te fabula narratur!'* And Marcuse used his chosen domicile of exile, the US, as the model for the onward march of one-dimensionality in 'advanced industrial society,' believing that this was the fate of the developed industrial world, first evident in the US. Future social theory may read Baudrillard and the Frankfurt School as telling successive phases of a story whose conclusion, and even narrative lines of development, are not yet clear to us.

19 The story concerns a former race-car driver who now delivers cars across the country for a corporation. For reasons not specified, he undertakes to drive a souped-up Dodge Challenger from Denver to San Francisco in 15 hours. The police soon engage in hot pursuit, and the film unfolds an existential drama of a high-speed trip across the desert of America, which highlights the decline of individuality in the contemporary era, and ends with the hero dying in a car explosion ignited by a crash into a police barricade.

20 See Paul Virilio, *Speed and Politics* (New York: Semiotext(e), 1987).

21 The 'desert' is Baudrillard's central metaphor for America and, as I suggest below, for the otherness of the object itself.

22 Jean-François Lyotard, *Économie libidinale*, p. 130.

23 Baudrillard's most ludicruous argument is that capital never took hold in the United States (*A*, pp. 158ff.), and that it is the relentless reproduction, intensification and realization of *models* which are the key constitutives of 'America.' Baudrillard overlooks the obvious point that it is precisely capital which has produced models and simulations in order to advance its own interests and hegemony. For an opposite reading of Los Angeles and Southern California from the standpoint of the vicissitudes of capital, see Mike Davis, 'The Streets of Los Angeles,' *New Left Review*, 164 (July–Aug. 1987), pp. 65–86.

24 Jean Baudrillard with Sylvère Lotringer, 'Forget Baudrillard' in *Forget Foucault* (New York: Semiotext(e), 1987). (hereafter *FB*).

25 Jean Baudrillard, *L'autre par lui-même* (Paris: Galileé, 1987) (hereafter *ALM*); translated into English as *The Ecstasy of Communication* (New York: Semiotext(e), 1988) (hereafter *EC*).

26 Martin Heidegger, *Nietzsche*, 3 vols (New York: Harper and Row, 1976, 1978 and forthcoming).

27 Friedrich Nietzsche, *The Anti-Christ* (London: Penguin, 1979). See especially the section 'Why I am a Fatality.' Nietzsche's concept of *amor fati*, love of fate, might also be significant with regard to Baudrillard's strange conversion to fatalism.

28 Jean Baudrillard, 'Forget Baudrillard,' p. 0; *ALM*, p. 0.

29 Jean Baudrillard, 'What Are You Doing After the Orgy?' *Artforum*, Oct. 1983, pp. 42–6; subsequent page references cited in text.

30 Baudrillard, 'Le cristal se venge,' p. 28.

CHAPTER 7 BEYOND BAUDRILLARD

1 I am using the term 'imaginary' in the sense derived from Lacan referred to earlier, and am also drawing on literature concerning political socialization and political cognitive mapping cited in Austin Ranney, *Channels of Power* (New York: Harper and Row, 1983) and on Fredric Jameson, *The Political Unconscious* (Ithaca, N.Y.: Cornell University Press, 1981).

2 E.g., Jean Baudrillard, *La gauche divine*. Interestingly, many of Baudrillard's critiques of the French Left remain untranslated, and one gets the impression from what English translations there are that Baudrillard is an uncompromising Leftist, although reading him in the context of contemporary French politics might lead one to other conclusions. Further critical studies of Baudrillard might interrogate his critiques of Marxism, Socialist and Communist parties, and feminism in the contemporary era within the context of his interventions in contemporary French culture and politics. For studies of French socialism which contain more empirical and balanced evaluation and critique, see George Ross, *Workers and Communists*, and the articles collected in *Telos*, 55 (Spring 1983), and *New Political Science*, 12 (Summer 1983).

3 Again one notes the crucial role of Bataille in Baudrillard's political imaginary. The term '*part maudite*' refers to the excess of a 'general economy' which must be wasted, sacrificed and used for nonutilitarian ends to satisfy human needs for expenditure, excess and so forth. See discussion in 2.2 below.

4 Baudrillard's vision is close to that of one of his 1980s heroes, Elias Canetti, who presents a basically negative view of 'the masses' in *Crowds and Power* (New York: Viking, 1962). Baudrillard also thematized masses and power somewhat differently from Canetti, and in the 1980s frequently cited Canetti's positions on 'the end of history' (see the discussion in 7.2).

5 Would it be unfair to suggest that Baudrillard has proclaimed the end of history precisely because he has nothing to contribute to contemporary history, because history has passed him by, because his politics have diverged to such an extent from contemporary politics that there is no possibility of convergence?

6   'Intellectuals, Commitment and Political Power: An Interview with Jean
    Baudrillard,' *Thesis Eleven* 10–11 (1984–5), pp. 166–73; subsequent page
    references cited in text.

7   Baudrillard is even harsher on the new philosophers in *Cool Memories*, where he
    indicates that their 'anti-Gulag' litany has become a 'dominant ideology. The
    priests of the anti-Gulag are equal to the torturers of the Gulag. Sheep have
    replaced the dogs of the apocalypse' (p. 168). Later he equates the new
    philosophers with the 'new romanticism' (p. 280).

8   In conversations in 1983, Baudrillard claims that his only 'references' at the time
    were Nietzsche, Bataille and Holderlin; see *Der Tod der Moderne*, p. 75, and 'Le
    cristal se venge,' p. 28. All these 'references,' along with Baudelaire and others
    whom Baudrillard cites, represent a view of the world which might be called
    'aristocratic aestheticism,' and all attribute great importance to signs.

9   Jean Baudrillard, *Cool Memories* (Paris: Éditions Galilée, 1987). Several people
    have described to me the enthusiastic reception of *Cool Memories* in France, and
    claim that they have seen Baudrillard on television during this time, promoting
    his book and his ideas.

10 Elias Canetti, *The Human Provence* (New York: Continuum, 1978). Canetti's
    book, frequently cited by Baudrillard, contains a series of reflections from the
    1920s to the 1980s, and Baudrillard's *Cool Memories* can be read as a –somewhat
    gamier – simulation in form and tone of Canetti's musings.

11 Arthur Kroker and Charles Levin, 'Baudrillard's Challenge,' p. 5.

12 Arthur Kroker, 'The Games of Foucault,' *Canadian Journal of Political and
    Social Theory*,' 11, no. 3 (1987, pp. 1–2, citing Baudrillard, *ALM*, pp. 83–4).
    Citation of this passage by Baudrillard becomes amusing when the editor of the
    English translation informs us that 'this summary, actually an excerpt from a
    review article by Guy Scarpetta, was inadvertently included by Baudrillard in
    manuscript form, but retained thereafter' (*EC*, p. 103).

3   Ursula Le Guin, *The Left Hand of Darkness* (New York: Ace, 1969),
    Introduction (no page number). Baudrillard carries out studies of science fiction
    himself in *S&S*, pp. 179ff., and in several texts uses the term 'science fiction' to
    characterize his own works. See Jonathan Benison, 'Jean Baudrillard on the
    Current State of SF' *Foundation*, 32 (Nov. 1984), pp. 25–42.

14 Jean Baudrillard, 'Forget Baudrillard.' p. 101.

15 Jean Baudrillard, 'Nuclear Implosion,' *Impulse*, Spring–Summer 1983, pp. 9–
    13.

16 Jean Baudrillard, 'L'an 2000 ne passera pas,' *Traverses*, nos. 33–4, p. 9;
    translated as 'The Year 2000 Has Already Happened' in *Body Invaders*, pp. 35–
    44; emphasis added.

17 For some characteristic totalizing panoramas, see *GD*, pp. 123ff., and
    Baudrillard's article 'Modernity.'

18 The coming of the year 2,000 and the fin de siècle is a major theme in both *GD*,
    pp. 133ff. and 161ff.; *CM*, pp. 216, 223, *passim*; and the essay 'The Year 2000.'

19 On the nineteenth century fin de siècle, see Roger Shattuck, *The Banquet Years*
    (New York: Random House, 1958); Mario Praz, *The Romantic Agony*
    (London: Oxford University Press, 1970); and Jean Pierrot, *The Decadent
    Imagination* (Chicago: University of Chicago Press, 1981). Matei Calinescu, in
    Five Faces of Modernity (Durham, N.C.: Duke University Press, 1987), pp.

151ff., describes the period of 'decadence' in France during the 1880s in ways that bring to mind Baudrillardian themes – a topic to which I will return in a subsequent study of the 1980s as the site of postmodernism.

20   Baudrillard, 'The Year 2000,' pp. 35ff.; subsequent page references cited in text.
21   Some of Baudrillard's most sympathetic commentators have become disillusioned with him, and have cited what they see as a decline of the quality of his work. Charles Levin wrote in a review of *De la séduction* that Baudrillard's first five books 'are sometimes brilliant. . . . Since then, he has been in a protracted slump' (*Telos*, 45 (Fall 1980), p. 198). More recently, Meaghan Morris has written:

> After producing over a dozen hefty books and a number of furious pamphlets in some 20 years as the professional *enfant terrible* of French sociology, Baudrillard has begun to work equally hard at playing the Disappearing Theorist. He has progressively and deliberately abandoned the protocols of systematic research, scrupulous argument, thesis formulation, 'critique,' – in favour of a style of personal *jotting* (and jaunting) about the world. For some, the result represents the emergence of a writer and thinker of great originality, while for others it epitomises the defeat of analysis by burble in the fashion-field of postmodernism. *New Statesman*, 113 (26 June 1987), p. 28

22   Jean Baudrillard, 'Softly, Softly,' *New Statesman*, 113 (6 Mar. 1987), p. 44.
23   In my 'Postmodernism as Social Theory,' I criticize Lyotard and other postmodern theorists for rejecting notions of totality and history, on the grounds that it is impossible to provide a theory of an epochal transformation from modernity to postmodernity without a global and totalizing theory of history.
24   Claus Offe, 'Technology and One-Dimensionality: A Version of the Technocracy Thesis?' in *Marcuse. Critical Theory and the Promise of Utopia*, ed. Robert Pippin et al. (South Hadley, Mass.: Bergin and Garvey, 1988), pp. 220ff.
25   Elias Canetti's *Crowds and Power*, treats two topics which increasingly come to concern Baudrillard. For an incisive critique of Canetti's work, see Tom Nairn, 'Crowds and Critics,' *New Left Review*, 17 (Winter 1962), pp. 24–33.
26   For further discussion of the relationship between critical social theory and history, see my book *Critical Theory, Marxism and Modernity*.
27   For a detailed analysis of this sort, see my *Television, Politics and Society* (Boulder, Colo.: Westview Press, forthcoming).
28   Jean Baudrillard, 'Panic Crash!,' in Arthur Kroker, Marilouise Kroker, and David Cook (eds), *Panic Encyclopedia* (New York: Saint Martin's Press, 1989), p. 67.
29   I attempt to chart out the 'secrets' (i.e. scandals) of the Reagan and Bush administration which were omitted by the mainstream media and reported by the investigative press in *Television, Politics, and Society*. While Baudrillard is taken as an 'authority' on the media, in fact most of what he writes on the media is highly problematical.

Bibliography

This bibliography is in no way definitive. Rather, I compiled it from references to Baudrillard's published work which I discovered cited in other articles, in computer information bases, or through my own research. The first section lists all of his major books and monographs that have appeared in the original French or in English, while the third lists translations by Baudrillard which I have discovered. The second section lists all of Baudrillard's articles in English which I was able to find and a selection of foreign language articles which contain material not published in his books, or which constitute an interesting text in their own right. Thus, while this is – to my knowledge – the most complete bibliography of his work yet to appear, there are no doubt many Baudrillardian texts circulating via marginal journals or sources that I missed.

I. BOOKS

Le système des objets (Paris: Denoel-Gonthier, 1968).

La société de consommation (Paris: Gallimard, 1970).

Pour une critique de l'économie politique du signe (Paris: Gallimard, 1972); translated as *For a Critique of the Political Economy of the Sign* (St Louis: Telos, 1981).

Le miroir de la production: ou, l'illusion critique du matérialisme historique (Tournail: Casterman, 1973); translated as *The Mirror of Production* (St Louis: Telos, 1975).

L'échange symbolique et la mort (Paris: Gallimard, 1976).

L'effet Beaubourg: Implosion et dissuasion (Paris: Éditions Galilée, 1977); translated in *October*, 20 (Spring 1982), pp. 3–13.

Oublier Foucault (Paris: Éditions Galilée, 1977); translated as *Forget Foucault* (New York: Semiotext(e), 1987).

L'ange de stuc (Paris: Éditions Galilée, 1978).

A l'ombre des majorités silencieuses, ou la fin du social (Fontenay-Sous-Bois: Cahiers d'Utopie, 1978); translated with other articles as *In the Shadow of the Silent Majorities* (New York: Semiotext(e), 1983).

Le P.C. ou les paradis artificiels du politique (Fontenay-Sous-Bois: Cahiers d'Utopie, 1979).

Jean Revol: peintures, dessins (France: Éditions Feudon-Béarn, 1980).

De la séduction (Paris: Denoel-Gonthier, 1979; 2nd edn with new preface, 1981).

Simulacres et simulation (Paris: Éditions Galilée, 1981).

A l'ombre des majorités silencieuses; Ou la fin du social; suivi de, L'extase du socialisme (Paris: Grasset, 1981).

Sophie Calle, *Suite venitienne*, with Jean Baudrillard, *Please Follow Me* (Paris: Éditions de l'Étoile, 1983), trans. with same title (Seattle: Bay Press, 1988).

Simulations (New York: Semiotext(e), 1983).

Les stratégies fatales (Paris: Grasset, 1983).

La gauche divine (Paris: Grasset, 1985).

Amérique (Paris: Grasset, 1986); trans. as *America* (London and New York: Verso, 1988).

L'autre par lui-même (Paris: Éditions Galilée, 1987); translated as *The Ecstasy of Communication* (New York: Semiotext(e), 1988).

Forget Foucault (New York: Semiotext(e) 1987).

Cool Memories (Paris: Éditions Galilée, 1987).

The Evil Demon of Images (Annandale, Australia: Power Institute Publications, 1987).

Jean Baudrillard: Selected Writings, edited by Mark Poster (Cambridge and Palo Alto: Polity Press and Stanford University Press, 1988).

The Revenge of the Crystal: A Baudrillard Reader, edited by Mick Carter (London: Pluto, 1989).

II.   ARTICLES AND INTERVIEWS

'Compte rendu de Marshall McLuhan: Understanding Media: The Extensions of Man' *L'homme et la société*, no. 5 (1967), pp. 227–30.

'Conversations à bâtons (in-)interrompus avec Jean Baudrillard,' *Dérive* 5–6 (1976), pp. 70–97.

'La Réalité dépasse l'hyperréalisme,' *Revue d'ésthétique, no 1 (1976), pp. 139–48.*

'Rituel – loi – code,' in *Violence et Transgression*, ed. Michel Maffesoli and André Bruston (Paris: Éditions Anthropos, 1979), pp. 97–108.

'Desert for Ever,' *Traverses*, 19 (1980), pp. 54–8.

'Beyond the Unconscious: The Symbolic,' *Discourse*, 3 (1981), pp. 60–87.

'Fatality or Reversible Imminence: Beyond the Uncertainty Principle,' *Social Research*, 49, no. 2 (1981), pp. 272–93.

'Il mormorio della rete' (an interview with Dominique Wahiche) *Media e messaggi*, 1 :1981), pp. 146–52.

'Estasi dell'oggetto puro,' in *Le Rovine del Senso*, ed. Paolo Meneghetti and Stefano Trombini (Bologna: Cappelli, 1982), pp. 117–18.

'Circuiti e cortocircuiti,' in *Oggi l'arte e un carcere*? ed. Luigi Russo (Bologna: Il Muline, 1982).

Interview in *Cinematographie* 80 (July/Aug. 1982), pp. 39–40.

'Domande a Jean Baudrillard, a cura di Giuseppe Bartolucci,' in *Paesaggio Metropo*, ed. Giuseppe Bartolucci et al. (Rome: Feltrinelli, 1982).

'De la croissance à l'excroissance,' *Le débat*, 23 (Jan. 1983).

'What Are You Doing After the Orgy?,' *Artforum*. Oct. 1983, pp. 42–6.

'Is Pop an Art of Consumption? *Tension*, 2 (1983), pp. 33–5.

'The Ecstasy of Communication,' in Hal Foster, ed., *The Anti-Aesthetic: Essays on Post-modern Culture* (Port Townsend, Wa.: Bay Press, 1983), pp. 126–34.

'Le cristal se venge: une entrevue avec Jean Baudrillard,' *Parachute*, June–Aug. 1983, pp. 26–33.

'Nuclear Implosion,' *Impulse*, Spring–Summer 1983, pp. 9–13.

Interview in *Magazine litteraire* (March 1983, pp. 80–5).

'Sur le "Look Generation",' interview in *Le nouvel observateur* (Febr. 18, 1983), p. 50.

Interview in *Psychologie* (May 1983), pp. 65–8.

Review of *Zelig, Skrien* (Winter 1983/4), p. 14.

Interview in *Cinema 84* 301 (Jan. 1984), pp. 16–18.

'Astral America,' *Artforum*, Sept. 1984, pp. 70–4.

'Interview: Game with Vestiges,' *On the Beach*, 5 (Winter, 1984), pp. 19–25.

'On Nihilism,' *On the Beach*, 6 (Spring, 1984), pp. 38–9.

'Jean Baudrillard,' interview in *Cuadernos del Norte*, 5, no. 26 (1984), 10–13.

'Une conversation avec Jean Baudrillard,' *UCLA French Studies*, 2–3 (1984–5), 1–22.

'Intellectuals, Commitment, and Political Power: An Interview with Jean Baudrillard,' *Thesis Eleven*, 10–11 (1984–5), pp. 166–73.

'Der Ekstatische Sozialismus,' *Merkur*, 39, no. 1 (1985), pp. 83–9.

'The Masses: The Implosion of the Social in the Media,' *New Literary History*, 16, no. 3 (1985), pp. 577–89.

'The Child in the Bubble,' *Impulse*, 11, no. 4 (1985), p. 13.

'L'an 2000 ne passera pas,' *Traverses*, nos. 33–34 (1985), pp. 8–16; translated as 'The Year 2000 Will Not Take Place,' in *Futur*Fall: Excursions into Post-Modernity* (Sidney, Australia: Power Institute of Fine Arts, 1986), pp. 18–28, and as 'The Year 2000 Has Already Happened,' in *Body Invaders*, ed. Arthur and Marilouise Kroker (New York: St Martin's, 1987), pp. 35–44.

'Clone Boy,' *Z/G*, no. 11 (1986), pp. 12–13.

'The Realized Utopia, America,' *French Review*, 60, no. 1 (1986), pp. 2–6.

—— in *Masses et postmodernite*, edited by Jacques Zylberberg (Quebec: Presses de l'Universitate Laval, 1986).

Interview in *Franzosische Philosophen in Gesprach*, edited by Florian Rotzer (Munchen: Klaus Baer Verlag, 1986).

'Au-dela du vrai et du faux, ou le malin genie de l'image,' *Cahiers internationaux de sociologie* (Jan–June 1987), pp. 139–45.

'A Perverse Logic & Drugs as Exorcism,' *UNESCO Courier*, 7 (1987), pp. 7–9.

'Amérique,' *Literary Review*, 30, no. 3 (1987), pp. 475–82.

'Video, culto al cuerpo y "Look",' *Fahrenheit, 450*, no. 2 (1987), pp. 23–5.

'When Bataille Attacked the Metaphysical Principle of Economy,' *Canadian Journal of Political and Social Theory*, 11, no. 3 (1987; orig. 1976), pp. 57–62.

'Modernity,' *Canadian Journal of Political and Social Theory*, 11, no. 3 (1987; orig. 1985), pp. 63–73.

'Softly, Softly,' *New Statesman*, 113 (6 Mar. 1987), p. 44.

'USA 80's' and 'Desert Forever,' in *Semiotext(e) USA* (New York: Autonomedia, 1987), pp. 47–50 and 135–37.

'Hunting Nazis and Losing Reality,' *New Statesman*, 19 Febr. 1988, pp. 16–17.

'Places of Urban Ecstasy,' *Die Zeitschrift fur Kunst und Kultur* 12 (1988), pp. 92–5.

'Panic Crash!,' in Arthur Kroker, Marilouise Kroker, and David Cook (eds), *Panic Encyclopedia* (New York: Saint Martin's Press, 1989), pp. 64–7.

III.   TRANSLATIONS

Brecht, Bertolt *Dialogues d'exilés* (Paris: L'Arche, 1965).

Weiss, Peter *Marat/Sade* (Paris: Éditions du Seuil, 1965).

Weiss, Peter *Discours sur la genèse et le déroulement de la très longue guerre de libération du Vietnam: illustrant la necéssité de la lutte armée des opprimés contre leurs oppresseurs* (Paris: Ains, 1968).

Muhlmann, Wilhelm E. *Messainismes révolutionnaires du tiers monde* (Paris: Gallimard, 1968).

Index

compiled by Chris McKay